From Votes
to
Victory

From Votes to Victory

WINNING AND GOVERNING
THE WHITE HOUSE
IN THE TWENTY-FIRST CENTURY

Edited by Meena Bose

Texas A&M University Press | College Station

This paper meets the requirements
of ANSI/NISO z39.48-1992
(Permanence of Paper).
Binding materials have been chosen for durability.

Library of Congress Cataloging-in-Publication Data

From votes to victory : winning and governing the White House in the twenty-first
century / edited by Meena Bose. — 1st ed.
p. cm.
Includes bibliographical references and index.
ISBN-13: 978-1-60344-226-8 (e-book)
ISBN-10: 1-60344-226-X (e-book)
ISBN-13: 978-1-60344-227-5 (pbk. : alk. paper)
ISBN-10: 1-60344-227-8 (pbk.)
1. Presidents—United States—Election—History—21st century.
2. Presidents—United States—Election—2008.   3. United States—
Politics and government—21st century.   4. Political campaigns—
United States—History—21st century. I. Bose, Meenekshi, 1970–
JK528.F76   2010
324.973'093—dc22
2010050699

*Underwriting and Web hosting for the Open Access edition of this volume were provided by
the Peter S. Kalikow Center for the Study of the American Presidency, Hofstra University.*

Contents

Acknowledgments

In November 2005, Hofstra University announced that it would establish an endowed chair in presidential studies, and that it would seek to establish a center for scholarship and discussion about the American presidency. Less than three years later, Hofstra's Peter S. Kalikow Center for the Study of the American Presidency hosted its first symposium, titled "From Votes to Victory: Winning and Governing the White House in the Twenty-first Century." This volume represents the scholarly results of that project.

In organizing the symposium, the Kalikow Center received indispensable assistance and support from many sources. Special thanks to Hofstra University professor emeritus of political science and former department chair Mark L. Landis, and political science department chair and associate professor of political science Rosanna Perotti, for serving as panel chairs; the Hofstra Cultural Center and the Office of University Relations, for coordinating and publicizing the event; presidential scholars Stephen J. Wayne of Georgetown University, Martha Joynt Kumar of Towson University, and James P. Pfiffner of George Mason University, for serving as panel discussants; and political strategist Charlie Cook, for delivering the keynote address.

Publication of this volume is due to Hofstra's appreciation of the importance of scholarship on the American presidency. Special thanks to President Stuart Rabinowitz, Provost Herman A. Berliner, and Dean Bernard J. Firestone of Hofstra's College of Liberal Arts and Sciences for their steadfast support. The Kalikow Center has worked closely with Texas A&M University Press on this project, and appreciates the efforts of Director Charles Backus and Editor-in-chief Mary Lenn Dixon in bringing it to fruition.

The symposium, the volume, and the Center itself are all due to Peter S. Kalikow's dedication to the advancement of presidency studies. Hofstra thanks Mr. Kalikow for his enthusiastic and continuing engagement in the Center's analyses of the American presidency

From Votes
to
Victory

Introduction

MEENA BOSE

This volume examines the challenges of winning the White House and becoming president in the twenty-first century. It presents a comprehensive analysis of the path from campaign to governance, beginning with the resources candidates must secure to gain their party's nomination, continuing through the general election campaign, and concluding with the challenges that the victor will face upon taking office. In addressing these topics, it focuses closely on the 2008 presidential race, with attention to earlier presidential campaigns as well.

The 2008 race is an important case study for understanding recent changes in presidential elections for several reasons. It was an election of firsts: A Mormon candidate was in sustained contention for the Republican Party's nomination; a former First Lady ran for president and nearly won the Democratic Party's nomination; and the country elected its first African American president. In addition to these historic events, neither an incumbent president nor vice president was seeking election for the first time in eighty years. Consequently, this contest provided an unparalleled opportunity for candidates to recast the national agenda with new initiatives. Yet at the same time, the hurdles to winning nomination and election were great.

Candidates raised hundreds of millions of dollars to wage an effective campaign for a major-party nomination, and they dispersed those resources widely to be competitive across the many states that moved up their primaries or caucuses. In campaigning for the nomination, candidates endured a grueling schedule of frequent intra-party debates, twenty-four-hour news coverage, and continual efforts to define their agenda before it was defined by analysts or competitors for them. After the party conventions, the two nominees continued to battle over campaign resources and media coverage, all with an eye toward garnering the necessary 270 votes in the Electoral College. After the election, the incoming president faced several pressing tasks, including developing a legislative strategy to work with Congress to enact campaign promises, and defining the U.S. national security agenda in the ongoing battle against terrorism. Other topics, most notably the financial meltdown in the fall of 2008, were also highly significant, but did not drive the critical battles in the nominating contests, where the campaign process has evolved most in recent years.

To examine these topics about presidential campaigns and governance in the twenty-first century, the contributors—whose diverse intellectual backgrounds include history, political science, American studies, and political communication—first participated in a symposium at Hofstra University on April 3, 2008. Presidential scholars Stephen J. Wayne, Martha Joynt Kumar, and James P. Pfiffner served as commentators and provided valuable advice and insights on the analyses. Contributors then revised their articles to incorporate the 2008 election results and the implications for American politics, focusing on how presidential campaigns and governance have evolved in recent years.

Running for President

The basic constitutional requirements for presidential selection have remained unchanged since 1787, but the political process would be virtually unrecognizable to the framers of the Constitution. Article II states that candidates must be thirty-five years old, natural-born citizens of the United States (or citizens at the time of the Constitution's ratification, which applied, of course, to the early presidents), and residents of the United States for at least fourteen years. The Twelfth Amendment, ratified in 1804, instituted separate balloting for presidential and vice presidential candidates, to avoid repetition of the 1800 election tie, in which Thomas Jefferson and Aaron Burr received the same number of Electoral College votes, and the House of Representatives had to choose the victor. The Twentieth Amendment, ratified in 1933, shortened the transition period from four to just over two months by moving up the inauguration from March 4 to January 20. Eligibility, electoral procedures, and dates aside, presidential selection has undergone significant transformations in American politics, beginning with the party nominating contests.

Perhaps the most important change in presidential nomination processes is the shift from party-centered campaigns to candidate-centered contests.[1] The development of political parties early in American history resulted initially in congressional leaders choosing their party nominees, but by the 1830s, nominating conventions assumed that responsibility, with state and local party officials directing the competition. In the 1970s, primaries and caucuses supplanted party conventions as the means of allocating delegates to candidates, which meant that potential nominees could bypass state and local party officials to appeal directly to voters. Lara M. Brown assesses the significant consequences of these changes for party nominations. She presents a theory of "aspirant opportunism" that finds political experience has less importance for candidates than it did previously, while front-loaded contests and early momentum in those contests have become highly significant factors in a candidate's success.

As presidential candidates have tied their political fortunes increasingly to their own efforts rather than to party leaders, their ability to raise financial fortunes is an essential component of their campaign. Campaign legislation in the 1970s imposed dollar limits on campaign contributions, and the 2002 Bipartisan Campaign Reform Act (also known as the McCain-Feingold law) updated those limits and closed some loopholes in the earlier rules, most significantly through banning so-called "soft money," or unlimited contributions to political parties.[2] Before the 2008 nominating contests began, analysts had predicted that a successful candidate would require approximately $100 million in funds, and indeed, the final two competitors for the Democratic nomination, Hillary Rodham Clinton and Barack Obama, each had raised more than that amount by the end of 2007.[3] Victoria A. Farrar-Myers examines how financial "viability" in presidential nominating contests has shifted in the early twenty-first century, with public financing falling by the wayside as candidates compete earlier than ever to build their political war chests.

Along with a campaign funding strategy, presidential candidates must develop a communications strategy to cultivate public support and garner votes. (Long gone are the days when candidates would rely on a "front-porch" campaign to meet the public.[4]) Media coverage enables candidates to reach voters through interviews with reporters and participation in events that are deemed newsworthy by the media. Candidates supplement media coverage with their own campaign advertisements and websites, and the 2008 presidential campaign illustrates the importance of using the World Wide Web (WWW) to expand a candidate's political base.

The constant news cycle is especially challenging for presidential candidates today because of the ever-lengthening campaign period. The 2008 race began just after the November 2006 congressional midterm elections, and by the spring of 2007, the top two contenders for the Democratic nomination, Hillary Rodham Clinton and Barack Obama, and eventual Republican nominee John McCain, had declared their candidacies. Lori Cox Han analyzes what she calls the "'not-so-invisible' invisible primary of 2007," referring to media coverage of the candidates before the nominating contests begin. Han examines how often major newspapers mentioned each presidential candidate in 2007, and she then focuses particularly on how significant certain demographic characteristics, namely, gender, race/ethnicity, and religion, were in coverage of four presidential candidates—Clinton, Obama, Bill Richardson, and Mitt Romney. Surprisingly, given how important some of these issues became during the nominating contests, they received little attention in 2007, and Han discusses the positive as well as cautionary lessons of this finding for American politics.

Once the nominating contests officially began, candidates had multiple venues for reaching potential supporters, and vice versa, from rallies to campaign websites to other online sources such as YouTube and blogs. Diane J. Heith examines the online resources that candidates used in the 2008 nominating contests to reach voters, and finds that they presented a significant opportunity to convey information directly and receive feedback. Candidates cannot ignore traditional media outlets, but in the twenty-first century, they must supplement that news coverage with their own initiatives to reach voters through the power of the WWW.

Winning the White House

After winning their party nomination, presidential candidates must expand their campaign strategy to prevail in the general election. Three subjects are of particular importance in this area: creation of a campaign organization and agenda; participation in presidential debates; and development of a strategy to win a majority of votes in the Electoral College.

Shirley Anne Warshaw examines how presidential candidates develop their campaign staff and policy initiatives, and she shows how the 2000 presidential race fundamentally shaped the 2008 campaign. She identifies six lessons from George W. Bush's first campaign for the White House that the Obama campaign followed closely in 2008. In particular, beginning a campaign as early as two years before election, developing a roster of well-established, experienced advisers, and identifying a short policy agenda with one overarching theme are essential strategies for candidates to develop name recognition and broad public support.

During the general-election campaign, the two major-party presidential nominees have their most visible joint performances in the debates sponsored since 1988 by the nonpartisan Commission on Presidential Debates.[5] The famous four debates between Richard M. Nixon and John F. Kennedy in 1960 received much publicity, but presidential-election debates were not repeated until 1976, when President Gerald R. Ford, in a close contest with Democratic candidate Jimmy Carter, agreed to participate in three debates (to his detriment, as it turned out, when he declared in the second debate that he did not believe Poland was under Soviet domination).[6]

Since then, presidential candidates have met at least during the campaign for a general-election debate. In recent elections, the standard has been three presidential debates—one on domestic policy, one on foreign policy, and one town-hall meeting—and one vice presidential debate, and the debates have become major campaign and media events.[7] Historian David Greenberg traces the evolution of presidential debates, and concludes that while they do not provide a road map to a candidate's agenda and leadership style, they do engage voters in learning more about the candidates and the issues at stake.

Election Day reveals how voters evaluate the presidential candidates, but the popular vote does not select the victor because of the intermediary institution of the Electoral College. This institution is unique in democratic politics worldwide, and has been the subject of much debate and criticism since the contested election of 2000, in which George W. Bush lost the popular vote to Al Gore but narrowly won the Electoral College vote after the Supreme Court case *Bush v. Gore* ruled that he should be awarded Florida's ballots. But hurdles to reform are high, as most changes would require a constitutional amendment, and many states, smaller ones in particular, have a vested interest in the current system, which gives them a voice greater than population alone would grant.[8] John C. Fortier and Timothy J. Ryan evaluate how presidential candidates can work most effectively within the current system by identifying trends in party identity in competitive "swing" states, and developing their campaign strategies accordingly.

Governing in the White House

Although presidential candidates must focus foremost on winning the election, they must give some consideration in the campaign period to how they would govern, if elected. To enact their agendas, they will have to work with Congress, and advance planning for how they will approach a Congress governed by their own political party versus a Congress governed by the opposition is necessary. In the post-9/11 era, defining U.S. national security interests and developing a strategy for combating terrorism also is essential. While other topics, such as selecting a White House staff, organizing the cabinet, developing a budget, and so forth, also merit attention in the campaign period, working with Congress and establishing a counter-terrorism strategy are particularly important in the twenty-first century.

Partisan polarization in national politics demonstrates the need to prepare a legislative strategy that accounts for variations in political control of Congress.[9] Presidential candidates will not know definitively whether their political party will govern either or both chambers of Congress until the elections, and therefore they must prepare for political obstacles as well as windows of opportunity. David A. Crockett evaluates how opportunities for presidential leadership are constrained or expanded depending on whether the new president faces unified or divided government.

In national security, determining how to protect the United States and U.S. interests at home and abroad is a fundamental concern that shapes all other priorities. During the Cold War, President Dwight D. Eisenhower's New Look strategy stated that the United States needed to combat the external threat of communism as well as the internal threat of devoting so many resources to this challenge that American values, institutions, and economic capabilities weakened.[10] This challenge of balancing national security demands with other needs continues today.[11] Christopher A. Preble analyzes the central challenge that every presidential candidate in the twenty-first century must face in identifying a long-term strategy for combating terrorism.

The comprehensive and interdisciplinary analyses presented here ground recent elections in a broader study of the enduring obstacles and challenges that presidential candidates in the twenty-first century face in running for and winning office. Together, the articles illustrate how presidential elections have evolved in recent years and the consequences of that evolution for future White House campaigns.

Notes

1. For an explanation of the evolution of presidential nominations, see John H. Aldrich, *Before the Convention: Strategies and Choice in Presidential Nomination Campaigns* (Chicago: University of Chicago Press, 1980); and Marty Cohen, David

Karol, Hans Noel, and John Zaller, *The Party Decides: Presidential Nominations Before and After Reform* (Chicago: University of Chicago Press, 2008).

2. An excellent analysis of the effects of the McCain-Feingold legislation is Michael J. Malbin, *The Election After Reform: Money, Politics, and the Bipartisan Campaign Reform Act* (New York: Rowman & Littlefield Publishers, 2006).

3. See Thomas B. Edsall and Chris Cillizza, "Money's Going to Talk in 2008," *Washington Post*, March 11, 2006. For 2007 funding totals for Clinton and Obama, see Table 3 of Victoria Farrar-Myers's article in this volume.

4. "Front-porch campaign" refers literally to presidential candidates greeting people and giving speeches on their front porches; this strategy was employed by a few presidential candidates in the nineteenth century, and presidential candidate Warren G. Harding did the same in 1920. For a vivid description of Harding's campaign, generally considered to be the last with this approach, see Frank Parker Stockbridge, "That Ideal Campaign Front Porch," *New York Times*, June 20, 1920, published in *The New York Times on the Presidency, 1853–2008*, ed. Meena Bose (Washington, D.C.: CQ Press, 2009).

5. For an explanation of the Commission's creation and its role in hosting presidential debates, see Newton N. Minow and Craig L. LaMay, *Inside the Presidential Debates: Their Improbable Past and Promising Future* (Chicago: University of Chicago Press, 2008). Also see Alan Schroeder, *The Presidential Debates: Fifty Years of High-Risk TV*, 2nd ed. (New York: Columbia University Press, 2008).

6. Minow and LaMay, *Inside the Presidential Debates*, 51.

7. When Hofstra University hosted the third debate between John McCain and Barack Obama on October 15, 2008, approximately 3,500 representatives from local, national, and international media covered the event. For more information on the many speakers and events that Hofstra hosted in connection with the debate, under the title Educate '08, see http://www.hofstra.edu/academics/educ8/index.html.

8. To understand the history and functioning of the Electoral College as well as debates about its usefulness today and proposals for reform, see Stephen J. Wayne, *The Road to the White House 2008*, 8th ed. (Boston: Thomson/Wadsworth, 2008).

9. Scholarly studies of the consequences of unified versus divided government include Keith Krehbiel, *Pivotal Politics: A Theory of U.S. Lawmaking* (Chicago: University of Chicago Press, 1998); David R. Mayhew, *Divided We Govern: Party Control, Lawmaking, and Investigations, 1946–2002*, 2nd ed. (New Haven: Yale University Press, 2002). For an analysis of how party control of Congress shapes policy making, see Gary W. Cox and Mathew D. McCubbins, *Setting the Agenda: Responsible Party Government in the U.S. House of Representatives* (New York: Cambridge University Press, 2005). The scholarly debate over political polarization is addressed in Barbara Sinclair, *Party Wars: Polarization and the Politics of National Policy Making* (Norman:

University of Oklahoma Press, 2006); and Morris P. Fiorina, with Samuel J. Abrams and Jeremy C. Pope, *Culture War? The Myth of a Polarized America*, 3rd ed. (New York: Longman, 2010).

10. For an analysis of the evolution of Eisenhower's national security strategy, see Meena Bose, *Shaping and Signaling Presidential Policy: The National Security Decision Making of Eisenhower and Kennedy* (College Station: Texas A&M University Press, 1998), ch. 1 passim.

11. John L. Gaddis presents an early assessment of the George W. Bush administration's post-9/11 national security strategy in "A Grand Strategy of Transformation," *Foreign Policy* (October/November 2002).

Navigating Presidential Nominating Contests

Inside Parties

The Politics of Earning the Presidential Nomination

LARA M. BROWN

If you see a turtle on a fence post,
chances are it didn't get there by accident.
—President William J. Clinton

Attaining the presidency involves winning two contests: a party nomination and a general election. These contests, however, are not discrete events. As John Aldrich explains, "The standard line that anyone can grow up to be president may be true, but it is true only if one grows up to be a major party nominee."[1] Given this, the question for many presidency scholars is how does a presidential aspirant win his or her political party's nomination?

Prior to the 1970s reforms, political parties were understood to be strong organizations that were directed by elites (high-level officeholders and party bosses) whose work involved knitting together a broad coalition of interests and rousing excitement among partisans.[2] Every four years, these elites—who controlled the delegate votes at the national party conventions—bestowed the presidential nomination upon an aspirant thought to be not only acceptable to a large majority of partisans and key interest groups, but appealing to the national electorate. In short, strong parties tended to favor "insiders," even when those insiders were "dark horses," or consensus solutions to deadlocked conventions (for example, James Polk in 1844). Hence, aspirants won their party's presidential nomination by being loyal to their party and its elites. This process of elite-conferred party nominations, begun in the 1830s and sustained for over a century, came under fire in Chicago in 1968.

Even though Vice President Hubert Humphrey (an insider) won his party's nomination with the support of President Lyndon Johnson and the Democratic convention delegates, he did not have the support of Democratic activists or the antiwar (Vietnam War) wing of the party.[3] Consequently, his nomination sparked protests and riots outside the convention hall, displaying to all of America—courtesy of national television coverage—not only the factional differences, but also the lopsided distribution of power (favoring elites) within the Democratic Party. The convention delegates, who understood the importance of a united party for winning the White House, attempted to appease dissenters by forming a commission to consider and propose new nomination rules. Senator George McGovern, a presidential aspirant who had challenged Humphrey for the nomination after Senator Robert F. Kennedy was assassinated in June of 1968, was named the chair. The McGovern-Fraser Commission (Representative Donald Fraser took over when McGovern decided to run for the 1972 presidential election) came forward with recommendations in 1970 that required states to ensure that delegates were chosen in the same year as the convention, give "adequate public notice" about delegate selection, include individuals as delegates who had traditionally been discriminated against (affirmative action), and use proportional representation in the awarding of pledged delegates to candidates in primaries and caucuses. In the decade following the commission's report, most states adopted presidential primaries because they ensured that the composition of the state's delegation would not be challenged by the national party as violating the "fair reflection rule."[4] The changes made to the Democratic Party's nomination process affected the Republicans because during the 1970s, the Democrats controlled many of the state legislatures that passed these laws. By 1976, more than 70 percent of national convention delegates were awarded in these types of contests.[5]

In the immediate aftermath of the reforms, an "anti-establishment" aspirant—Senator George McGovern—earned the Democratic Party's presidential nomination in 1972, and an "outsider"—Governor Jimmy Carter—gained the party's 1976 nomination. After observing these two rather raucous contests, scholars began to argue that the reforms had forced the major political parties to take a back seat to "candidate-centered campaigns," which were thought to be self-interested endeavors propelled by money, media coverage, and momentum.[6] Over time, scholars revised their analyses to incorporate the effects of front-loading (the phenomenon of more and more states moving their nominating contests earlier and earlier in the electoral cycle) and to account for the significant advantage apparently held by the "front-runners" in these nomination races.[7] Hence, aspirants in the post-reform period won their party's nomination by raising substantial sums of money, garnering favorable media attention, and winning early primary contests, like New Hampshire. Even as later studies argued that parties are "endogenous institutions"[8] directed by elites (officeholders and office-seekers), the perception that candidate-centered campaigns had weakened the parties in the post-reform period persisted.

Others—more recently—have challenged this conception of "weak" political parties being overrun by ambitious candidates and powerful national media. They have taken the position that parties are as strong as ever and that since at least the 1980 presidential election, parties have been successful in directing resources (money and endorsements, specifically) toward their "favored" presidential aspirants, thereby ensuring those aspirants their party nomination.[9] In other words, parties were only weak while they were adapting to the new nomination rules (1972 and 1976). As Cohen et al. explain: "Every nomination is a struggle, but in the past quarter century, parties have usually been able to determine the particular candidate who wins and—perhaps even more important—have never been saddled with a standard-bearer unacceptable to key constituencies within their coalition."[10] More generally, they argue that while parties are strong, they are not driven by elites (office-seekers and officeholders), but instead are directed and shaped by important activists and interest groups (stakeholders) who make demands upon the elites. As such, both before and after the reforms, presidential aspirants won their party's nomination by becoming the "favorite" of key constituents and interest groups within their party's coalition.

While all of these theories identify and describe critical elements in the presidential nomination process, none addresses a central question, which is not only the focus of this essay but turns out to be the bridge between these competing claims: If party "insiders" (variously named party "favorites," "front-runners," and in earlier eras, "dark horses") tend to win nominations more often than "outsiders," then how does a presidential aspirant become a party "insider"? This essay offers an answer, which serendipitously was one of the major themes of the 2008 presidential nomination contest: political experience. Extending and applying some of David Rohde's findings about "progressive ambition" among congressional members[11] to presidential aspirants, it presents a few quantitative models that suggest that while an aspirant's political experience matters, specific types of experiences matter more than others. While this study does not delve deeply into what it means conceptually for successful aspirants to be "opportunists,"[12] it does assert that opportunists, aspirants possessing at least half as much breadth (number of positions sought and held) as depth (number of years of service) of political experience, fare better in presidential nomination contests than those who are not opportunists. Hence, even though presidential nomination contests are often riotous affairs, the experiential profiles of the presidential aspirants provide some clues as to the identity of the likely winners, and the 2008 presidential nomination contest was no exception.

Understanding Aspirant Opportunism through Political Experience

Considering the structure of opportunities in the political system alongside Schlesinger's ambition theory,[13] it seems appropriate to assume that the vast majority of presidential aspirants prior to the 1970s reforms were much like today's aspirants—inordinately ambitious individuals who were aiming toward the White House from nearly the time they entered politics.[14] Even a somewhat cursory reading of history supports this intuition.[15] If we assume, however, that all presidential aspirants are ambitious and that they have been working for years to become a party insider, then what differentiates the successful aspirants from the unsuccessful ones? Who makes it to the inside?

Reflecting back on the elections and considering only those who ran, presidential aspirants appear to have differed in their ability to perceive and capitalize on the electoral conditions and political events which occur during their political careers. Those most capable of turning exogenous factors and unforeseen occurrences to their favor seem to have been the most likely to succeed. Those most able to "control the political definition of their actions" and alter the "terms of debate"[16] before they reached the presidency seem to have been the most likely to earn their party's nomination. In this sense, these "opportunists" seem to have been practiced "heresthicians" who, as William H. Riker described, "win because they have set up the situation in such a way that other people will want to join them—will feel forced by circumstances to join them—even without any persuasion at all."[17]

More broadly then, the relationship between aspirant ambition and opportunism appears similar to that which exists between intelligence and wisdom. Ambition appears to be necessary, but not sufficient to win.

In sum, presidential aspirants appear to vary on their level of opportunism, not their level, amount, or type of ambition. While some are likely innate opportunists (perceptive, creative, flexible, resilient), it seems more reasonable to conclude that most acquire their abilities over time, through practice—and, at times, through failure. But as Riker aptly notes: "The novice heresthetician must learn by practice how to go about managing and manipulating and maneuvering to get the decisions he or she wants. Practice is, however, difficult to engage in, especially since one often must win often enough to become a political leader before one has much opportunity to practice."[18] Thus, while an aspirant's prior political experience or career path may not provide a complete portrait of his or her level of opportunism, this essay posits that it may yet help explain an aspirant's electoral success or failure.[19]

David Rohde's study on "risk-bearing and progressive ambition" further suggests how one might measure an aspirant's level of opportunism, using political experience: "House members seeking higher office served about one and one-half terms less than the average House member."[20] Said another way, politicians who pursue political opportunities—even potentially risky ones—tend not to possess particularly high levels of institutional seniority. Whether these politicians leave their positions "prematurely"— take risks—because they perceive lower risks in the environment or they are willing to accept higher risks than others is unclear. Nevertheless, they do appear to systematically spend less time in their positions than others. Combining this fact with another idea offered in the same article by Rohde, that "it is possible to employ previous behavior as an indicator of risk taking,"[21] this study hypothesizes that the aspirants who win their party's nomination are "opportunists," or those who possess at least half as much breadth (number of positions sought and held) as depth (number of years of service) of political experience. Defined more precisely, "opportunists" possess a level of opportunism (breadth of experience relative to his or her depth of experience) that is at or above the mean level of opportunism for all presidential aspirants (0.50).

Operationalizing Aspirant Opportunism

Given that the interest of this research is what type of aspirant wins, rather than who runs or which office most leads to success, the data set consists of those who actively sought the presidency or were acknowledged presidential aspirants between 1796 and 2004, including some third-party candidates.[22] There are a total of 353 presidential aspirants: 191 Democrats, 144 Republicans, and 18 independent or third-party aspirants.[23] Since the data set is comprised of presidential aspirants some individuals have multiple entries (for example, Henry Clay was a presidential aspirant in five elections and he has five separate entries). As major-party nominations are the focus of this essay, the quantitative analyses presented exclude independent or third-party aspirants.[24] Prior to discussing the variables and reviewing the estimates, Table 1 provides a few summary statistics, including the mean level of opportunism and the percentage of opportunists in different groups of presidential aspirants. Evident from these numbers are the patterns that emerge: as the electoral cycle progresses and the number of aspirants are winnowed down to the "finalists" (major-party nominees) and the "winners" (presidents), the mean level of opportunism and the percentage of opportunists within those cohorts also increase. Hence, the electoral cycle appears to favor aspirant opportunism.

As has been alluded to previously, the dependent variable employed below is a dummy variable for winning or losing a party's presidential nomination (1 = won, 0 = lost). While the cross-tabulations show the probabilities of winning and losing associated with being an opportunist, the nomination models explore the effects of seven independent variables on winning: breadth of political experience, depth of political experience,

Table 1 – Descriptive Statistics of the Presidential Aspirants, 1796–2004

Cases 1796–2004 Percent (%) Opportunists	N Mean (SD)	Breadth Mean (SD)	Depth Mean (SD)	Opportunism Mean (SD)
All aspirants 48.7	353	7.2 (3.9)	16.1 (9.4)	0.50 (0.3)
Major-party aspirants 49.3	335	7.4 (3.8)	16.2 (9.2)	0.51 (0.3)
All nominees 65.3	121	8.0 (4.2)	15.0 (9.5)	0.59 (0.3)
Major-party nominees 68.6	105	8.4 (4.1)	15.5 (9.2)	0.63 (0.3)
All presidents 75.0	52	91 (4.4)	16.0 (8.9)	0.64 (0.3)

Source: Data compiled by author.

Note: The above table omits five cases that were outliers (beyond +/- three standard deviations from the mean) on the opportunism variable in the data set because they were not included in either the cross-tabulations or the regression models presented below (for further explanation, see note 11).

whether or not the aspirant was an opportunist, the level of aspirant opportunism, whether or not the aspirant was the incumbent president, whether or not the aspirant had made a run for the presidency before (incumbents were excluded from this measure), and whether or not the aspirant was or had been either a vice president, a cabinet member, or a governor.[25]

Political experience is measured two ways—breadth and depth. Breadth of political experience is operationalized as the total number of political positions sought and held by an aspirant prior to running for the presidency.[26] It includes an aspirant's electoral campaigns, whether won or lost (but not reelections) along with appointed and elected political positions at the federal and state level (mayors are the only local office included). Campaigns are included in this breadth measure because aspirants gain political experience by running for office, even when they lose. Reelections (aside from incumbent presidential campaigns) are not counted because they rarely provide aspirants with either a significant challenge or a substantial amount of new information about politics.[27] Hence, an aspirant earns one point of breadth for running and one point for serving, meaning that an aspirant who runs for governor and wins, receives two points of breadth, while an aspirant who runs and loses, receives one point of breadth. Depth of political experience is measured as the total number of years of service in the above described political offices. This means that in the above example of the governor who won, assuming that he served a four-year term before he ran for president, he would have two points of breadth and four years of depth. This depth variable counts any fractional years of service (months) as one year, in part because for many aspirants the exact dates of political service were not available.

Opportunism is derived from these experience variables and it is operationalized as an aspirant's breadth of experience relative to his or her depth of experience (breadth/depth). As one might imagine given the brief discussion about the concept of opportunism and Rohde's findings, there are both theoretical and technical reasons for coding opportunism in this manner. On the technical side, it allows for a more thorough examination of the data because as one would expect, breadth and depth are significantly correlated (Pearson's $r = 0.59$, $p < 0.01$). It also allows for a comparison of presidential aspirants across political eras because it standardizes the political experience of all aspirants, which is important given that over time, both the breadth and depth of experience among presidential aspirants have declined. For example, aspirants who ran prior to the Civil War (n = 78) possessed a mean breadth of about ten points and a mean depth of about twenty-one years, while aspirants who ran between 1972 and 2004 (n = 114) possessed a mean breadth of less than six points and a mean depth of less than fifteen years.[28] On the theoretical side, it captures three substantive claims, directly relevant to the larger concept of aspirant opportunism: (1) that those aspirants who have more breadth than depth are more adept in politics because they have experience from multiple vantage points and, as such, are more likely to perceive political opportunities and be capable of turning events and conditions to their favor;[29] (2) that the longer one remains in office, the more secure one is of holding it (incumbency advantage), and as a result, aspirants who have this type of experience (for example, long-serving senators who have run for the presidency) may be less likely to perceive opportunities or turn them to their advantage; and (3) that the more breadth an aspirant has, the more he or she might be considered a "risk-taker," or a politician who is more inclined to attempt success, rather than avoid failure, and that being a "risk-taker" helps one win. Hence, successful aspirants are those who would rather be—paraphrasing Theodore Roosevelt—in the arena, losing, than on the sidelines, watching without even the possibility of winning before them.[30] That said, the number of political positions sought and held relative to the number of years of service in those positions is an imperfect measure of opportunism because it does not account for other natural abilities of the aspirants (for example, resiliency, flexibility, and creativity) or acquired abilities (for example, fundraising prowess, rhetorical eloquence, negotiating expertise, mastery of procedural rules, and codes of conduct). Still, it is an objective and replicable measure that allows for an initial exploration into a much broader, richer concept and provides some insight into the level of opportunism of the presidential aspirants (temperament and behavioral inclination). As mentioned previously, an opportunist is defined in this study as an aspirant who possesses a level of opportunism at 0.50 or above (opportunist = 1, non-opportunist = 0), which is the mean level for all presidential aspirants in the data set.[31]

Incumbent presidents were coded with a dichotomous variable (1 = incumbent, 0 = non-incumbent). Similarly, a dummy variable (1 = yes, 0 = no) was created for those aspirants who had made previous attempts to win the office. So that it captured a phenomenon other than incumbency, incumbents were excluded—coded as zero—on this measure. This, however, does not mean that once an aspirant has been president, they are always coded as zero. Both Grover Cleveland and Theodore Roosevelt alternated between zeros and ones over the course of the data set. In 1884, Cleveland received a zero because he had not run before; in 1888, he received a zero because he was the incumbent; and in 1892, he received a one because he had run before, but was no longer the incumbent. Theodore Roosevelt's numbers were similarly assigned.

Another dummy variable serves to distinguish the prior offices attained by the aspirant. Given the history of numerous vice presidents, cabinet members, and governors succeeding to the presidency, it seemed appropriate to try to capture the advantage enjoyed by aspirants who either are or were in one of those three positions. This measure did not attempt to distinguish between those currently in office and those who had formerly held the office or those who had served in more than one of these offices, nor did it aim to sort out the possible differential advantages of these positions. It simply served to divide the dataset into two groups of aspirants: those who may be considered the "most qualified" successor to the current incumbent by virtue of their office and historical tradition, and those aspirants who are challenging that paradigm (1 = yes, 0 = no). Though dummy variables were constructed for senators (1 = yes, 0 = no) and members of the House of Representatives (1 = yes, 0 = no), when they were included in the models, the coefficients were not statistically significant and they were omitted from the models presented here.[32] A few additional variables related to an aspirant's background that were suggested by previous studies on "progressive ambition"[33] (for example, size and competitiveness of the aspirant's home state) were either tested and omitted because they were not significant in the models, or they were not included because of how they were constructed in those studies.[34]

The Impact of Political Experience and Aspirant Opportunism on Elections

The overall findings suggest that the political experience and level of opportunism of the aspirants matter in presidential nominations. Table 2 presents the cross-tabulations of the nomination by opportunist variables. Table 3 presents the coefficients from three logistic regression models where the dependent variable is again whether or not the aspirant won the nomination: one equation includes breadth and depth of experience variables, the second equation uses the dichotomous opportunist variable, and the third equation includes the level-of-opportunism variable.[35]

Table 2 – Cross-tabulations of Nomination by Opportunist
(major-party aspirants)

Nomination	Opportunist (Dichotomous)		
	Yes (N)	No (N)	Totals (N)
Yes	69%	31%	31%
	(72)	(33)	(105)
No	40%	60%	69%
	(93)	(137)	(230)
Totals	100%	100%	100%
	(165)	(170)	(335)

Note: Statistics do not include John Quincy Adams in 1824 because he was not the
"King Caucus" nominee (William Crawford earned the nomination).
Nomination statistics (SPSS generated):
     Pearson chi-square = 22.83**
     Likelihood ratio: 23.23**
     Somer's d with nomination (0 = no; 1 = yes) as dependent = 0.24 (t = 4.93)
* = significant to the 0.05 level (two-tail test), ** = significant to the 0.01 level (two-tail test)

    The findings from the cross-tabulations in Table 2 reveal that there are statistically significant differences between opportunists and non-opportunists in terms of the likelihood of winning the nomination. Even though there were nearly an equal number of opportunists and non-opportunists (165 and 170, respectively) in the data, approximately 69 percent of the 105 winners are opportunists, while about 60 percent of the 230 losers are not opportunists. Hence, a nomination winner is about 38 percent more likely to be an opportunist than a non-opportunist; a nomination loser is approximately 20 percent more likely to be a non-opportunist than an opportunist. These statistics are especially interesting when one considers that less than one-third (105) of the 335 major party aspirants win.

    In Table 3, all of the independent variables in the three models reach statistical significance with the exception of the aspirant's office variable in Models 2 and 3. In Model 1, breadth of experience, incumbency, a previous presidential run, and the aspirant's office (vice president, governor, or cabinet member) are all positively correlated with winning the nomination, while depth of experience is negatively correlated. The constant is also negative and statistically significant, suggesting that an aspirant is more likely to lose his or her party's nomination than to win. This should not

Table 3 – Effects of Political Experience on Winning the Nomination

Variable Name	Model 1 (Major-party Members, 1796–2004)	Model 2 (Major-party Members, 1796–2004)	Model 3 (Major-party Members, 1796–2004)
Dependent variable: Dummy variable measuring winning or losing the party's nomination			
Constant	1.39*** (0.32)	-2.01*** (0.25)	-2.46*** (0.32)
Breadth of Experience	0.10** (0.05)		
Depth of Experience	(0.02)	0.06***	--
Opportunist (dichotomous)	-- (0.28)	0.83***	--
Opportunism (ratio)	--	--	1.65*** (1.04)
Incumbent President	3.56*** (0.61)	3.37*** (0.58)	3.46*** (0.58)
Previous Presidential Run	0.87*** (0.30)	0.88*** (0.30)	0.94*** (0.30)
Aspirant's Office (Governor, Vice President, Cabinet Member)	0.52* (0.29)	0.43 (0.29)	0.38 (0.29)

Percent of cases correct:	77.6	75.5	78.2
Number of cases:	335	335	335
-2 Log Likelihood:	336.97	338.57	334.02
Cox and Snell r-squared:	0.21	0.21	0.22

NOTE: Figures are logistic regression coefficients (SPSS generated). Standard errors are in parentheses.

* = significance at $p < 0.10$, ** = significance at $p < 0.05$, *** = significance at $p < 0.01$ (two-tailed tests)

be surprising given that there were 335 major-party aspirants and 230 of them lost their party's nomination.[36] The magnitude of the incumbency variable is the largest at 3.56 ($p < 0.01$), suggesting that incumbents are substantially favored to win their party's nomination.

The breadth of political experience coefficient is positive and statistically significant (0.10, $p < 0.05$), suggesting that an aspirant who has held and sought more political positions is more likely to win his or her party's nomination than an aspirant who has sought and held fewer political positions. Aligning with Rohde's findings,[37] the depth of political experience coefficient is negative and statistically significant (-0.06, $p < 0.01$), meaning that an aspirant who has served for longer periods in political offices is less likely to win his or her party's nomination than one who has served for shorter periods.[38] Though the magnitudes of these variables are relatively small, when the means and the standard deviations are considered, these coefficients likely possess more substantive impact. Model 2 replaces these experience variables with the dichotomous opportunist variable in the equation. As expected, it is both positive and statistically significant (0.83, $p < 0.01$). Model 3 substitutes the dummy opportunist variable for the ratio level-of-opportunism measure. Contemplating this latter equation further, it is intriguing that aside from the constant and the incumbency variables, the level-of-opportunism variable is the next largest in magnitude.

Taken together, the findings from the three models suggest that breadth of experience is an asset, while depth is a liability and that a favorable ratio (including, especially, one above the mean of 0.50) between these two types of political experiences helps an aspirant win his or her party's nomination. As mentioned earlier, it may be that depth of experience promotes rigidity and narrow-mindedness, while breadth of experience encourages flexibility and agility. It also may be that those who are more opportunistic—flexible, creative, perceptive—are also more likely to self-select into more positions, pursuing more breadth and less depth in their careers. Either way, which neither Rohde's data nor mine can answer (because the motivations driving the behavior are hidden), those aspirants who have sought and held more positions, and held them for relatively shorter periods, appear to be advantaged when they run for their party's nomination.

In all three models, the coefficients for having run for the presidency before are also fairly large and statistically significant (0.87, $p < 0.01$; 0.88, $p < 0.01$; and 0.94, $p < 0.01$, respectively), meaning that an aspirant who made a previous attempt is more likely to win his or her party's nomination than one who has not. The substantive implications of this may be that: (1) successful aspirants learn from their mistakes, and (2) previous attempts may help them to become more known outside of their home state or the nation's capital, or both. Interestingly, this suggests that winning a party's presidential nomination is a challenging task and that only those aspirants who tenaciously, even resiliently, pursue their ambitions are likely to achieve them. While the aspirant's office variable reaches statistical significance in Model 1, it does not appear to be a significant variable in either Model 2 or Model 3. Overall, these equations imply, albeit tentatively and inconclusively, that the *actual* experience of an aspirant (a previous presidential run, whether or not he or she is an opportunist, and level of opportunism) matters more than the *perceived* experience of an aspirant (whether or not an aspirant was a governor or vice president or cabinet member), leaving aside incumbents who may benefit from both their actual and perceived level of experience. Thus, opportunism appears to matter.

Opportunistic Aspirants and the 2008 Presidential Nomination Contests

Since the reforms of the 1970s, the modern presidential nomination process has been marked by one major unintended consequence, stemming from the proliferation of primaries: front-loading, or the propensity of more and more states to schedule their nomination contests early in the electoral cycle.[39] Front-loading tends to increase the cost of elections, stretch the length of the electoral cycle, compress the decisive time frame, and depress turnout in the states that come later in the process. As was noted, it also helps lock in party "favorites" (often party insiders) who lead in the early public opinion polls, amass large numbers of elite endorsements, receive ample media coverage, and raise substantial sums during the period known as the "invisible primary."[40] Thus, aspirants in today's system must start early to become a party "favorite" and be fast on their feet—opportunistic—in order to maintain their "front-running" position.

While the 2008 presidential nomination races were more competitive than they had been in decades, each party's "favorite" who garnered favorable momentum from media coverage and early contest wins still won. While neither party's presidential nominee (Senators John McCain and

Table 4 – The Experiential Profile of the 2008 Major-party Aspirants*

	Breadth (points)	Depth (years)	Prior Run for President	Party for President	"Favorite"
Republicans					
Giuliani	4	16	0.25	X	
Huckabee	4	14	0.29		
Hunter	2	28	0.07		
McCain	5	28	0.18	X	X
Romney	3	4	0.75	X	
Thompson	2	8	0.25		
Democrats					
Biden	3	36	0.08	X	
Clinton**	6	16	0.38	X	X
Dodd	4	34	0.12		
Edwards	4	6	0.67	X	X
Kucinich	6	15	0.40	X	
Obama	5	12	0.42	X	
Richardson	7	25	0.28		

Source: Calculated from the "career" data available at CNN Election Center 2008, http://www.cnn. com/ELECTION/2008/primaries

* = Republican aspirant Ron Paul and Democratic aspirant Mike Gravel have been omitted from the above table because neither aspirant was considered a serious contender.

** = Senator Clinton's past service as First Lady are included in her breadth and depth scores, and her husband's election and reelection to the presidency are counted as though she had been the candidate.

Barack Obama) were officially "opportunists" (with level-of-opportunism scores above 0.50), both possessed experiential profiles, which at the outset of the race should have suggested to interested observers that they would be formidable aspirants in their respective fields (see Table 4).

On the Republican side, Senator John McCain secured his party's nomination. Early on, he was thought the front-runner because he had support from several of incumbent President George W. Bush's former campaign staff, but after some initial missteps (namely not raising enough money and spending too much of what was raised) he fell from the top spot.

While he remained a Republican favorite, few thought that his campaign reorganization would be sufficient. Senator McCain, however, had run for president before and as the model above suggests, his prior political experience may have helped him overcome the setback. Embracing the opportunities in the political environment, he capitalized on his newly acquired underdog status in the media, the fractured and somewhat dispirited conservative electorate (who were split between former governors Mike Huckabee of Arkansas and Mitt Romney of Massachusetts), and his relatively inexperienced political opponents.[41] While McCain was propelled forward by momentum after his win in the New Hampshire primary, he was also prepared to move beyond New Hampshire. He reached out to military families and with their help he prevailed in South Carolina, which became a turning point in the Republican race.[42] Thus, Senator McCain's path to the nomination appears to fit with both what we know about the front-loaded dynamics of modern contests[43] and about the types of aspirants—opportunistic party insiders—who tend to win their party's nomination.[44]

On the Democratic side, Senators Barack Obama and Hillary Clinton competitively fought through June of 2008 for the party's presidential nomination. While Senator Obama appeared to have benefited more from momentum than Senator Clinton (his standing in national polls increased by about 20 percent from the time he began winning contests in January), both candidates enjoyed bursts of momentum at different stages of the contest. For example, Senator Clinton's campaign rebounded after her win in New Hampshire, while Senator Obama's campaign was boosted after his win in South Carolina. Not insignificantly, when one considers these aspirants' level-of-opportunism scores and the Democratic field more broadly, it is clear that both were in the Democratic top tier (see Table 4). Senator Obama's level-of-opportunism score (0.42) ranks second to former senator John Edwards who had been the Democratic Party's vice presidential nominee in 2004. Further, Senator Clinton, as the spouse of former president Bill Clinton, had been intimately involved with two prior presidential campaigns that were successful ("First Lady" is included in her breadth and depth scores as though it were the equivalent of a cabinet member position). In short, while her level-of-opportunism score (0.38) is only slightly above the mean score of the 2008 Democratic field (0.34), like Senator McCain, her experience in previous presidential contests probably provided her with a leg up on some of her opponents, including Governor Bill Richardson of New Mexico. Beyond this, it was clear from the beginning that Senators Clinton (the "front-runner") and Obama, and former senator Edwards were the favorites of different demographic factions within the Democratic Party's coalition (Jacksonian traditionalists; well-educated liberal elites and minorities concentrated in urban areas; and ideological progressives particularly concerned with social justice issues, respectively). Senators Clinton and Obama developed substantial campaign organizations before the lead-off contest in Iowa, which included each of them raising over $100 million in 2007. Thus, it is not surprising that the nomination race came down to Senators Clinton and Obama, or that former senator Edwards effectively placed third.

While the level-of-opportunism scores for the aspirants in Table 4 incorrectly suggest that former governor Romney and former senator Edwards should have prevailed in their contests (they not only have high scores, but they are the only two in both fields of aspirants who would be classified as "opportunists"), both were serious contenders for their party's nomination, coming in third overall (behind Huckabee and Clinton, respectively). Moreover, had Romney and Edwards won the Iowa caucuses rather than each of them placing second (as they both had intended), a strong case could be made that these individuals would most probably have secured their respective party nominations. The only other level of opportunism score that does not fit comfortably with the historical outcomes is that of Representative Dennis Kucinich of Ohio (0.40). Representative Kucinich possesses an experiential profile that suggests that he should have done quite well (he had run before and his level of opportunism score ranks third—above Senator Clinton). Unfortunately, the experiential profile of the aspirants does not include a variable measuring ideological extremism, which would likely improve significantly the predictive capacity of the above models and is likely one of the major reasons for Representative Kucinich's failure.

One of the few surprises from the 2008 nomination cycle was how moderate the boosts of momentum were, given how front-loaded the contests were across the country. Five states (not including Florida and Michigan, whose contests were not sanctioned by the national parties) [45] held contests in January, and more than twenty contests were held on February 5, or Super Tuesday. By the end of February, forty-three contests had taken place. This is vastly different from the 2000 election, when only twelve contests had been held by that time. It was long assumed that the compactness of the 2008 calendar would mean that the nomination races would wrap up by early February—weeks earlier than they had in years with competitive races. This, however, did not occur. In fact, during the month of January, on the Republican side, three different aspirants—Huckabee, McCain, and Romney—won the first five contests. Similarly, Senators Obama and Clinton alternated wins throughout the month.

While Super Tuesday winnowed the Republican field down to Senator McCain, it did little to clarify the winner on the Democratic side. Senator Clinton handily won most of the large states (for example, New York, New Jersey, Massachusetts and California), while Senator Obama won more states overall. The popular vote was nearly evenly split, as were the number of delegates. Senator Obama went on to win eleven contests (including "Democrats abroad") during the month of February. While Senator Clinton came back to win Ohio and Texas in March and Pennsylvania in April, Senator Obama eventually drew the majority of superdelegates to his candidacy by the final contests in June. Even though Senator Obama was not an "opportunist," like McCain, he engaged in several opportunistic maneuvers throughout the contests. Not only did he and his campaign realize early on that if he won the "small" state, lower-turnout, caucus contests (for example, Idaho and North Dakota) and placed second within the "big" state, larger-turnout primaries (for example, Ohio and Pennsylvania), he would secure as many, if not more, pledged delegates than if he did the reverse. He and his campaign also realized that the cumulative total of his wins in the larger number of small states would be perceived as him running a successful campaign, and that those wins would sustain his momentum until he had secured the nomination through the delegate math. Further, he and his campaign worked in the background to secure the support of former senator Edwards and Governor Richardson after they dropped out of the contests, and to ensure that the Democratic Party's elites waited to resolve the Michigan and Florida controversy until the end of the nomination period.[46] Thus, Senator Obama's relatively high level of opportunism (0.42 and ranking second in the 2008 Democratic field of aspirants) accurately suggests that political observers should have known that he was an aspirant to watch from the time he entered the race.

Conclusions

After reviewing some of the scholarly debate in the literature on political parties, this essay has presented findings from a few quantitative models that offer some insights into the intra-party competitions that surround the presidential nomination contests. The equations suggest that the political background of an aspirant—that is, the breadth and depth of political experience, the level of opportunism, the offices held, the incumbency status, and a prior presidential run—matters in terms of who wins and who loses their party's nomination. More specifically, the models indicate that depth of political experience—if it is not tempered with sufficient breadth of political experience—may negatively affect an aspirant's chances of securing the nomination. Further, they tentatively suggest that the *actual* experience of an aspirant (a previous presidential run and his or her level of opportunism) matters less than the *perceived* experience of an aspirant (whether or not an aspirant was a governor or vice president or cabinet member), leaving aside incumbents who may benefit from both their actual and perceived level of experience.

This essay has also discussed the 2008 nomination contests within the context of the models, and asserted that while the competition over the course of this cycle has been greater than in most years, the front-runners and/or the top-tier candidates (party insiders) were still favored. Importantly, those aspirants' political backgrounds also indicate that they should have been favored in the nomination contests because they possessed some experiential advantages that their opponents did not. Senator McCain had run before. Senator Clinton had viewed the political system from several different vantage points (spouse of a governor, spouse of a presidential aspirant, First Lady, and U.S. senator from New York—only former representative, ambassador, energy secretary, and governor Bill Richardson had viewed the political system from a similar number of places). Senator Obama had approximately twelve years of political experience combined with three unique campaigns during that period of time (state senate, U.S. House, and U.S. Senate), which suggests that he possesses a rather high propensity for risk-taking, especially when compared with the depth of experience of his fellow senators Joseph Biden of Delaware and Christopher Dodd of Connecticut. Moreover, the experiential profiles of the aspirants also reveal those who were likely to fare poorly in the nomination contests, like Representative Duncan Hunter of California and Senator Dodd. Thus, while the intra-party competition for the presidential nomination between aspirants is often riotous, with continual jockeying and gamesmanship, the experiential profiles of the presidential aspirants provide some early clues as to the identity of the likely winners.

Acknowledgments

The author wishes to thank James Pfiffner for his ongoing and invaluable support with this research; Todd Belt, Victoria Farrar-Myers, Lilly Goren, Wayne Steger, and Stephen Wayne for their feedback on earlier and related drafts; Ellen Meeker for her research assistance, and James Lo for his assistance with the statistical tests of the quantitative models. I would also like to thank Meena Bose for organizing the conference at Hofstra University and for editing the resultant volume, along with the anonymous peer reviewers for Texas A&M University Press, who provided constructive feedback, which helped me revise and condense the salient analyses. Some portions of this essay overlap with my previously published work and my forthcoming book, see Brown (2008). I would like to further acknowledge both *Congress and the Presidency* and Cambria Press for granting the copyright permissions.

Notes

Former president Bill Clinton invoked the saying quoted in the chapter epigraph numerous times over the course of his political career. See, for example, Douglas Jehl, "The Campaigner in Chief Alternately Defends His Record and Looks Ahead," *New York Times*, November 6, 1994.

1. John H. Aldrich, *Before the Convention: Strategies and Choices in Presidential Nomination Campaigns* (Chicago: University of Chicago Press, 1980), 5.

2. For example, see V. O. Key, *Politics, Parties, and Pressure Groups*, 5th ed. (New York: Crowell, 1964); Frank Sorauf, *Party Politics in America* (Boston: Little, Brown, 1964); Samuel J. Eldersveld, *Political Parties: A Behavioral Analysis* (New York: Wiley, 1964) and *Political Parties in American Society* (New York: Basic Books, 1982); and Barbara Hershey and Paul Allen Beck, *Party Politics in America*, 10th ed. (New York: Longman, 2003).

3. On the final ballot, Humphrey earned over one thousand delegates more than Senator George McGovern and Senator Eugene McCarthy (both antiwar candidates) combined.

4. The reform commission proposed "a rule requiring that all states represent these particular groups (African Americans, women, and youth) in reasonable relationship to their presence in the state population . . . [while the rule] was subsequently modified . . . beginning with its 1980 nominating convention, the party required that each state delegation be equally divided between the sexes," according to Stephen J. Wayne,

The Road to the White House, 2004: The Politics of Presidential Elections (Belmont, Cal.: Thomson/Wadsworth Learning, 2004), 106.

5. Larry Bartels, *Presidential Primaries and the Dynamics of Public Choice* (Princeton, N.J.: Princeton University Press, 1988), 20.

6. For example, see Aldrich, *Before the Convention*; Thomas E. Patterson, The *Mass Media Election: How Americans Choose Their President* (New York: Praeger, 1980); Nelson W. Polsby, *Consequences of Party Reform* (New York: Oxford University Press, 1983); Gary R. Orren and Nelson W. Polsby, eds., *Media and Momentum: The New Hampshire Primary and Nomination Politics* (Chatham, N.J.: Chatham House, 1987); Alan I. Abramowitz, "Candidate Choice Before the Convention," *Political Behavior* 9 (1987), 49–61; and Bartels, *Presidential Primaries.*

7. For example, see William G. Mayer, "The Basic Dynamics of the Presidential Nomination Process: Putting the 2000 Races in Perspective," *Presidential Studies Quarterly* 33, no.1 (March 2003), 72–100; William G. Mayer, ed., *The Making of the Presidential Candidates 2004*, (New York: Rowman & Littlefield, 2004); William G. Mayer and Andrew E. Busch, *The Front-Loading Problem in Presidential Nominations* (Washington, D.C.: Brookings Institution Press, 2004); and Nelson Polsby and Aaron Wildavsky, *Presidential Elections: Strategies and Structures of American Politics*, 11th ed. (Lanham, Md.: Rowman & Littlefield, 2004). Andrew Busch and William Mayer aptly note: "Of all the candidates who have been nominated since 1980, every one of them can plausibly be regarded as, if not the frontrunner, at least one of the top-tier candidates" (*The Front-Loading Problem*, p. 23).

8. John H. Aldrich, *Why Parties? The Origin and Transformation of Political Parties in America* (Chicago: University of Chicago Press, 1995), 4.

9. Marty Cohen, Hans Noel, David Karol, and John Zaller, "Polls or Pols: The Real Driving Force behind Presidential Nominations," *Brookings Review* 3 (Summer 2003), 36–39; Cohen, et al., "Political Parties in Rough Weather," *Forum* 5 (2008), Issue 4, Article 3, available at: http://works.bepress.com/martin_cohen/1; Cohen, et al., *The Party Decides: Presidential Nominations Before and After Reform* (Chicago: University of Chicago Press, 2008).

10. Cohen, et al., "Political Parties in Rough Weather," 1.

11. David Rohde, "Risk-Bearing and Progressive Ambition: The Case of Members of the United States House of Representatives." *American Journal of Political Science* 23, no. 1 (February 1979), 1–26.

12. See Lara M. Brown, *Jockeying for the American Presidency: The Political Opportunism of Aspirants* (Amherst, N.Y.: Cambria Press, forthcoming).

13. Joseph A. Schlesinger, *Ambition and Politics: Political Careers in the United States* (Chicago: Rand McNally, 1966).

14. John H. Aldrich concludes similarly that aspirants have not changed. See

his "Presidential Selection," in *Researching the Presidency: Vital Questions, New Approaches*, George C. Edwards III, John H. Kessel, and Bert A. Rockman, eds. (Pittsburgh: University of Pittsburgh Press, 1993), 173.

15. For a brief description of each presidential campaign until 1960, and the presidential aspirants who were involved, see Rexford Tugwell, *How They Became President: Thirty-five Ways to the White House* (New York: Simon & Schuster, 1964).

16. Stephen Skowronek, *The Politics Presidents Make: Leadership from John Adams to George Bush* (Cambridge: Harvard University Press, 1993), 19–21.

17. William H. Riker, *The Art of Political Manipulation* (New Haven: Yale University Press, 1986), ix.

18. Ibid.

19. For a more thorough discussion of the concept of aspirant opportunism, see Lara M. Brown, *Jockeying for the American Presidency*.

20. Rohde, "Risk-Bearing and Progressive Ambition," 20.

21. Ibid., 14.

22. The eighteen third-party and independent candidates included in this study were those who either earned electoral votes or were more successful than was expected in earning popular votes. They were: John Floyd (1832), William Wirt (1832), Millard Fillmore (1856), John Bell (1860), James Weaver (1892), Theodore Roosevelt (1912), Robert La Follette (1924), Strom Thurmond (1948), Harry Byrd (1960), George Wallace (1968), John Schmitz (1972), John Hospers (1972), John Anderson (1980), Ross Perot (1992), Ross Perot (1996), Ralph Nader (2000), Patrick Buchanan (2000), and Ralph Nader (2004).

23. For coding purposes, Republicans include Federalists, National Democrats, and Whigs. Democrats include Jeffersonian Republicans. Also, despite the many varied ideological claims of independent and third-party candidates over the course of history, all of them were coded as though they were members of one party. While the data set actually possesses a total of 358 aspirants, when one reviews the distribution of the opportunism variable, it has a positive skew. The mean is 0.527; the median is 0.477; and the modes are 0 and 0.50 (twenty cases at each mode). There are five cases that are outliers (beyond +/- three standard deviations from the mean, or between -0.559 and 1.613). While some have suggested transforming the variable to reduce the positive skew, it makes more sense from a theoretical perspective to omit the five outliers, and then proceed with the analysis, which is what this study has done. Once this is done, the distribution of the opportunism approaches normal (mean is 0.504; the median is 0.492; and the modes are 0 and 0.50 (twenty cases at each mode). The reason is that those cases of high levels of opportunism (all five cases have values of 2.00 or more) are owing to the fact that those individuals each possessed one year in government, but had two (or more) points for breadth. For example, California

governor Ronald Reagan in 1968 was considered an aspirant for the Republican nomination. His opportunism score that year is "2.00" because while he had run successfully for governor in 1966, which gave him "2" points of breadth, he had only served in office since January 1967. Hence, as attractive as he may have been at the time to some partisans as a Republican "comer," he was mostly a "celebrity," which this variable is not aiming to capture (see related discussion about military service in note 26).

24. Quantitative models describing the general elections are found in Brown, *Jockeying for the American Presidency.* While some models are also offered in Brown, "Around Closed Doors and through Open Windows: A Theory of Aspirant Opportunism, 1796–2004," *Congress and the Presidency* 36, no. 1 (March 2008), 1–26, the models have been revised, taking into account the five outliers that had previously distorted some of the findings. Thus, the models included in this study and in Jockeying for the American Presidency should take precedence over earlier versions found in Brown (see "Around Closed Doors" and "The Presidential Problem: Presidential Aspirants and the Disconnect in the Modern Selection Process," paper presented at the American Political Science Association Annual Conference in Chicago, August 30–September 2, 2007).

25. Other "aspirant trait" variables were explored and the findings were not significant. As such, they were omitted from the analysis.

26. The data on the breadth and depth of political experience of the presidential aspirants come from one main biographical reference: James T. Havel's *U.S. Presidential Candidates and Elections, a Biographical and Historical Guide,* two volumes (New York: Macmillan Library Reference, 1966), but some other sources were useful as well, including Joseph Nathan Kane, *Facts About the Presidents,* fifth ed. (H. W. Wilson, 1989); Irving Stone, *They Also Ran: The Story of the Men Who Were Defeated for the Presidency* (New York: Signet Books, 1966[1943]), and the Biographical Directory of Congress (bioguide.comgress.gov). These variables include service as a delegate at a national party convention and service as a presidential elector. These offices were included because they are suggestive of an aspirant's prior level of partisan involvement. It does not include commission membership (for example, Presidential Commission for Relief in Belgium), military service, or local political office, unless the local office served was mayor. These offices are omitted because the credit individuals receive for them and the political skills they develop either attaining or serving in them are difficult to assess consistently across aspirants (especially as an interval-level statistic) and because, at least with respect to the military, it is not altogether clear that these individuals were chosen by their party for any reason other than their celebrity, which is not something that this measure is attempting to capture. Military service is also not counted because the military is hierarchically organized and it does not rest on

a doctrine of separation of powers, or checks and balances. As such, it seems fair to conclude that military experience is more akin to business experience than it is to political experience.

27. Reelection to the presidency is counted because of the significant challenge involved, even if one is an incumbent.

28. For more on historical trends, see Brown, *Jockeying for the American Presidency.*

29. This is an extension of the idea that "where one stands depends a great deal on where one sits." In essence, if one has sat in many positions, one may be able to see more than one way to stand.

30. Theodore Roosevelt gave a speech at the Sorbonne in Paris on April 23, 1910, in which he famously implored the young, privileged university students to step "into the arena." The full text of the speech is available at http://www.theodore-roosevelt.com/trsorbonnespeech.html (accessed on February 18, 2008).

31. While this is a somewhat unsophisticated construction of opportunism, the value of it being replicable and objective should not be overlooked. Many presidential studies (see especially James David Barber, *Presidential Character: Predicting Presidential Performance in the White House* [Englewood Cliffs: Prentice-Hall, 1972]) rely on psychological typing or character descriptions as the basis of their analyses, making them difficult to apply to presidents (and aspirants) who were not included in those studies. This measure could easily be created for future aspirants.

32. While the coefficients were negative, as one would expect given the history, neither variable proved statistically significant.

33. See, for example, Paul Abramson, John Aldrich, and David Rohde, "Progressive Ambition among U.S. Senators, 1972–1988.," *American Journal of Political Science* 49 (1987), no. 1, 3–35; Michael Nelson, "Who Vies for President?" in *Presidential Selection*, Alexander Heard and Michael Nelson, eds. (Durham: Duke University Press, 1987); Aldrich, "Presidential Selection"; Barry Burden, "United States Senators as Presidential Candidates," *Political Science Quarterly* 117 (2002), 81–102; and Randall Adkins, Andrew Dowdle, and Wayne Steger, "Progressive Ambition and the Presidency, 1976–2008," prepared for presentation at the Midwest Political Science Association Conference, Chicago, April 20–23, 2006.

34. Some of the variables tested or considered were the size of the aspirant's home state (measured as a percentage of electoral votes), the competitiveness of the aspirant's home state (dichotomous dummy variable based on the size of the popular-vote margin between the two political parties in that state), and the influence of accidental presidents (dichotomous dummy variable), "liabilities index" (gender, age, minority status), "risk-taking" propensity (whether aspirants ran against an incumbent or not to win their seat), and ideological positioning. For further discussion on why these variables were omitted, see Brown, "The Presidential Problem."

35. Other equations that were tested broke the pool of aspirants down by party (Democrats in one and Republicans in another). The findings from these models were largely consistent with Adkins, Dowdle, and Steger, "Progressive Ambition," and D. Jason Berggren, "Two Parties, Two Types of Nominees, Two Paths to Winning a Presidential Nomination, 1972–2004," *Presidential Studies Quarterly* 37, no. 2 (June 2007), 203–27, which showed some partisan differences in which characteristics were more important in each nomination race. They were omitted here due to space constraints, but they can be provided upon request.

36. Although John Breckinridge in 1860 earned the nomination from the Southern Democrats, only Stephen Douglas who earned the nomination from the Northern Democrats was coded as the Democratic "nominee" from that cycle.

37. Rohde, "Risk-Bearing and Progressive Ambition."

38. Transforming the variable to reduce the positive skew of the distribution, while it did slightly decrease the magnitude of the coefficient, did not alter the sign in the regression models. Since a transformed variable's effect is more difficult to describe and understand, it seemed prudent to use the original interval-level count in the models.

39. William G. Mayer, ed., *In the Pursuit of the White House* (Chatham, N.J.: Chatham House, 1996); "The Basic Dynamics"; *The Making of the Presidential Candidates.*

40. Journalist Arthur Hadley coined this phrase, which refers to the campaign period before the contests get underway. See Arthur T. Hadley, *The Invisible Primary* (Englewood Cliffs, N.J.: Prentice Hall, 1976). See William G. Mayer and Andrew E. Busch, *The Front-Loading Problem in Presidential Nominations.* See also Andrew E. Busch and William G. Mayer, "The Front-Loading Problem," and William G. Mayer, "The Basic Dynamics of the Contemporary Nomination Process: An Expanded View" in Mayer, ed., *The Making of the Presidential Candidates 2004* (Lanham, Md.: Rowman & Littlefield, 2004), 1–43, 83–132. See also Nelson W. Polsby and Aaron Wildavsky, *Presidential Elections: Strategies and Structures of American Politics,* 89–115. See also Stephen J. Wayne, *The Road to the White House 2004: The Politics of Presidential Elections* (Belmont, Cal.: Wadsworth/Thomson Learning, 2004), 103–58. See also Michael J. Goff, *The Money Primary: The New Politics of the Early Presidential Nomination Process* (Lanham, Md.: Rowman & Littlefield, 2004). See also Marty Cohen, David Karol, Hans Noel, and John Zaller, "Beating Reform: The Resurgence of Parties in Presidential Nominations, 1980–2000" (paper presented at the Annual Meeting of the American Political Science Association, 2002).

41. Even though McCain's level of opportunism was much lower than many of his competitors (0.18), the mean level of opportunism for the Republican field was

only 0.21, excluding Romney whose score (0.75) was more than double his nearest Republican competitor (Huckabee at 0.29).

42. For further discussion about McCain's opportunistic maneuvering after his campaign reorganization, see Brown, *Jockeying for the American Presidency.*

43. See Mayer, *In the Pursuit of the White House*; "The Basic Dynamics"; *The Making of the Presidential Candidates 2004.*

44. See Brown, *Jockeying for the American Presidency.*

45. The Democratic National Committee penalized both Michigan and Florida by stripping the states of all of their convention delegates, and they did not reinstate some of these votes until a Rules and Bylaws Committee meeting on May 29, 2008. The Republican National Committee penalized these two states by stripping them of half of their convention delegates.

46. See Brown, *Jockeying for the American Presidency.*

Donors, Dollars, and Momentum

*Lessons for Presidential Candidates in Waging
a Viable Campaign for the Nomination*

VICTORIA A. FARRAR-MYERS

In the 2008 presidential primary cycle, presidential candidates raised campaign funds at unprecedented levels. Barack Obama established a record for most contributions raised from individuals before his party's convention ($338 million)—over $100 million more than the previous record (George W. Bush with $236 million in 2004).[1] Hilary Clinton ($210 million) raised as much money as John Kerry did four years before, but still lost the Democratic nomination to Obama. John McCain raised more money ($125 million) than any other Republican presidential candidate in history other than Bush in 2004. Other candidates like Mitt Romney ($65 million), Rudy Giuliani ($62 million), John Edwards ($40 million), and even Ron Paul ($35 million) received contributions that a mere eight years before would have put them at levels competitive with or ahead of other candidates, but in 2008 left them underfinanced to wage an effective, viable campaign throughout the entire primary season.

Therefore, the 2008 presidential election season demonstrated that the cost of being a viable candidate for a party's nomination has increased dramatically as compared to past election cycles. Even though financial viability is just one component of determining a candidate's overall viability, it is one of the most important criteria, particularly for candidates to make strategic decisions during the pre-primary period. This chapter begins by surveying the changing nature of financial viability in the evolving world of presidential campaign finance. Next, it examines what is meant by "financial viability" in the current financing environment and what are the key components of financial viability. Finally, in analyzing the 2008 election, this chapter considers how these components of financial viability enable candidates to build sufficient momentum during the pre-primary period to enter the primary season as viable potential choices for their party's nomination.[2]

The Changing Nature of Financial Viability

In the context of presidential selection, the concept of viability could be reduced to the simple perception of how likely it is that a particular candidate will win his or her party's nomination.[3] Such a perception is forward-looking from any given vantage point—that is, based on the information obtained to date, can we project outward to determine this candidate's chances of being the party's standard-bearer in November? Certainly, once the caucuses and primaries get underway, determinations about candidate viability become easier to make for the candidates themselves, political pundits, and scholars alike. During the pre-primary period, however, political analysts are left trying to evaluate whether each candidate has a good combination of the various ingredients that comprise a viable campaign.

The viability of a candidate's campaign is based on both tangible and intangible ingredients.[4] Among the tangible ingredients, which the candidate is better able to affect and others are better able to objectively evaluate, are money, name recognition, network/support, campaign organization, backing of the party (often indicated by key endorsements by prominent party leaders), credibility on key issues, and résumé. Intangible ingredients, which are outside the candidate's control but can be used to her or his advantage, include political timing, political environment and mood, and desire for change. At the center of waging a viable campaign, particularly during the pre-primary period, lies financial viability: "Money is a threshold factor for establishing a viable campaign. With it, candidates can promote their message, operate their campaign simultaneously in multiple states, and be seen as having a groundswell of support behind their candidacies—in fact, being able to raise campaign fund is sometimes seen as viability itself."[5]

Conventional wisdom dictates that "presidential candidates raising the greatest total receipts during the months preceding the Iowa caucuses and New Hampshire primary tended to win the party nomination."[6] Conventional wisdom and tendencies, though, do not always hold true and can change, particularly in the context of twenty-first-century presidential elections. Presidential campaign finance from 1976–1996 was premised on a system of public financing, in which candidates could (and in fact did) tailor their fund-raising activities and adopt strategies geared toward the goals of maximizing the funds received through public financing and becoming eligible to obtain public funding as quickly as possible.

Candidates initially qualified to receive matching funds by raising $100,000 from contributions of $250 or less, with a minimum of $5,000 being raised in at least twenty states. Once qualified, a candidate received (but not before January 1 of the election year) public funds matching dollar for dollar the first $250 of every individual contribution, up to one-half of the federal spending limit for that election cycle. One result of this system is that it could easily become a central point in a candidate's campaign strategy. The potential of "free money" often led struggling candidates to stay in the race in the hope that once they had additional funds, they would better deliver their message. In some cases, candidates needed to stay in the race to obtain matching funds if for no reason other than to pay off previously borrowed funds.[7] In other cases, public funding enabled front-runners to turn a moderate cash advantage into a more sizable one, thereby helping them secure victory.[8]

Receiving public funding, however, also meant having to accept certain restrictions that came along with such funding. In the 2000 primary season, George W. Bush gambled in opting out of the public financing system that he would be successful in raising funds in excess of the amount that they would otherwise receive through public funding. His gamble proved to be successful, as he raised as much in individual contributions ($91.3 million) as Democrats Al Gore ($49.2 million) and Bill Bradley ($42.1 million) combined received in total funds, *including* public funding. In the two election cycles since 2000, the top candidates (Bush, Kerry, and Dean in 2004; Romney, McCain, Giuliani, Obama, and Clinton in 2008) have generally also chosen to follow Bush's path and not to accept public funding and the associated restrictions that come with such money.[9]

The amount of contributions that these candidates have raised alone tells only part of the significance of opting out of the system. The fact that candidates could and did raise such enormous amounts, and the way they went about doing so, in and of themselves became news stories. As a result, the candidates often received a double benefit: not only did they receive campaign funds, they received increased media coverage during their quest to meet certain goals. For example, in 2004, Bush, backed by his group of "Rangers" (those who helped raise more than $200,000), "Pioneers" (raising more than $100,000), and "Mavericks" (in excess of $50,000), raised substantially more money in 2003 alone than he did during his run in

2000. Similarly, when John Kerry had only a few million dollars on hand in late March 2004, he set out on an ambitious fund-raising schedule to obtain $80 million in the eighty days before the Democratic Convention, and beat that goal by raising $89 million. Likewise, Howard Dean rose in the polls in 2003 on the strength of his "Deaniacs" who contributed substantial funds by means of the Internet.

Public financing of presidential elections is effective so long as the public funds that a candidate receives exceed what he or she could otherwise expect to raise outside of the system. The strategic decision boils down to a simple cost-benefit analysis. For a candidate to be willing to accept the spending limits and other restrictions required under the public finance system, he or she must expect the benefits of additional public funds to outweigh those restrictions. With few exceptions, most notably independently wealthy candidates Ross Perot and Steve Forbes who opted out of the public finance system to make use of their personal fortunes, candidates during the 1976–1996 era generally wanted the benefits of public financing. What was once an exception—a candidate opting out of the public finance system—looks like it has become the rule, at least for those candidates who wish to be seen as legitimate contenders for their party's nomination.[10] A candidate conceivably could be hampered by accepting public funding as that decision could send a signal to potential contributors (and voters) that even the candidate does not believe enough in his or her campaign to think that he or she could raise sufficient funding outside the public finance system. As a result, in its current form the public finance system could be obsolete as a means for affecting the outcome of presidential nominations. Furthermore, the fact that Barack Obama did not accept public funding for his general election campaign in 2008 (the first time for a major-party candidate) yet continued his fund-raising successes adds additional evidence of the erosion of the public financing system.[11]

As a result of this fundamental change in presidential campaign fund-raising strategy, the environment of presidential campaign financing has been less predictable since 2000. As Table 1 shows, if the pre-2000 conventional wisdom held true from 2000–2008 based on the money raised from individual contributions during the six months preceding the Iowa caucuses, cases could be made that Bill Bradley and Howard Dean should have faced George W. Bush in 2000 and 2004 respectively; or that in November 2008, Hillary Clinton would have been facing Mitt Romney, Rudy Giuliani, Fred Thompson, or even Ron Paul, but certainly not John McCain.

Table 1: Contributions from Individuals Raised in the Year Prior to the Election Year

		Third & Fourth Quarter	*Cumulative—Year Before Election*	*Key Election Wins (IA, NH, & Nom.)*
2000	REPUBLICANS	1999	1999	
	Bush	$29,250,380	$65,390,923	IA, Nom
	McCain	$9,121,330	$13,205,337	NH
	Bauer	$3,368,294	$6,785,120	
	Forbes	$2,535,327	$5,247,606	
	Hatch	$1,950,029	$1,950,029	
	Keyes	$1,587,016	$3,501,628	
	Dole	$1,542,550	$4,935,202	
	Quayle	$782,332	$4,083,023	
	Alexander	$293,650	$2,301,747	
	Smith	$30,040	$1,522,128	
2000	DEMOCRATS	1999	1999	
	Bradley	$15,519,856	$27,223,397	
	Gore	$10,388,825	$27,843,861	IA, NH, Nom
	LaRouche	$1,247,775	$2,049,293	
2004	DEMOCRATS	2003	2003	
	Dean	$30,413,276	$40,921,455	
	Clark	$13,661,556	$13,661,556	
	Gephardt	$6,610,808	$13,656,622	
	Kerry	$6,121,723	$19,405,997	IA, NH, Nom
	Lieberman	$5,619,284	$13,610,337	
	Edwards	$3,817,601	$15,686,646	
	Kucinich	$3,002,247	$4,709,604	
	LaRouche	$1,844,747	$6,385,860	
	Moseley Braun	$247,687	$461,796	
	Sharpton	$237,527	$395,142	
2008	DEMOCRATS	2007	2007	
	Clinton	$51,194,290	103,709,204	NH
	Obama	$42,841,849	101,429,472	IA, Nom
	Edwards	$11,684,785	34,742,977	
	Richardson	$8,889,051	22,023,040	
	Biden	$3,694,158	8,092,961	

Table 1: continued next page

Table 1: *Cont.*

	Dodd	$2,930,550	9,770,744	
	Kucinich	$2,727,264	3,843,866	
	Gravel	$130,598	305,778	
2008	REPUBLICANS	2007	2007	
	Paul	$25,026,060	28,028,878	
	Giuliani	$24,795,271	58,122,655	
	Thompson, F.	$21,395,995	21,395,995	
	Romney	$19,788,681	52,546,120	
	McCain	$11,995,557	36,534,073	NH, Nom
	Huckabee	$7,641,834	8,917,190	IA
	Hunter	$988,777	2,258,785	

Source: Compiled by author from Federal Election Commission data available at
http://www.fec.gov.
Note: Table 1 contains contested primaries only; thus, the uncontested Republican nomination in

With obtaining public financing no longer being at the core of presidential campaign financing, candidates are faced with having to develop
different fund-raising strategies to establish and maintain their financial
viability during the pre-primary period. As noted above, a key question
to consider, then, is what is meant by "financial viability" in the current
financing environment. Just as campaign viability can be broken down into
several different ingredients, so too can the concept of financial viability.
Not all dollars are created equal in the ever-evolving world of presidential
election fund-raising, and certain types of money raised may provide a
better harbinger than others of a candidate's potential success during the
actual primary season.

The Ingredients of Financial Viability

Although the concept of financial viability can be broken down into its
key ingredients, the nature of the ingredients of financial viability does
not lend itself easily to identifying critical thresholds that, once met,
would allow candidates to be deemed to be financially viable. Financial
viability is contextual and fluid. It depends not just on the funds any individual candidate raises, but also on how much the other candidates in
that primary-election year have raised and the ways in which they do so.

As noted at the outset of this chapter, what might constitute a financially viable level of fund-raising in one election year may not be sufficient in another year. Further, just as different chefs can combine the same ingredients to create different-tasting dishes, so too can individual candidates achieve financial viability by a different mixture of the ingredients set forth below. With this in mind, let us examine the key ingredients of financial viability, how they can be used to achieve financial viability in any given election cycle, and what may happen if a candidate is lacking one or more of these ingredients.

Ingredient 1: Comparatively Big Money

Even though recent elections have shown that the candidate who raises the most money in the months immediately preceding the primary season does not necessarily win the nomination, overall funds raised nevertheless constitute the first ingredient to establishing financial viability. One should resist the temptation, though, to rank order the winners of the "Money Primary" (that is, "the competition of candidates for financial resources contributed by the partisan elites before the primaries begin") as one would do in an election.[12] Instead, the key factor for assessing this ingredient of financial viability is whether a candidate has raised enough money to be competitive with other candidates—that is, whether the candidate in question is able to proceed through the pre-primary period and enter the primary season as one of the top challengers for the party's nomination.

Keep in mind that those situations in which the same candidate wins in Iowa and New Hampshire and then goes on to win the party's nomination occurs less frequently than having two separate candidates win in the first caucus and primary (see, for example, Table 1). Of the eighteen primary seasons between 1976 (the first presidential election conducted under the current campaign financing regime put in place by the Federal Election Campaign Act) and 2008, five saw one candidate win in Iowa and in New Hampshire, and receive the party's nomination (Ford, 1976; Carter, 1976; Carter, 1980; Gore, 2000; and Kerry, 2004), and nine saw multiple winners (Republicans, 1980; Democrats, 1984; Republicans, 1988; Democrats, 1988; Democrats, 1992; Republicans, 1996; Republicans, 2000; Republicans, 2008; and Democrats, 2008).[13]

Just as more than one candidate from each party can enter the primary season as viable candidates, so too can more than one candidate raise sufficient funds to achieve financial viability. To do so, however, a candidate

Table 2: Funds Raised and Cash on Hand as of December 31 in the Year Prior to the
Election Year Relative to the Party Leader

		Contributions from Individuals Percentage of Party Leader*	Total Contributions Percentage of Party Leader*	Cash on Hand Percentage of Party Leader*
2000	REPUBLICANS	1999	1999	1999
	Bush	$65,390,923	$67,567,934	$31,384,042
	McCain	20%	23%	5%
	Bauer	10%	14%	0%
	Forbes	8%	50%	3%
	Dole	8%	7%	0%
	Quayle	6%	8%	1%
	Keyes	5%	7%	3%
	Alexander	4%	5%	0%
	Hatch	3%	3%	1%
	Smith	2%	2%	1%
2000	DEMOCRATS	1999	1999	1999
	Gore	$27,843,861	$27,847,334	69%
	Bradley	98%	99%	$8,320,942
	LaRouche	7%	7%	0%
2004	DEMOCRATS	2003	2003	2003
	Dean	$40,921,455	$40,959,621	$9,647,361
	Kerry	47%	61%	17%
	Edwards	38%	40%	3%
	Clark	33%	33%	35%
	Gephardt	33%	40%	17%
	Lieberman	33%	34%	6%
	LaRouche	16%	16%	1%
	Kucinich	12%	15%	27%
	Moseley Braun	1%	1%	0%
	Sharpton	1%	1%	0%
2008	DEMOCRATS	2007	2007	2007
	Clinton	$103,709,204	$114,674,923	$37,947,874
	Obama	98%	88%	50%
	Edwards	34%	30%	21%
	Richardson	21%	19%	5%

Table 2: continued next page

Table 2: *Cont.*

	Dodd	9%	13%	7%
	Biden	8%	9%	5%
	Kucinich	4%	3%	1%
	Gravel	0%	0%	0%
2008	REPUBLICANS	2007	2007	2007
	Giuliani	$58,122,655	69%	$12,776,812
	Romney	90%	$88,313,366	19%
	McCain	63%	43%	23%
	Paul	48%	32%	61%
	Thompson	37%	24%	17%
	Huckabee	15%	10%	15%
	Hunter	4%	3%	2%

* Within each category, the actual amount for the party leader (i.e., contributions from individuals, total contributions, and cash on hand) is listed;
values for all other candidates are shown as a percentage of the party leader's amount.
Source: Compiled by author from Federal Election Commission data available at http://www.fec.gov.

must be within striking distance of the winner of the Money Primary (that is, the top fund-raiser from the party). To assess what "within striking distance" means, Table 2 shows the total funds raised from individual contributions, overall funds raised (thus, including funds contributed or loaned by the candidate's personal wealth—such as Steve Forbes in 2000 or Mitt Romney in 2008—or transferred over from previous campaigns for other offices—such as Hillary Clinton in 2008, all discussed more fully below), and remaining cash on hand, in each case at the end of the year prior to election year as a percentage relative to the party's leader that year.

Even if a candidate did not win any of these key aspects of the Money Primary, some of those who maintained a double-digit percentage (that is, at least 10 percent) of the party's leader in each category managed to attain some success in early primaries and perhaps their party's nomination itself. Kerry in 2004 and McCain in 2008 went on to electoral success despite finishing behind the leaders of the Money Primary in their respective years. Even Mike Huckabee pulled out a victory in the Iowa caucus despite raising about only one-tenth of the party leaders in 2008. On the flip side, though, George W. Bush's victory for the 2000 Republican nomination can be traced to the significant advantage he built up in fund-raising compared to other candidates, most notably Elizabeth Dole, who despite having strong credentials in terms of other ingredients of overall viability was unable to establish financial viability vis-à-vis Bush.[14]

Table 2 also reflects, though, that what constitutes "striking distance" can vary. Perhaps this variability is most noticeable in comparing the Republican and Democratic primaries in 2000. Bill Bradley compared more favorably to Al Gore than McCain did to George W. Bush. Whereas Bradley was able to raise virtually the same amount that Gore did during the pre-primary period and had the advantage in terms of cash on hand at the end of the year, McCain raised slightly over 20 percent of what Bush raised and had only 5 percent of the amount of cash on hand that Bush did. Yet McCain managed to win one early primary (New Hampshire), while Gore proceeded to beat Bradley in the earliest contests and for the nomination. Even though comparative financial strength may not produce a direct correlation with electoral outcome, the relationship is strong enough to constitute one of several ingredients necessary for a candidate to establish financial viability.

Ingredient 2: Early Money

As noted above, Table 1 shows that the candidate who raises the most from individual contributors in the last half of the year prior to the election year does not necessarily win once the votes are counted. Instead, *early money* is one of the keys in establishing financial viability. The amount of money raised in the first quarter of the year prior to election year (when many aspirants first announce their candidacy for the presidency) sends many signals to the electorate, analysts, and the candidates. These funds demonstrate a strong base of support, allow the candidate to distinguish himself or herself from others, and may lead to a candidate being deemed the "early front-runner"; conversely, a distinct lack of funds raised during this period presents a significant hurdle to overcome. Certainly a candidate could do so, much like Howard Dean did in 2004: he went from sixth in the Money Primary during the first quarter of 2003 to second at the end of the second quarter. Unless a candidate is able to make up significant ground like Dean did during the months of April–June 2003, the prospects of achieving financial viability—and, thus, being seen as a viable candidate overall during the pre-primary period—are very dim after a poor showing in fund-raising at a time that is still up to a year before the first caucus vote is tallied in Iowa.

Table 3: Contributions from Individuals at the End of the First and Second Quarters of the Year Prior to the Election Year

		At End of First Quarter	At End of Second Quarter	Total Funds Year Before Election
2000	REPUBLICANS	1999	1999	1999
	Bush	$7,474,082	$36,140,543	$67,567,934
	Quayle	$2,024,112	$3,300,691	$5,631,291
	McCain	$1,678,335	$4,084,007	$15,544,828
	Bauer	$1,366,886	$3,416,826	$9,744,651
	Dole	$668,753	$3,392,652	$5,061,399
	Alexander	$657,150	$2,008,097	$3,085,631
	Smith	$226,474	$1,492,088	$1,614,198
	Forbes	$16,538	$2,712,279	$33,942,652
	Keyes	$0	$1,914,612	$4,432,756
	Hatch	$0	$0	$2,281,029
2000	DEMOCRATS	1999	1999	1999
	Gore	$8,881,976	$17,455,036	$27,847,334
	Bradley	$4,364,671	$11,703,541	$27,451,329
	LaRouche	$162,021	$801,518	$2,051,190
2004	DEMOCRATS	2003	2003	2003
	Kerry	$7,501,390	$13,284,275	$25,057,443
	Edwards	$7,398,836	$11,869,045	$16,235,455
	LaRouche	$3,704,005	$4,541,113	$6,389,182
	Gephardt	$3,353,928	$7,045,813	$16,488,049
	Lieberman	$2,961,023	$7,991,053	$13,823,407
	Dean	$2,932,262	$10,508,179	$40,959,621
	Kucinich	$172,695	$1,707,356	$6,227,898
	Sharpton	$107,456	$157,615	$408,342
	Moseley Braun	$72,451	$214,109	$492,069
	Clark	$0	$0	$13,699,256
2008	DEMOCRATS	2007	2007	2007
	Clinton	$25,805,109	$52,514,914	$114,674,923
	Obama	$25,665,688	$58,587,623	$101,429,497
	Edwards	$14,021,284	$23,058,192	$34,742,977
	Richardson	$6,177,407	$13,133,989	$22,271,369
	Dodd	$3,748,257	$6,840,194	$15,142,497

Table 3: continued next page

Table 3: *Cont.*

	Biden	$2,084,290	$4,398,803	$10,125,106
	Kucinich	$356,980	$1,116,602	$3,863,378
	Gravel	$34,670	$175,180	$363,896
2008	REPUBLICANS	2007	2007	2007
	Romney	$20,596,399	$32,757,439	$88,313,366
	Giuliani	$15,936,337	$33,327,384	$60,562,227
	McCain	$13,351,443	$24,538,516	$38,092,097
	Paul	$638,389	$3,002,818	$28,046,802
	Huckabee	$526,957	$1,275,356	$8,974,483
	Hunter	$469,601	$1,270,008	$2,386,058
	Thompson, F.	$0	$0	$21,564,300

Source: Compiled by author from Federal Election Commission data available at http://www.fec.gov.

Table 3 shows the funds raised from individual contributions at the end of the first and second quarters prior to the election year. From this table, several important lessons emerge for establishing financial viability and, as a result, the viability of a candidate's overall campaign. Winning the "Early Money Primary" would appear to be tied to electoral success during the next year. For example, Gore in 2000 and Kerry in 2004 were the Early Money Primary winners who went on to get the Democratic Party's nomination despite being outpaced in fund-raising by Bradley and Dean respectively in the second half of the year prior to the election year. Similarly, the closeness of Clinton's and Obama's fund-raising efforts in the Early Money Primary appears to have been a harbinger of their battles in the 2008 caucuses and primaries.

The one exception to this connection shown in Table 3 is John Mc-Cain in 2008, who finished third in the Early Money Primary. Borrowing from the first ingredient for financial viability discussed above, though, McCain managed to garner comparatively big money during the Early Money Primary, ending the first quarter and second quarter having raised approximately 65 percent and 75 percent respectively of the amount that Mitt Romney, the Early Money Primary winner, raised. Also, compared to the funds contributed to the other Republican candidates like Mike Huckabee, Duncan Hunter, and Ron Paul, as well as other candidates who were considering runs for the presidency during 2007 (for example, Tommy Thompson and Sam Brownback), McCain was clearly more aligned with Romney and Rudy Giuliani as early front-runners.

The importance of the Early Money Primary places an increasing emphasis on the use of the Internet as a key fund-raising tool. During the 2000 nomination season, John McCain became the first presidential candidate to make the Internet a prominent part of his campaign. He invested personnel and other resources early to develop the infrastructure needed to maximize the impact of utilizing the electronic medium, and from doing so reaped benefits. For example, immediately after beating George W. Bush in the New Hampshire primary, McCain saw his website collect donations at a reported rate of $30,000 an hour. Overall, McCain raised $6.4 million during the 2000 campaign through the Internet.[15] In the two election cycles since, other candidates have made similar investment in developing a Web fund-raising presence, leading to such benefits as raising more money, creating more expansive databases of supporters or potential supporters, and reaching a broader array of voters.

The immediacy of the Internet enables it to be an important campaign and fund-raising tool. Establishing an Internet presence has a relatively low-cost barrier to entry, as a candidate can readily develop a forum for attracting potential supporters even without first having raised a large amount of campaign funds. The Internet also allows candidates to get their message out quicker to a wider target audience—including people who may not have traditionally been fund-raising targets for standard appeal letters, such as younger voters and workers using the Internet at their jobs. The Web also provides a more efficient means of enabling a potential contributor to make a donation of any size (important for reaching critical small donors as discussed below). Further, by continuing to add fresh content to the candidate's Web site, supporters can be driven back to the site, thus providing repeat opportunities for contributors to make additional donations (to the extent they have not already contributed the maximum amount allowed by law).

Compared to the traditional method of planning a widespread mailing, printing the appeal letters, relying on the post office to deliver the appeal, and then waiting for a check to arrive, candidates can now take a much more streamlined approach toward campaigning and fund-raising. For example, after some particular newsworthy event, a candidate within a few hours can send out an e-mail message complete with color graphics and touting the candidate, and providing a link so that the recipient can make a contribution using his or her credit card. Candidates can create a suggestive sale or impulse-buy opportunity. Instead of asking "do you want fries with that?" they are selling themselves and their candidacy to a willing consumer at a time when the consumer may be most motivated to buy into the candidate. In doing so, candidates are laying the groundwork for success in the Early Money Primary and beyond.

Another lesson embedded in Table 3 deals with the emergence of an unknown or late-arriving candidate. The correlate of having to win (or at least be highly competitive in) the Early Money Primary is that candidates do not have time to build a grassroots campaign or name recognition. They must appear to be among the front-runners by no later than the end of June, and more likely by the end of March, in the year before the election. "Surprise" or "dark horse" candidates may emerge because they outperform expectations during the Early Money Primary and are able to sustain their financial and overall viability during the pre-primary period. Candidates who may win an early primary in a surprise fashion without having the benefit of previously being seen as viable alternatives over the previous year run the risk of being considered nothing more than a "flash in the pan."

Consider, for example, the 2004 Democratic primary season. Going into the Early Money Primary, one would have thought that Richard Gephardt and Joe Lieberman would have appeared to be among the more viable candidates, taking into account the other ingredients of viability discussed above. With Gephardt having served as the Democratic Party leader in the House of Representatives and having run for president in 1988, and Lieberman having been Al Gore's vice presidential running mate in the 2000 election, they both had name recognition, a strong résumé, backing of party leaders, and presumably access to a network of support and a competent campaign organization. Yet, John Edwards, a relatively unknown and unaccomplished first-term senator, raised more than double the amounts raised by each of Gephardt and Lieberman by the end of the first quarter of 2003. Further, although Gephardt and Lieberman closed the gap a little during the second quarter of 2003, Edwards maintained his lead in the Early Money Primary over the other two. In 2004, both Gephardt and Lieberman bowed out of the race early, while Edwards established a presence in Democratic race and later parlayed it into being the party's vice presidential nominee.

A related aspect to consider involves a late-arriving candidate, such as Wesley Clark in 2004 or Fred Thompson in 2008. Both joined the race for their party's nomination in the third quarter of the year before the election and did comparatively well in the Money Primary during the second half of the year. Clark finished second in the Money Primary during this period and raised more than twice than what eventual nominee John Kerry raised. Thompson finished third and brought in more from individual contributions than Early Money Primary front-runners Romney and McCain. Yet they were trying to establish the viability of their campaigns—both financial viability and overall—at a time when several other candidates had already done so. The foundation for future electoral success can be laid as early as the first quarter in the year prior to the primary season. As a result, candidates who wait until the third quarter to wedge themselves into a crowded race against others who are already seen as viable may have simply waited too long.

A third lesson drawn from Table 3 is that while success in the Early Money Primary may be a necessary condition to establishing financial viability, alone it is not sufficient. A candidate must not only have early success in fund-raising, but (as alluded to above) must be able to generally sustain it throughout the pre-primary period. Consider the percentage of funds raised by Kerry in 2004 and Clinton and Obama in 2008 as compared to their overall funds raised in the pre-primary season. All were successful fund-raisers early, but did not dry up their sources of contributions at the outset. Table 3 shows that of the contributions that John Kerry eventually received by December 31, 2003, he had raised slightly over half (53 percent) by June 30, with the remaining 47 percent during the second half of the year—in other words, his fund-raising efforts were fairly well balanced throughout the pre-primary period. Similarly, Table 3 shows that Hillary Clinton raised 46 percent of her pre-primary funds by June 30, meaning that she raised more (54 percent) in the second half of 2007 than the first, although (like John Kerry) she was fairly well balanced between the first and second halves of the year. While Obama's 58 percent reflects that his fund-raising dropped off during the second half of the year compared to the first, one should note that the approximately $32.8 million he raised during the second quarter of 2007 represents a record for the largest amount of individual contributions raised in a calendar quarter during the pre-primary season by a candidate in a contested election.[16]

John Edwards in 2004 and 2008 provides an interesting contrast to Kerry, Clinton, and Obama. Despite his early success in 2004, Edwards raised 46 percent of all the funds he would raise during all of 2003, from individual contributions in the first quarter alone; this number goes to 73 percent by the end of the second quarter. He repeated this performance in 2007, with 40 percent and 66 percent raised by the end of the first and second quarters respectively. In both election cycles, he was unable to sustain his initial success, indicating that although he had a strong core group of support, he had difficulty broadening this base. John McCain's performance in 2007 is very comparable to Edwards: McCain raised 35 percent and 64 percent by the end of the first and second quarters respectively. Heading into the primary season, the viability of McCain's overall candidacy was being questioned, in part based on the shaky ground on which his financial viability stood. As will be discussed in more detail below, though, the weight given to financial viability in determining a candidate's overall viability changes once the voting begins, and McCain appears to have benefited from this change.

Table 3 focuses on contributions by individuals, both because it is generally the largest source of funds a candidate receives as well as being important in determining financial viability (to be discussed below). A candidate, however, can utilize money from other sources to help fund his or her campaign. Steve Forbes, for example, used over $43 million of his own money in 2000 and over $37 million in 1996 to finance his runs for the Republican nomination. In the 2004 race, John Kerry infused over $5.5 million into his campaign through self-contributions and transferring funds raised during his previous campaigns for Senate.[17] Similarly, during the first quarter of 2007, Hillary Clinton transferred $10 million from her senatorial campaign coffers to her presidential campaign, including a transfer in the amount of $8,750,000 on March 30, 2007. Mitt Romney loaned $2.35 million to his campaign in 2006 alone and over $35 million cumulatively during the pre-primary period. Early money from candidate-controlled sources is useful to help kick-start a campaign. Such financing provides a valuable resource to enable the candidate to quickly develop the organizational infrastructure to facilitate more widespread fund-raising and campaigning efforts. However, it is a resource that has no correlation to whether the candidate has support among donors and potential voters in his or her quest for the White House. For that reason, such financing may promote a candidate's financial independence, but it should not be considered as an ingredient in determining viability—financial or otherwise.

Ingredient 3: Small-donor Contributions

Part of the reason that financial viability serves as a surrogate for overall candidate viability is because it is the most precise measure during the pre-primary period as to whether voters will support the candidate when it comes time to cast their ballots. Instead of expressing their preference in the voting booth, however, potential voters are doing so through their donations. As noted above, candidates can obtain funds through various means, such as their own wealth, leftover funds from previous campaigns, party committees, or PACs. None of these sources, though, provide contributions directly from the people who will be deciding the party's nominee. For this reason, the analysis herein has focused largely on contributions from individuals.

The third ingredient of financial viability, though, focuses on a specific type of contribution—those from small donors. Table 4 examines the contributions that candidates received from individuals as of the end of the third quarter in the year prior to the election year for the smallest contributors ($200 or less) and largest contributors ($1,000 or $2,000+ depending on the election year).[18] At first blush, one might not think of small-donor contributions as being a driver in determining financial viability. For example, the contributions that George W. Bush received from the smallest donors ($200 or less) equaled approximately 8 percent of his overall funds raised as of September 30, 1999. John Kerry and Hillary Clinton each raised 12 percent of their funds from small donors at the same point in their campaigns. Even the more successful populist-oriented fund-raisers received more funds from the largest donors than small donors. For example, as of September 30, 2007, John Edwards, Barack Obama, and John McCain raised 28 percent, 26 percent and 22 percent from small donors and 44 percent, 47 percent, and 53 percent, respectively, from the largest donors. Howard Dean, perhaps the most successful populist-oriented fund-raiser in recent years, collected just over 50 percent of the funds he raised from small donors.

Nevertheless, small-donor contributions constitute an important indication of financial viability because small donors represent the breadth of support of likely voters come primary or caucus election time. Although a candidate may have an easier time raising $2,000 from one large donor than from twenty small donors giving $100 a piece, he or she will have an easier time garnering twenty votes from those small donors. Table 4A recasts the information presented in Table 4 in a new light—by the estimated number of contributions made within each category (see the note at the end of Table 4A explaining how the estimated number of contributions was determined). Recasting the information in this way uncovers the importance of small-donor contributions. Those candidates who emerged as front-runners or the eventual nominee, or both, typically had an advantage over other potential front-runners in the number of contributions received, both from small donors specifically and, as a result, overall.

In 1999, the small overall fund-raising advantage that Al Gore had over Bill Bradley turned out to be an approximately 2.5-to-1 estimated advantage in the number of small contributions. A similar pattern can be found in the Democratic race in 2007–2008. Despite the closeness of the Money Primary race between Obama and Clinton, Obama is estimated to have held an over 2-to-1 advantage in the number of small contributions, and over 110,000 contributions overall. Along the same lines, although McCain trailed Romney and Giuliani in terms of funds raised, he held a slight lead over Romney and a sizable lead over Giuliani in terms of number of small contributions. Even George W. Bush, who drew an extraordinary number of large contributions in 2000, still had the largest number of his contributions come from the small-donor pool.

As with winning the Early Money Primary, success in the "Small Donor Money Primary" is a necessary but not sufficient condition to achieve financial viability. This fact is most noticeable in the race for the 2004 Democratic nomination. As of the end of the third quarter in 2003, eventual nominee John Kerry was not only trailing Howard Dean by an estimated 6.75-to-1 margin in the number of small donor contributions, he was behind Lyndon LaRouche and Dennis Kucinich in the estimated number of small-donor contributors, as shown in Table 4A. Likewise, although McCain would maintain his lead in the Small Donor Money Primary over Romney and Giuliani, by the end of 2007 he lagged behind both Ron Paul and Fred Thompson in terms of money raised from small-donor contributors. The advantage that Kerry had over Dean and that McCain had over Paul and Thompson, however, is that they also had significant support among the larger donors and thus, presumably, a wider range of appeal among the electorate.

One should also keep in mind that the information in Table 4A does not necessarily translate into votes. Donors can change their minds after making an early contribution to one candidate, and vote for another. Also, contributors can hedge their bets and make donations to more than one candidate. For example, actors Tom Hanks and Paul Newman each made contributions to both Barack Obama and Hillary Clinton in their 2008 race for the Democratic nomination.[19]

In addition, a person could make a series of small contributions to a candidate instead of a single large donation, thus potentially skewing the numbers reflected in Table 4A. This fact, however, emphasizes another important point regarding small donors—they constitute a possible and likely source of future contributions. A donor who has already given the

Table 4: Individual Contributions (in Dollars) by Size of Contribution as of the End of Third Quarter in the Year Prior to the Election Year

Through September 30, 1999	Total Contributions from Individuals	Smallest Donors Contributions: $200 or Less		Largest Donors Contributions: $1,000	
		Dollars	Percentage	Dollars	Percentage
Gore	$24,291,738	$4,815,709	20%	$15,288,000	63%
Bradley	$19,017,244	$1,932,921	10%	$13,604,000	72%
Bush	$55,898,279	$4,602,731	8%	$39,873,000	71%
Bauer	$5,351,142	$3,020,445	56%	$936,000	17%
McCain	$7,078,511	$2,228,531	31%	$3,106,000	44%
Quayle	$4,131,588	$1,898,748	46%	$1,450,000	35%
Dole	$4,705,711	$865,998	18%	$2,775,000	59%
Alexander	$2,323,497	$53,100	2%	$1,879,000	81%

Through September 30, 2003	Total Contributions from Individuals	Smallest Donors Contributions: $200 or Less		Largest Donors Contributions: $2,000+	
		Dollars	Percentage	Dollars	Percentage
Dean	$25,326,097	$13,733,047	54%	$2,184,000	9%
LaRouche	$5,425,745	$2,821,851	52%	$28,000	1%
Kucinich	$3,367,231	$2,175,330	65%	$278,000	8%
Kerry	$17,220,464	$2,034,892	12%	$7,936,000	46%
Gephardt	$10,840,983	$1,309,431	12%	$5,096,000	47%
Clark	$3,484,108	$1,212,054	35%	$942,000	27%
Lieberman	$11,585,316	$944,104	8%	$5,208,000	45%
Graham	$4,327,942	$403,878	9%	$2,088,000	48%
Edwards	$13,989,880	$395,125	3%	$7,878,000	56%
Moseley	$328,201	$79,532	24%	$92,000	28%
Braun					
Bush	$82,843,770	$9,521,150	11%	$57,516,000	69%

Table 4: continued next page

Table 4: *Cont.*

Through September 30, 2007	Total Contributions from Individuals	Smallest Donors Contributions: $200 or Less		Largest Donors Contributions: $2,000+	
		Dollars	Percentage	Dollars	Percentage
Obama	$78,915,482	$20,850,080	26%	$36,960,300	47%
Clinton	$77,867,063	$9,448,527	12%	$51,282,070	66%
Edwards	$29,935,179	$8,467,811	28%	$13,129,621	44%
Richardson	$18,259,372	$3,533,420	19%	$8,949,516	49%
Kucinich	$2,107,157	$1,481,284	70%	$225,750	11%
Biden	$6,070,510	$551,490	9%	$3,518,076	58%
Dodd	$8,198,082	$281,581	3%	$5,488,521	67%
Gravel	$305,778	$185,044	61%	$25,416	8%
McCain	$29,858,910	$6,565,405	22%	$15,691,866	53%
Romney	$43,703,533	$6,046,245	14%	$26,732,164	61%
Thompson, F.	$12,612,568	$4,223,042	33%	$5,140,103	41%
Paul	$8,191,285	$4,105,409	50%	$1,394,256	17%
Giuliani	$44,293,657	$3,771,359	9%	$30,552,303	69%
Hunter	$1,750,896	$952,218	54%	$394,500	23%
Huckabee	$2,297,261	$584,976	25%	$863,109	38%

Source: Compiled by author from Federal Election Commission data available at http://www.fec.gov.

maximum amount to a candidate allowed under federal law obviously cannot give any more during the primary season; a small donor, on the other hand, can give more and may represent a more likely prospect than others who have not made any contributions to the candidate. Despite the various limitations discussed above, Table 4A reflects the overall importance of small-donor contributions in establishing both the financial viability and overall viability of a candidate, as a broad base of financial supporters more than likely will reflect and turn into a broad base of electoral supporters.

Bringing The Ingredients of Financial Viability Together
To achieve financial viability, candidates must "use the ingredients they have to create the proper recipe for success" and may do so in one of several ways.[20] Like George W. Bush in 1999, a candidate can simply raise far and away more funds than his or her opponents, including within the Early Money Primary or the Small Donor Money Primary. Alternatively,

John McCain did not excel in any of the three ingredients of financial viability. However, he did well enough to keep his candidacy afloat and to enter the primary season among the group of candidates seen as viable candidates for the Republican nomination. On the other hand, though, the absence of a key ingredient of financial viability can be a forewarning of a future lack of success once voting starts. The analysis above offers several examples of the importance of having each ingredient of financial viability present—whether it was John Edwards's inability to sustain his strong showing in the Early Money Primary in 2003, Fred Thompson's decision to enter the race late and therefore miss the Early Money Primary in 2007, or Rudy Giuliani's relative lack of success with small donors in the same year.

Unpacking financial viability into the three key ingredients also may offer insight on the eventual electoral outcomes that looking at the Money Primary on a macro basis does not. In the race for the 2000 Democratic primary, for example, Bill Bradley would have appeared to be competitive with Al Gore heading into the primary season. He had raised money comparable to that which the vice president had raised, and in fact had financial momentum in the second half of 2003 by out-fund-raising Gore during that period. Yet Gore outperformed Bradley within each ingredient of financial viability; an advantage that Gore carried through the primary season, winning every caucus and primary.

Although financial viability is often used as a surrogate for overall campaign viability during the pre-primary period and unpacking financial viability can provide clues to future electoral outcomes, financial viability is not the same as electoral viability. The performance of Howard Dean in the 2004 Democratic primary demonstrates this. Despite a few shortcomings in Dean's mix of financial-viability ingredients—a slow start in the Early Money Primary and not having sufficient breadth of appeal to attract large donors as well as the small ones—Dean entered the primary season on strong financial footing. Dean's financial successes did not translate into overall viability of his campaign, thus leading to the question of how a candidate can maintain and use financial viability once established within the strategic calculus of campaign decision-making to enhance the candidate's overall viability.

Financial Viability, Candidate Viability, and the Calculus
of Campaigning in the Primary Season

Once the Iowa caucus is held, the evidence used to assess the viability of a candidacy changes. Prior to the primary season, financial viability often suffices as an indicator of overall viability because it provides an objective measure of potential electoral support and success of a candidate. It helps establish a basis for determining who will enter the primary season as viable candidates (that is, with overall viability, not just financial viability). Also, understanding the components of financial viability laid out above provides insights into the strategic choices that a candidate has made to position himself or herself to be viable throughout the primary process. Understanding financial viability during the pre-primary process and the strategic decisions underlying it, though, comprises only one aspect of viability once the voting begins. During the primary season, one can look to the most direct determinant of viability—vote returns. In addition, the analysis starts to get framed in terms of actual finish, expected finish, delegate counts, margin of victory, and other factors tied into voting.

During this period, even though the weight given to financial viability in determining whether a candidacy is viable changes and to some degree diminishes, it does nonetheless remain an important criterion in evaluating overall viability. Questions surround candidates as to whether they will have enough money to stay in the race until the next primary, or whether they are able to build on the momentum from one or more primary victories by increasing the rate by which they are receiving contributions. Further, the influx of money during the early primary period provides additional evidence of the kind of appeal that a candidate may have as well as provide the resources to wage the kind of campaign that he or she seeks to wage.

The 2008 primary season offers an excellent opportunity to examine how candidates maintain and strategically use their financial viability once the voting begins. It also allows us to test the boundaries of looking at financial viability in the pre-primary process as an indicator of overall viability during the primary process. The nominations of both parties were being contested, and no clear front-runner emerged in the pre-primary period. Although what may be seen as the uniqueness of the 2008 primary season in both parties may limit the ability to draw generalizations from it, the continued erosion of the public financing system among the top-level candidates in the 2008 primaries connects it with the two election cycles that preceded it and thus helps us understand the emerging trends in presidential campaign finance in the current environment.

The front-loading of caucuses and primaries early in the year, starting with the Iowa caucuses on January 3, 2008, provided a clear demarcation between the pre-primary period (ending December 2007) and the primary period (starting January 2008). This demarcation also coincided with the candidates' reporting requirements of campaign finance data with the Federal Election Commission (FEC)—candidates had to file their year-end report for activity through December 31, 2007, as well as a monthly report for activity through January 31, 2008. Along with enhanced and more timely publishing of key campaign finance data (compared to prior election cycles) by the FEC through its website, candidates and analysts were able to get a quicker and more complete assessment of each candidate's continued financial viability.

Table 5 reflects the financial activity of presidential candidates during January 2008 (the first month of the primary season), including funds raised, expenditures, and changes in their cash on hand as compared to December 31, 2007, and helps highlight the differences between financial viability and overall viability once voting starts. On the Republican side, Table 5 reflects John McCain's solidification as the party front-runner. Entering the primary season, McCain was a marginally financially viable candidate compared to Romney and Giuliani. As noted above, though, despite some well-documented financial limitations, he had performed well enough in the pre-primary period to have entered the primary season with a legitimate shot at securing the GOP nomination. He was able to capitalize both on his victory in the New Hampshire primary and strategic and other shortcomings of his primary competitors throughout the rest of January. He received more contributions than any other Republican candidate and drew more support from small donors than any other candidate except Ron Paul. McCain improved his standing in terms of the ingredients of financial viability, reflecting his growing strength as a viable candidate and the Republican Party's presumptive presidential nominee.

Ron Paul represents an interesting side story in terms of financial and candidate viability. From July 1, 2007, to January 31, 2008, Paul raised more campaign contributions from individuals than any other Republican candidate, and was the clear winner in the Small Donor Money Primary among GOP hopefuls. Based on the estimates shown in Table 4A, Paul had a much larger contributor pool from which to draw for voters, yet

Table 4A: Individual Contributions (in Estimated Number of Contributions) by the Size of Contribution as of the End of the Third Quarter in the Year Prior to the Election Year*

Through September 30, 1999		Smallest Donors Contributions: $200 or Less		Largest Donors Contributions: $1,000	
	Total Contributions from Individuals	Est. No. of Conts.	Percentage	Est. No. of Conts.	Percentage
Gore	70,425	48,157	68%	15,288	22%
Bradley	38,734	19,329	50%	13,604	35%
Bush	104,938	46,027	44%	39,873	38%
Bauer	33,465	30,204	90%	936	3%
McCain	28,298	22,285	79%	3,106	11%
Quayle	21,742	18,987	87%	1,450	7%
Dole	13,210	8,660	66%	2,775	21%
Alexander	3,062	531	17%	1,879	61%

Through September 30, 2003		Smallest Donors Contributions: $200 or Less		Largest Donors Contributions: $2,000+	
	Total Contributions from Individuals	Est. No. of Conts.	Percentage	Est. No. of Conts.	Percentage
Dean	151,057	137,330	91%	1,092	1%
LaRouche	32,198	28,219	88%	14	0%
Kucinich	23,217	21,753	94%	139	1%
Kerry	31,593	20,349	64%	3,968	13%
Gephardt	20,319	13,094	64%	2,548	13%
Clark	14,298	12,121	85%	471	3%
Lieberman	17,801	9,441	53%	2,604	15%
Graham	7,241	4,039	56%	1,044	14%
Edwards	14,090	3,951	28%	3,939	28%
Moseley Braun	1,031	795	77%	46	4%
Bush	140,724	95,212	68%	28,758	20%

Table 4A: continued next page

Table 4A: *Cont.*

Through September 30, 2007	Total Contributions from Individuals	Smallest Donors Contributions: $200 or Less		Largest Donors Contributions: $2,000+	
		Est. No. of Conts.	Percentage	Est. No. of Conts.	Percentage
Obama	251,302	208,501	83%	18,480	7%
Clinton	138,743	94,485	68%	25,641	18%
Edwards	100,506	84,678	84%	6,565	7%
Richardson	46,278	35,334	76%	4,475	10%
Kucinich	15,448	14,813	96%	113	1%
Biden	9,249	5,515	60%	1,759	19%
Dodd	7,876	2,816	36%	2,744	35%
Gravel	1,983	1,850	93%	13	1%
McCain	82,305	65,654	80%	7,846	10%
Romney	86,343	60,462	70%	13,366	15%
Thompson, F.	48,386	42,230	87%	2,570	5%
Paul	45,121	41,054	91%	697	2%
Giuliani	64,105	37,714	59%	15,276	24%
Hunter	10,193	9,522	93%	197	2%
Huckabee	7,274	5,850	80%	432	6%

Source: Compiled by author from Federal Election Commission data available at http://www.fec.gov.
Note: For each election, the average amount of each contribution in the $200 or Less category was assumed to be $100.
For 1999, the average amount of each contribution in the $1,000 category was $1,000.
In subsequent elections, the average amount for the $2,000+ category was assumed to be $2,000.

this support did not materialize at the polls. Even though Paul was the last remaining Republican candidate other than John McCain, in the early contests he garnered no higher than a second-place finish in the Nevada and Montana caucuses. In some ways, Paul's 2007–2008 fund-raising and campaign experiences are like that of Howard Dean's four years earlier. Like Dean, who also handily won his party's Small Donor Money Primary, Paul relied extensively on the Internet, which allows a candidate to quickly and efficiently solicit and receive contributions. Further, like Dean, Paul suffered from having limited success in the Early Money Primary as well as difficulty reaching large donors. Dean, though, was at least seen as a potentially viable candidate entering the primary season. Paul, on the other hand, generally lacked the other ingredients of overall viability.

Table 5: Presidential Candidate Financial Activity, January 2008

	Individuals	Candidate	Other	Total	Disbursements	Change in Cash on Hand
Obama	$36,002,466	$0	$0	$36,002,466	$29,747,016	$6,113,911
Clinton	$13,702,517	$5,000,000	$85,700	$18,788,217	$27,645,660	($8,761,533)
Edwards	$3,906,334	$0	$0	$3,906,334	$4,648,694	($732,628)
Kucinich	$450,147	$0	$5,000	$455,147	$691,625	($235,778)
Richardson	$306,779	$0	$16,650	$323,429	$610,271	($977,576)
Biden	$76,405	$0	$0	$76,405	$462,511	($204,969)
Dodd	$58,436	$0	$2,750	$61,186	$486,292	($425,106)
Gravel	$0	$0	$0	$0	$0	$200
McCain	$11,587,744	$0	$76,402	$11,664,146	$10,364,914	$2,249,993
Romney	$9,612,128	$6,950,000	$23,902	$16,586,030	$10,249,998	$6,351,579
Paul	$4,406,490	$0	$578	$4,407,068	$6,250,119	($1,837,233)
Huckabee	$3,954,248	$0	($20,769)	$3,933,479	$4,931,449	($967,045)
Giuliani	$2,974,856	$0	$27,890	$3,002,746	$6,829,874	($3,800,313)
Thompson, F.	$2,027,881	$0	$7,050	$2,034,931	$2,478,813	($439,678)
Hunter	$0	$0	$0	$0	$0	$0

Table 5: continued next page

Table 5: *Cont.*

	Size of Donation				
	$200 and Under	$200.01-$499	$500-$999	$1000-$1,999	$2,000 and over
Obama	$16,282,635	$4,040,456	$3,928,379	$5,119,335	$7,170,756
Clinton	$4,589,418	$1,151,383	$1,253,872	$2,405,434	$4,438,319
Edwards	$2,738,670	$555,014	$209,271	$219,295	$234,000
Kucinich	$361,266	$17,977	$529,884	$19,300	$22,100
Richardson	$157,142	$562,051	$24,005	$31,636	$127,900
Biden	$44,805	$9,340	$6,750	$5,000	$11,500
Dodd	$37,285	$4,451	$4,000	$3,000	$8,900
Gravel	$0	$0	$0	$0	$0
Paul	$3,226,499	$334,020	$430,295	$256,056	$169,406
McCain	$3,052,651	$716,098	$1,370,930	$2,261,619	$4,395,120
Romney	$2,244,252	$642,514	$625,408	$1,085,235	$5,109,145
Huckabee	$2,009,154	$239,746	$451,501	$560,101	$706,844
Thompson, F.	$1,360,105	$282,668	$176,941	$134,100	$111,335
Giuliani	$508,084	$179,306	$274,744	$650,511	$1,552,020
Hunter	$0	$0	$0	$0	$0

Source: Compiled by author from Federal Election Commission data available at http://www.fec.gov.

This side discussion about Ron Paul emphasizes the weight attributed to financial viability as a criterion of overall viability once the primaries and caucuses take place. As McCain pulled away from other candidates in terms of votes and delegates, little attention was paid to campaign finance matters such as Paul's fund-raising successes and his competitiveness with McCain in terms of financial viability, nor to the fact that McCain ended January 2008 with limited resources for the next phase of his campaign (that is, starting to position himself against either Obama or Clinton in preparation for the general election campaign). McCain ended January with slightly over $5 million in cash on hand (an increase of over $2.2 million in cash on hand as of December 31, 2007). However, he had nearly $4 million in campaign loans scheduled to come due in May. Although McCain was appearing at large-event fund-raisers in an attempt to build his war chest, the approximately $12 million he raised in January 2008 and again in February paled compared to the funds raised in the same period by his then still-to-be determined Democratic opponent.[21]

The more interesting campaign finance and candidate viability stories in the 2008 primary season could be found within the Democratic race. As may have been expected based on the pre-primary financial viability, the race was narrowed down to Hillary Clinton and Barack Obama. The race between the candidates for votes and delegates was close and extended throughout the entire primary period—far longer than primary races have in recent presidential nomination cycles. Because of the closeness of the race and the fact that both candidates had established themselves as viable candidates for the party's nomination, campaign funding and financial viability remained important throughout the primary period in trying to distinguish the candidates and their respective momentum.

In January 2008, Obama raised an extraordinary amount (over $36 million), outspent Clinton, and ended the month in a better cash-on-hand position than he started. Clinton, on the other hand, showed signs of weakening financial viability. In addition to being outspent, she ended the month with nearly $9 million cash on hand less than she started January, and even loaned $5 million of her personal funds to her campaign. Stories abounded about how the Clinton campaign was running fewer television ads, particularly in caucus states, and how top campaign aides agreed to work without pay for a month. By comparison, Obama bought commercial time during television coverage of the Super Bowl (normally one of the highest-rated shows and most expensive ones in which to run ads) and during top-rated television shows like *American Idol*. Obama, in other words, used the financial advantage he developed during January to try to further distinguish himself from Clinton.

Clinton held her own in January in the race for voters and delegates, winning such delegate-rich states as California, New York, Massachusetts, and New Jersey. Yet, analysts were starting to question the overall viability of Clinton's candidacy, which again brings into the discussion the ingredients of Clinton's financial viability during January 2008. Consider, for example, the first ingredient—comparatively big money. By many standards, the $13.7 million Clinton raised in January would be very strong. Her level of fund-raising during January, however, has been characterized as "weak,"[22] primarily because it paled in comparison to the $36 million that Obama raised. By out-raising his opponent in terms of contributions from individuals by over a 2.5-to-1 ratio during January, Obama separated himself from Clinton despite the closeness of the race at the polls.

Perhaps to suppress the speculation regarding Clinton's diminishing financial viability, her campaign announced a few days before the critical March 4 primaries in Texas and Ohio that she had raised almost $35 million during the month of February. She utilized these funds in very visible ways, undertaking an aggressive advertising campaign (the "Red Phone" ads), for example, to contend that Obama was not prepared to handle international crises as president, a factor that reportedly influenced late-deciding voters in the Ohio and Texas primaries. Interestingly, two days after losing the primary votes in both large states, the Obama campaign announced that it had raised a record $55 million during the same month, and noted other staggering statistics: $45 million had been raised over the Internet; these funds came from nearly 750,000 contributors, with over half making donations for the first time; and 90 percent of the contributions were in amounts of $100 or less (that is, the smallest of the small donors).[23] Obama maintained a comparable fund-raising advantage throughout the rest of the primary season. In March 2008, he raised more than twice the amount of funds Clinton did in the month—$41 million to almost $20 million. Likewise, for the last two full months of the primaries (April and May combined), Obama raised over $52 million compared to Clinton's total of almost $30 million.

Even though the outcome of the race for the Democratic nomination in 2008 hinged on far more than the fund-raising advantage that Obama had established and maintained, the discussion above does highlight the connection between fund-raising efforts and strategic campaign decisions. With additional resources at hand and employing more effective

campaigning techniques (for example, advertising and debate performances), Clinton was able at least temporarily to slow the momentum
Obama had been gaining during March and April. Nevertheless, the
steady success of Obama's fund-raising allowed his campaign to stand
strong in the face of the inroads that Clinton was threatening to make.
Obama did not need to change strategies, curtail activities for lack of
funds, or act in any way other than a viable candidate for the party's
nomination and the presidency.

The closeness of the race for delegates notwithstanding, what may have
been a key difference between the two candidates can be traced to the
Small Donor Money Primary, where Obama consistently outperformed
Clinton on a 2-to-1 basis (see Table 6). The importance of the Small Donor
Money Primary was recognized by the Obama and Clinton campaigns
themselves, as evidenced through their websites. The Clinton campaign's
website, for example, included stories and comments from contributors
about why they were making their $15, $25 or $50 donations. Obama's
website, for its part, ran a banner story, "Over One Million Own This
Campaign," with a continually updated count indicating that more than
one million people had made contributions to the Obama campaign. As
noted earlier, a broader base of support among small donors provides a
larger pool of likely supporters in the election booth, and Obama's pursuit
of support among voters who were likely to make small donations was
not just a part of his fund-raising strategy, but his overall campaign message. While Obama's small-donor fund-raising advantage did not directly
translate into a 2-to-1 voting edge, his ability to reach these donors—and
voters—played an important role in not only his garnering the Democratic
nomination in his race against Clinton, but also helped lead him to victory
over John McCain in the general election in November 2008.

The Multifaceted Nature of Money in Presidential Selection

Money in electoral politics is often treated as if it were of monolithic importance. Phrases like "money and politics" and "money and elections"
treat all money used in the political system as if its effects were uniform
and without any variation. By breaking down the concept of financial
viability into its three key ingredients, we have seen that the impact that
money has in the presidential selection process varies dramatically based
on the comparative amount of campaign funds raised, and when and from
whom such campaign funds were raised. Further, we saw that the weight

Table 6: Clinton and Obama Small-donor Fundraising, 2007–2008

	Obama Advantage			
	Clinton	Obama	Dollars	Percentage
Third Quarter 2007*	$9,448,527	$20,850,080	$11,401,553	221%
Fourth Quarter 2007	$4,622,401	$10,191,027	$5,568,626	220%
January 2008	$4,589,418	$16,282,635	$11,693,217	355%
February 2008	$17,409,642	$30,745,460	$13,335,818	177%
March 2008	$11,305,833	$24,147,928	$12,842,095	214%
April-May 2008	$21,070,588	$33,467,043	$12,396,455	159%
	$68,446,409	$135,684,173	$67,237,764	198%

Source: Compiled by author from Federal Election Commission data available at http://www.fec.gov.
* Includes all small-donor contributions raised during pre-primary period through the end of the Third Quarter 2007. Small-donor summary data for the first and second quarter of 2007 were not available. from the FEC Website.

given to campaign financing in determining overall candidate viability during the primary season changes once the votes start to be tallied.

Understanding financial viability in this way offers presidential candidates several strategic tips on running their campaign during the pre-primary period. First and foremost, candidates must be able to come out of the gate quickly and establish as early as the first quarter in the year before the election that they are an effective and strong fund-raiser. Certainly, Howard Dean was able to rebound from a slow start to be the top Democratic fund-raiser in 2003, and Mike Huckabee won the Iowa caucuses in 2008 even though he did not appear to be a financially viable candidate. Neither one, however, was able to sustain this momentum, particularly compared to the likes of George W. Bush, Al Gore, Barack Obama, and Hillary Clinton who, despite some ups and downs along the way, maintained their positions as financially viable candidates and actual or potential front-runners throughout the entire pre-primary period.

On a related point, candidates cannot wait too long to get into the race, as evidenced by the electoral performances of Wesley Clark and Fred Thompson. Despite a certain energy their presence brought once they did enter their respective races, neither was able to establish financial or overall viability because both were being compared to candidates who had already done so. On the flip side of the coin, candidates may not wish to stay in the race if they are unable to establish the basis of financial viability by the end of June in the year before the election. Some candidates have quickly realized that the uphill battle they have been fighting is just going to get worse, and have exited from a race before it even started. Elizabeth Dole in 1999 immediately comes to mind, and the 2007 pre-primary period saw its fair share of announced candidates withdraw early as well (Tom Vilsack, Sam Brownback, and Tommy Thompson, to name a few).[24]

One of the more significant implications of the findings herein is that not only should candidates not ignore small donors, they should embrace them. Critics of "big money" in politics often lament the importance given to large contributors. The Campaign Finance Institute, a Washington, D.C.-based think tank, has contended, "With Presidential Candidates Also Raising Record Amounts, Mostly from Large Donors, It's Time to Put Small Donors on the Agenda."[25] Yet small donors are one of the key drivers of financial viability in the pre-primary period and of candidate viability overall—not necessarily for the amount of money they contribute, but for the number of potential voters that they can bring into a candidate's tent of support.

The deconstruction of financial viability into its key components has shown a connection between these components and the likelihood of electoral success in garnering a party's nomination during the era of diminishing importance of public financing. This connection is clear in 2000 and 2004 when early voting returns broke along the lines with the key components of financially viability in the pre-primary period. The 2008 primary season—in which a marginally financially viable candidate emerged with one party's nomination and two financially viable candidates fought through the entire primary season before the race for the other party's nomination was determined—shows some of the limitations of this connection, though. What the 2008 election season does show is the important connection between successful fund-raising in the pre-primary period and strategic campaign decisions in both the pre-primary and primary periods.

Consider the relative positions of Hillary Clinton and Barack Obama at the outset of 2007. Clinton entered the race with many key ingredients of an overall viable campaign: name recognition, résumé, support from the party establishment, donor connections, campaign expertise and organization, and $10 million on hand transferred from her senatorial campaign to fund the start-up costs of her presidential campaign. Obama, lacking these built-in ingredients to a viable campaign, had to construct a different strategy. He promoted his campaign via the Internet, sought to establish grassroots movements in caucus states, and went after youth and other "unlikely" voters. Each of these elements proved to be interconnected fund-raising and electoral strategies. Obama utilized classic campaign techniques to build his money base, but his success in fund-raising also reached a broad range of voters that ultimately helped carry him to victory for the Democratic nomination and in the general election.

In the changing world of presidential campaign finance, where candidates must be more innovative in the void left by no longer pursuing a strategy based on obtaining public financing, the connections among financial viability in the pre-primary period, strategic decisions during both the pre-primary and primary seasons, and ultimate electoral success need to be further investigated. This chapter has shown that how candidates get money (for example, from small donors) and when they get money (for example, early money) are important determinants of financial viability, but this is just a start. The examination of fund-raising can be deconstructed further—perhaps on a daily or weekly basis, or an individual-contribution level instead of categorical groupings. Other strategic decisions—most notably, candidate expenditures, including when, how much, and for what purpose—should be examined in a similarly deconstructed manner to identify other lessons for presidential aspirants desiring to wage a viable campaign for their party's nomination. For this chapter has made one key lesson clear: candidates cannot wait to the primary season to make certain strategic choices, as they could in the era before 2000. Instead, these choices now must be made, or at least be rooted, in the pre-primary process. Candidates need to have their primary electoral strategy formed and implemented as part of their fund-raising efforts to become financially viable during the pre-primary period in order to become electorally viable once the voting begins.

Notes

1. All dollar amounts listed in this introductory paragraph are determined as of July 31 of the applicable election year.

2. Momentum and viability are related but different ways to measure how successful a candidate may be in winning his or her party's nomination. See Larry M. Bartels, *Presidential Primaries and the Dynamics of Public Choice* (Princeton, N.J.: Princeton University Press, 1988) for a more systematic analysis of momentum. As Bartels notes, "momentum" has at its heart the "possibility that [a candidate] might break out of the pack, leaving others to 'play catch-up'" (p. 4). As a result, a previously non-viable candidate could gain momentum to become a viable candidate in the primaries, or a viable candidate could gain momentum to become the clear front-runner.

3. Alan I. Abramowitz, "Viability, Electability, and Candidate Choice in a Presidential Primary Election: A Test of Competing Models," *Journal of Politics*, 51 (1989), 978.

4. See Victoria Farrar-Myers, "Money and the Art and Science of Candidate Viability," in *Rethinking Madam President: Are We Ready for a Woman in the White House?* Lori Cox Han and Caroline Heldman, eds. (Boulder, Colo.: Lynne Rienner Publishers, 2007). The paragraph in the primary text above summarizes the discussion found on pages 122–23.

5. Farrar-Myers, "Money and the Art and Science of Candidate Viability," 113.

6. Randall E. Adkins and Andrew J. Dowdle, "The Money Primary: What Influences the Outcome of Pre-Primary Presidential Nomination Fundraising?" *Presidential Studies Quarterly*, 32 (2002), 273. Similarly, Mayer developed a simple model to forecast presidential nominations with two independent variables: (1) the "percentage of party identifiers who supported each candidate in the last national Gallup poll before the Iowa caucuses" and (2) the "total amount of money each candidate raised before the election year, divided by the largest amount of money raised by any candidate in that party's nomination race." See William G. Mayer, "Forecasting Presidential Nominations or, My Model Worked Just Fine, Thank You," *PS: Political Science and Politics* 36 (2003), 153; see also R. Lawrence Butler, *Claiming the Mantle: How Presidential Nominations Are Won and Lost before the Votes are Cast* (Cambridge, Mass.: Westview Press, 2004), 62, for a simple graphic depiction of this model.

7. For example, see Herbert Alexander, "Money and the Presidential Nominating Process," in Kenneth W. Thompson, ed., *The Presidential Nomination Process: Constitutional, Economic and Political Issues* (Lanham, Md.: University Press of America, 1984). Alexander (p. 64) once noted that in the race for the 1984 Democratic presidential nomination, neither Alan Cranston nor Gary Hart could "afford to quit" the race before receiving public funding, since "a new infusion of money . . . will enable them to pay off their debts and perhaps to compete in the early primaries and caucuses."

8. See Clyde Wilcox, "Financing the 1988 Prenomination Campaigns," in Emmett H. Buell, Jr. and Lee Sigelman, eds., *Nominating the President* (Knoxville: University of Tennessee Press, 1991). Wilcox (p. 92) noted the different experiences of Bruce Babbitt and Michael Dukakis during the pre-primary period for the 1988 Democratic nomination. By the time public funds were released in January 1988, Babbitt had little cash on hand and needed the money to repay existing loans. Dukakis, by comparison, had $4,000,000 in the bank, was debt-free, and was able to use the influx of public funds for the strategic development of his campaign.

9. In 2007–2008 primary season, John McCain ended up not receiving public funds. He did file the requisite paperwork to receive public financing, only to rescind his request prior to receiving any money. John Edwards initially indicated that he would

not seek public funding, but ended up receiving public funds when his fundraising lagged behind his Democratic competitors Clinton and Obama.

10. Political columnist George Will speculated as early as 2004 on what the political landscape might be like in 2008: "Then there may be two tiers of candidates—those who accept public funding and the spending (i.e., speech) limits that come with it, and those who do not. Only the latter will be serious candidates." See his "Kerry Drops a Good Idea." *Newsweek*, June 7, 2004, 86.

11. Shortly after the 2008 general election, one political analyst wrote: "By raising more than $640 million for his presidential race—in effect burying his opponent in cash—Barack Obama probably also laid to rest the concept of public financing for presidential campaigns. After all, why would any candidate adept at raising such vast sums surrender the advantage in return for $84 million in government support?" See Shawn Zeller, "Vantage Point: Trends and Forecasts in Government, Commerce and Politics." *CQ Weekly*, November 17, 2008, 3070.

12. See, for example, Adkins and Dowdle, "The Money Primary." The definition of "Money Primary" above is found on Adkins and Dowdle, 257.

13. The remaining primaries—Reagan, 1984; Bush, 1992; Clinton, 1996; and Bush, 2004—saw an incumbent president running unopposed. As for the five instances in which the same candidate won the early contests and the nomination, note that two include incumbent presidents facing a challenge within their party (Ford, 1976; Carter, 1980), and a third case (Carter, 1976) is included despite the fact that Carter, who received 28 percent of the vote in Iowa, actually came in second to "Uncommitted" with 37 percent.

14. At the time Elizabeth Dole dropped out of the race in October 1999, she had raised less than one-tenth of the amount George W. Bush had—$5 million to $57 million, respectively. Dole also trailed Steve Forbes ($20 million, although $16 million was self-funded) and John McCain (nearly double Dole's amount) in the Money Primary.

15. Michael Cornfield and Jonah Seiger, "The Net and the Nomination," in William G. Mayer, ed. *The Making of the Presidential Candidates 2004* (Lanham, Md.: Rowman and Littlefield, 2004), 209.

16. When George W. Bush ran unopposed for the 2004 nomination, he raised $33.7 million, $49.2 million, and $46.7 million in individual contributions during the second, third, and fourth quarters of 2003, respectively.

17. Chris Dodd (over $4.7 million), Rudy Giuliani ($1.95 million), Joe Biden ($1.9 million), and John McCain (over $1 million) also made significant transfers of leftover funds from previous campaigns to their presidential campaigns.

18. Limited availability of data required focusing on contributions as of the end of the third quarter of the year prior to the election year in order to have comparable data across the three election cycles presented in Table 4. The maximum amount

that an individual could contribute to a candidate during the primary season under federal campaign finance laws changed with the passage of the Bipartisan Campaign Reform Act in 2002. For the 2000 election cycle, the maximum amount was $1,000. For 2004, the maximum amount was increased to $2,000, and then adjusted upward in subsequent years based on inflation. To simplify the presentation of Table 4 and Table 4A, data for the groupings of contributions between $200.01—$999 (all elections) and $1,000—$1,999 (2004 and 2008 elections) were omitted.

19. See each candidate's profile at CNN Election Center, http://www.cnn.com/ELECTION/2008/candidates (accessed March 1, 2008).

20. Farrar-Myers, "Money and the Art and Science of Candidate Viability," 128.

21. Jim Kuhnhenn, "Clinton, Obama Far Ahead of McCain in Fund-Raising," *Atlanta Metro News*, http://www.ajc.com/news/content/news/stories/2008/03/01/pemoney_0302.html (accessed March 8, 2008).

22. "Clinton Lent $5 Million to Her Campaign before Super Tuesday," CNN Election Center, http://www.cnn.com/2008/POLITICS/02/06/election.clinton/index.html (accessed March 1, 2008).

23. John McCormick, "Barack Obama's February Haul: $55 million," ChicagoTribune.com, http://weblogs.chicagotribune.com/news/politics/blog/2008/03/barack_obamas_february_haul_ne.html (accessed March 8, 2008).

24. Vilsack withdrew from the race fifteen days after declaring his candidacy, in part because of his inability to raise the money necessary to compete.

25. "The Ups and Downs of Small and Large Donors: A Campaign Finance Institute Analysis of Pre- And Post-BCRA Contributions to Federal Candidates And Parties, 1999–2006," Campaign Finance Institute, 2007, http://www.cfinst.org/books_reports/SmallDonors/Small-Large-Donors_June2007.pdf (accessed March 1, 2008).

The Virtual Primary Campaign

Connecting with Constituents in a Multimedia Age

DIANE J. HEITH

Since 1992, candidates' own words have appeared less and less within election coverage in nightly news broadcasts.[1] Instead, reporters' preference for their own interpretations dominates transmission of candidates' platform, language, and opinion, according to Farnsworth and Lichter. Not surprisingly, candidates seek alternate ways to get their message to citizens unfiltered. Interestingly, citizens appear as frustrated with the mainstream media as the candidates do. Poll after poll has reported anger and aggravation with the coverage provided by mainstream media as well as the increasing preference for gathering information online.[2]

Dissatisfaction with mainstream media offerings and the ubiquity of the Internet in daily life coalesced during the 2008 pre-primary and primary campaign season. The seven major candidates (as of January 1, 2008), Democrats Hillary Clinton, John Edwards, and Barack Obama, and Republicans Mike Huckabee, Rudy Giuliani, John McCain, and Mitt Romney, each had well-developed, content-rich websites.

The campaign of 2008 magnified the consequences for the Internet in politics: the diminishment of mainstream media gatekeeping and the inclusion of a younger, active polis. Even with a front-loaded calendar, media attempts to manage the race were evident as early as August 2007 when Senator John McCain's campaign was considered "dead in the water" and Senator Hillary Clinton was considered the "inevitable" Democratic nominee. However, the uncontrolled and unfiltered flow of information from the candidates to citizens as well as the free flow of information between citizens online created alternate mechanisms for campaign narratives and enabled outsider candidacies. Thus, the traditional gatekeepers could not dominate the debate or outcomes by narrowing the race early.

In the 2008 primary process, there was an outpouring of participation tracked in traditional measures (rally numbers and increased vote turnout) and in nontraditional measures (website traffic and donations online). Via the Internet, citizens and candidates increased their connections without increasing traditional media input. Via websites, blogs, and YouTube, citizens and candidates reached beyond media-controlled campaigns and expanded both citizen and candidate options.

Meeting Citizens Online

The premier question for candidates and campaign consultants since 2004 might have been how can we advantage (or avoid falling victim to) multiplatform media. Candidates for president in 2008 have the same simple, yet gargantuan, tasks that candidates always face. Candidates need to have a message and they need to be able to deliver their message. They need to respond to critics and supporters alike, be they pundits, reporters, or opponents. Candidates also need to create a sustainable organization. The organization needs to encourage supporters to vote. The organization needs to convert opponents into supporters or, alternatively, to suppress interest in turning out for an opponent. Most importantly, each candidate needs to raise money to fund all aspects of the campaign.

The traditional mechanisms that candidates have used since the 1950s to reach voters with their message and reach donors' checkbooks are both exclusive and inclusive. Exclusive voter and donor enterprises have included targeted mailings, invitation-only dinners, and meetings. Inclusive voter and donor exercises have included large events and rallies, fundraising phone calls to less-personal lists, and phone calls urging support and turnout. Inclusive message outreach has primarily involved the mainstream media but has also included narrower media outlets to both broadcast and narrowcast the candidate's message via interviews, debates, faxing, poll-data dissemination, and of course, television and radio advertising.

For the 2008 campaign, candidate outreach for both inclusive and exclusive purposes relied heavily on new media mechanisms. Following the example of earlier presidential campaigns,[3] the 2008 presidential candidates employed candidate websites, candidate e-mail, and online fundraising. New in 2008, the candidates also ventured off their own sites to optimize non-campaign-dominated websites such as YouTube, Facebook, and MySpace.

The Campaign Online

In recognition of the changing media marketplace, all candidates running for president in 2008 offered campaign websites. Presidential campaigns since 1996 have been online.[4] However, having a page is no longer enough, websites need to work for the candidate. In 2004, Howard Dean showed the political world that candidates could raise money online as well as meet volunteers and voters.[5] As Williams, Trammell et al. argue, "a modern campaign now requires websites that are interactive and invite user participation."[6] Campaign 2008 demonstrates that candidates who embraced the online world increased opportunities and maximized support.

Website Comparisons

When a potential voter, pundit, reporter, or scholar visits a candidate's website, judgments about the site and thus the candidate are almost immediate. Since all candidates have websites, the issue for comparison is no longer Web presence, but rather the quality, quantity, and appeal of these sites.

The entire slate of candidates in 2008, Republican and Democrat, mainstream and fringe, crafted effective websites. The clearest evidence of how integral an online campaign is stems from the money spent in the virtual world. Campaigns spent heavily on online advertising, e-mail, and texting, as well as Web content and design. Gone are the days where the Web budget was a minor subset of marketing. In 2007–2008, Hillary Clinton's campaign spent $503,120 on Web advertising while Barack Obama spent almost $3 million in the same time frame.[7] The attention to the Web builds on the efforts of both parties and both major candidates in 2004. The candidates employed their Web presence to address their issue agendas, although their blogs dealt with slightly different issues in 2004.[8]

On the surface, all candidates provided similar information on their websites. The sites all highlighted pictures of the candidates, their families, and an U.S. flag from some vantage point.[9] More importantly, each website provided information about the candidate. Viewers could watch videos of the candidates speaking. Site visitors could learn about the candidates' issue positions and even in some cases compare issue positions. Moreover, since 2004, candidates have made their websites interactive, via the Web log, commonly known as a blog.[10]

In terms of overall traffic, the Barack Obama website was the most

Table 1: Rank of Website*

Obama	3,018.0
Clinton	11,088.0
Edwards	46,570.0
Mcain	27,677.0
Huckabee	23,177.0
Romney	33,318.0
Giuliani	3,588,812.0

*From Alexa.com rankings of site traffic; the smaller the number the more highly visited. Google.com is number one.

highly viewed and utilized. According to Alexa.com, the website-ranking website, Barack Obama's campaign site was over three times more popular than that of his nearest competitor.[11] As Table 1 demonstrates, there was a tremendous difference in Web traffic between the top seven candidates. Alexa.com's model could not count visits to Rudy Giuliani's website in some viewing categories because citizens so infrequently utilized it.[12]

Moreover, Web traffic closely mirrored the fluctuations of the 2008 primary and pre-primary process. Barack Obama's website was always the most trafficked one, as early as April 2007.[13] However, between June and July of 2007, Hillary Clinton's site observed a dramatic increase in viewership, mimicking the increased mainstream media attention. Traffic then ebbed until the campaign began in earnest. Obama dominated campaign Web traffic, outpacing his competition by more than double, peaking at a fivefold traffic comparison in mid-February 2008.[14] Moreover, Tables 2 and 3 demonstrate that Obama's reach (number of users) and rank (three months of aggregated historical traffic data) was considerably higher than any of the other candidates.[15]

The basic biographic Web page as well as the ability to blog was available in 2000 and 2004, but the interactive nature of the websites as well as the expectation of interaction sets campaign 2008 apart. Williams, Trammell et al. note that in 2004, candidates were reluctant to link to outside material.[16] Websites now allowed interested citizens to make connections with the candidates. Some candidates did this well while others lagged behind. In fact, the effort put forth by the candidates reveals much about the candidates' constituency strategies. The web pages are like paid advertising in that they are devoid of media commentary. Thus, candidates determined what they wanted citizens to see, and structured their pages around what aspects they wanted to highlight and the individuals to whom they wished to appeal.

The norms that govern what websites would and would not do, evolved significantly during the 2008 campaign cycle. The mechanisms used within the sites did not vary considerably, as all campaigns recognized what they wanted to get from citizens and what they wanted to provide to them. The variation between the candidates centered on how the candidates extended their campaign outside their own websites.

Candidate Website Design and Content

The seven major candidates (as of January 1, 2008), Democrats Hillary Clinton, John Edwards, and Barack Obama, and Republicans Mike Huckabee, Rudy Giuliani, John McCain, and Mitt Romney, used their websites for the typical campaign tasks that existed long before the Internet. These candidates distinguished themselves from their opponents, identified and encouraged likely voters, and raised money to support their candidacies.

A campaign website, like any website, serves two constituencies: the user and the provider. In thinking about website design, the campaigns clearly focused on their users' needs as well as their own. All of the campaigns during the primary period featured a "layered top story area" which allowed the changing of headlines.[17] The blogosphere appeared to inspire the campaign websites in terms of layout and design, with similar features for searching for content.[18] However, the Obama website was much denser and content-rich than the sites of his opponents; the Obama site required 1.2MB of storage space while the Hillary Clinton page required 422KB.[19] In addition, the Obama campaign had an incredibly simple mechanism for collecting e-mail address and cell-phone numbers for texting, which they then converted to an incredibly sophisticated machine to contact individuals.

There was nearly universal agreement as to what a website needed to provide its users (see Table 2). Since 2000, all candidates provided information like *candidate bios* and stands on relevant *issues*.[20] Additionally, candidates since 2004 provided a *media* page, references to candidate appearances in the mainstream media. Evolving from the exponential blossoming online of interest in blogs, all seven candidates' websites provided a *candidate blog* which typically provided a daily statement, response, or comment on some occurrence in the campaign. John McCain's blog on February 28, 2008, featured posts by the campaign manager: "Former President Bush Endorses McCain"; "John McCain Sweeps Chesapeake

Primary." A click on each link took the viewer to a short article explaining the headline. By definition, blog entries are brief, almost diary-like updates.

The remaining links on candidate websites listed in Table 2 are all opportunities for connection that highlight what the Internet does well: linking people, transmitting information, and facilitating purchases. All seven candidates used their websites to allow individuals to *join a group*, online or in their geographic area. All seven candidates encouraged interested individuals to *volunteer* for the campaign, serving in person, online, or by phone. The 2008 campaign websites excelled in offering things for purchase online, opportunities to *buy* bumper stickers, hats, and shirts from the campaign store. All seven candidates also gave individuals the opportunity to *donate* to the campaign online.

The one area of difference on these candidate websites came in the form of activation. With the exception of Rudy Giuliani, the difference fell along party lines. The Clinton, Edwards, Giuliani, and Obama websites contained links for individuals to *register* to vote. The Huckabee, McCain, and Romney websites did not provide any opportunity to register.

These site links were not equally used. Using the traffic rankings by Alexa.com, Table 3 reveals that only Obama and Clinton's campaign attracted significant traffic within their websites.[21] On John McCain's website, 95 percent of visitors went to the main page; only 5 percent then to other areas within the site. In contrast, on Obama's website, 44 percent went to

Table 2: Opportunities to Connect

Opportunities

Candidates	blog	register	join	volunteer	donate	purchase	read media	read about issues	read bios
Clinton	√	√	√	√	√	√	√	√	√
Edwards	√	√	√	√	√	√	√	√	√
Guiliani	√	√	√	√	√	√	√	√	√
Huckabee	√		√	√	√	√	√	√	√
McCain	√		√	√	√	√	√	√	√
Obama	√	√	√	√	√	√	√	√	√
Romney	√		√	√	√	√	√	√	√

The assessments of the candidate websites arises from a review of the web pages between January 1, 2008 and March 10, 2008.

Pages under review: www.barackobama.com; www.hillaryclinton.com; www.johnedwards.com; www.mittromney.com; www.johnmccain.com; www.mikehuckabee.com; www.rudy2008.com.

Table 3: Sites Visited within the Websites*

Obama	
my.barackobama.com	44%
barackobama.com	42%
store.barackobama.com	6%
origin.barackobama.com	2%
donate.barackobama.com	1%
factcheck.barackobama.com	1%
action.barackobama.com	1%
Other websites	3%
Clinton	
hillaryclinton.com	89%
connect.hillaryclinton.com	3%
contribute.hillaryclinton.com	2%
blog.hillaryclinton.com	2%
tools.hillaryclinton.com	2%
links.hillaryclinton.com	1%
Other web sites	1%
McCain	
johnmccain.com	95%
Other websites	5%

* From Alexa.com tracking of site traffic

their own page created within the Obama website, my.barackobama.com. Those visitors outranked visitors to the main page (42 percent) suggesting that Obama was not only attracting people to the site but also keeping them, as they returned to their own personalized pages. Both Obama and Clinton saw traffic on their pages; for joining and donating, although Obama's store of T-shirts and other paraphernalia was more popular.

Beyond the Candidate Web Page

What separates the 2008 campaign usage of the Internet from previous efforts is the effort to manage a campaign's presence on the Internet to the extent that it is possible. Journalists, citizens, and campaign workers made use of the blogosphere in 2004; however, Howard Dean's campaign was first to recognize and make use of social networking websites like MeetUp.[22] The Dean campaign piggybacked on outside organizations' efforts to organize via the Web. Between 2004 and 2008, social networking sites went mainstream as part of the social landscape, but were not part of the political process. In 2008, the political campaign included a role for social networking sites within the political process.

In contrast to the fear of the outside links in 2004, the 2008 candidates for the Democratic and Republican nominations all recognized the value of linking their websites to other highly trafficked sites. Putting an icon of a social networking site on a candidate's website offered a link to alternative views of the candidate in a familiar format, and the icon also indicated which sites (and thus which participants) the campaigns deemed valuable.

In contrast to the similarity of website organization, there was much more variation in terms of the sites to which candidates linked. Only one site consistently appeared on all seven candidates' websites during the primaries: YouTube (see Table 4). YouTube is not a social networking site; its primary function is the dissemination of videos. The unique role YouTube played in the 2008 primary races will be discussed below.

While all candidate websites linked to social networking sites, there was much variation in terms of the choice and number of linking icons. Six of the seven candidates had icons for MySpace, Facebook, and Flickr (see Table 4). John McCain's campaign did not link to any of those. As Table 4 demonstrates, there is wide variation in the number of social website with which the candidates chose to affiliate. Mike Huckabee and Rudy Giuliani linked their sites to two additional social networks. McCain connected only to Veoh while Romney connected to no additional sites beyond MySpace, Facebook, and Flickr. Democrats Clinton and Edwards were similar to their Republican counterparts. Clinton connected to two additional sites and Edwards to no additional sites. In contrast, as Table 4 demonstrates, Barack Obama had ten additional social networking sites listed in addition to MySpace, Facebook, and Flickr.

YouTube

While the social networking links are important, judging their ability to transmit campaign information is relatively difficult. If you click on the link to any of the social networking sites, the click takes you to the candidate's home page on that site. Typically, those pages offer stripped-down versions of the candidate's biographic information. Those pages also provide links to other web pages and interested users of the site. For example, Hillary Clinton had 188,952 individuals identify themselves as

Table 4: Hyperlinkages

	MySpace	Flickr	YouTube	Face-book	Eventful	Meetup	Veoh	Digg	Blip.tv
Candidates									
Clinton	√	√	√	√					
Edwards	√	√	√	√					
Guiliani	√	√	√	√				√	√
Huckabee	√	√	√	√	√	√			
McCain			√				√		
Obama	√	√	√	√				√	
Romney	√	√	√	√					

	iTunes	Eons	Black-Planet	Linke-dIn	Faith-Base	GLEE	Mi-Gente	Asia-nAve	
Clinton		√							
Edwards									
Guiliani	√								
Huckabee									
McCain									
Obama		√	√	√	√	√	√	√	
Romney									

	Party-Builder	Twit-ter							
Clinton		√							
Edwards									
Guiliani									
Huckabee									
McCain									
Obama	√								
Romney									

The assessments of the candidate websites arise from a review of the sites between January 1, 2008, and March 10, 2008.

"friends" on MySpace; Obama had 312,860.[23] However, it is difficult to discern how these links influence knowledge or political participation. The campaigns understood the difference between reaching Facebook users and connecting with Facebook friends. Rather than merely rely on their "friends," the candidates also bought ad space on the social networking sites as well as on Google, Yahoo, and other websites (Kaye, 2008).

In contrast, the video-broadcasting website YouTube offers an effective way to track knowledge because the video content reveals the information disseminated. There are multiple ways to find content on YouTube. An individual can search for content specifically, for content generally, or view suggested videos (for example, "videos being watched now," "featured videos," and "most popular"). A general search on YouTube for a campaign or campaign names reveals loose rankings of interest. As Table 5 reveals, YouTube searches for Ron Paul resulted in the most hits, with over 100,000, while Obama and Clinton trailed, with a little over 40,000 each.[24]

A more specific measure of interest stems from determining the most watched political videos: which clips attract interest, and how much interest. YouTube will reveal how many people have watched a video. This is useful for discerning the content and knowledge of those seeking political information online. The website does not distinguish the number of times a user views a video, unlike Alexa.com, which counts a user only once a day regardless of number of site visits.

According to Table 6, the most popular video on YouTube was made by a YouTube user, whose user name is Obama Girl. Over six and a half million viewers watched the video "I Got A Crush on You."[25] It was so popular that it spawned spin-offs and a lot of media attention for Obama

Table 5: YouTube References*

Candidates	General Hits
Clinton	42,500
Edwards	15,300
Guiliani	5,380
Huckabee	5,080
McCain	9,030
Obama	41,600
Romney	11,300
Campaign 2008	8,390
Paul	104,000

*As of February 28, 2008

Girl. This video did contain political content about candidate Barack Obama, albeit innocuous content. Similarly inoffensive videos included "John Edwards Feeling Pretty"; over one million people watched this one about John Edwards doing his hair.

The other videos viewed more than a million times were substantively content-rich. The most-popular-video list serves to highlight the important moments during the primary process, according to YouTube viewers. The popular videos provided by the candidates' reference issues like immigration and health care. Other popular videos included Obama's victory speech after winning Iowa; Clinton's substituting Obama's "yes, we can" slogan, for "yes, we will"; and John McCain answering the "How Do We Beat the B****?" question. The exchanges of significance between the candidates can be watched repeatedly, independent of media commentary.

What Table 6 also reveals is how the Internet, via sites like YouTube, provided an outlet for outreach for candidates the media deemed second-tier. Governor Mike Huckabee's campaign exemplifies how a relatively unknown candidate can connect with citizens without receiving traditional support via money for advertising or receiving free media coverage despite a website less sophisticated than those of other candidates. Since anyone can post on YouTube, and viewership determines popularity, citizens make a video popular and make a candidate noteworthy. Thus, when a candidate gets viral video attention (videos whose popularity spread them far and wide), the media is in the position of reporting the phenomenon, not creating one via its own attention. As Table 6 showcases, of the eighteen videos boasting viewership over one million, 22 percent relate to Huckabee; that is over eight million free references to the former governor.

Nonetheless, Mike Huckabee might not be the candidate most aided by the Internet. Fringe candidates come and go in campaigns. In campaign 2008, there were close to twenty candidates vying for the presidency in early 2007; the invisible primary of money, polling, and name recognition initially narrowed the race to about eight Democrats and Republicans. Republican Ron Paul remained in the race much longer than most second-tier candidates, despite falling short in the invisible primary. Paul's YouTube popularity propelled his candidacy. As Table 6 indicates, Paul only had four videos over the 500,000 viewership mark, totaling 2,904,372. However, he had eight videos under the 500,000 mark which averaged 212,000 viewers. Clearly, Paul had a following that used YouTube for information about their candidate, particularly rerunning media appearances.

Table 6: Most Watched Videos (over 500,000 times viewed, as of 2/28/08)

Candidate	Type of Video	Title of Video	Description	Views
Obama	Fan Made	"I Got A Crush on You," by Obama Girl	Song by Obama Girl	6,628,601.00
Clinton	Clinton Campaign	Hillary on the Choice	Senator Clinton: comparison of public service	4,614,593.00
Huckabee	Fan Made	Immigration Gumballs	Immigration Debate	2,536,761.00
Huckabee	Campaign	Huckabee Responds to Evolution	Answering the CNN debate question	2,445,103.00
Clinton	Clinton Campaign	Night Shift	Clinton on family policy	2,387,616.00
Clinton/Obama	Fan Made	Hillary Clinton Says, "Yes We Will"	Hillary copies Obama chant	2,245,814.00
Clinton/Obama	Fan Made	Clinton vs. Obama: Speeches Are More than Just Words	Hillary Clinton criticizing Obama	2,133,748.00
Huckabee	Fan-made	Chuck Norris Approved	Huckabee and Norris review facts	1,841,834.00
Clinton	Fan-made	The Shocking Video That Hillary Does NOT Want You to See	Hillary Uncensored, the unedited trailer that has been ranked the #1 video in Google's top 100	1,761,850.00
Clinton	News Station	Web Extra: Joyce Garbaciak Interviews Sen. Hillary Clinton	Clinton spends a few minutes answering questions from WISN 12 News Correspondent	1,604,538.00
McCain	Fan-made	John He Is . . .	Music video parody	1,410,016.00
Huckabee	Huckabee Campaign	What Really Matters	Governor Huckabee's holiday greeting	1,305,848.00
Obama	Fan-made	Fox Attacks Obama	*Fox News* criticizing Barack Obama	1,128,661.00
Edwards	Fan-made	John Edwards Feeling Pretty	Edwards doing his hair	1,127,098.00
Obama/Guiliani	Fan-made	Debate 2008: Obama Girl vs. Guiliani Girl	Song by Obama Girl	1,122,189.00
McCain	Fan-made	How Do We Beat the B**** Extended Version	Unedited footage of John McCain answering a question from a supporter on the campaign trail	1,081,815.00
Obama	Obama Campaign	Obama's Response to Bush's SOTU	Barack Obama responds to Bush's State of the Union Address	1,075,893.00

Table 6: continued next page

Table 6: *Cont.*

Obama	Obama Campaign	Obama's Victory Speech	Barack Obama speaks after winning the Iowa caucus	1,039,987.00
Paul	Campaign	Ron Paul Courageously Speaks the Truth	Answering questions on the CNN debate	934,741.00
Obama	Obama Campaign	Barack Obama: My Plan for 2008	Information on Obama's plan	839,312.00
Obama	Music Video	"Barack Obama: Yes We Can"	Obama-inspired Black Eyed Peas Song	785,090.00
Obama	Obama Campaign	Barack Obama Speaks at Dr. King's Church in Atlanta, Georgia	Speech delivered the day before Martin Luther King Jr. Day	692,439.00
Obama	YouTube	Barack Obama YouTube Spotlight	How can we make this country better? We want to hear your ideas!	689,828.00
Obama	Obama Campaign	America's Youth Come Together	Young voters from across America come together in support for Obama	677,678.00
Paul	Campaign	Ron Paul is Bill Maher's New Hero	Answering questions on the talk show	670,397.00
Paul	Campaign	Ron Paul Going the Distance	Message	669,609.00
Obama	Obama Campaign	Barack Obama on *Ellen*	Obama on the *Ellen Degeneres Show*	665,435.00
Clinton	Clinton Campaign	I Need Your Advice	Obama seeking advice	649,597.00
Obama	CNN	Barack Obama Strongest in November versus McCain	CNN breaks down why Obama is the strongest candidate	648,682.00
Clinton	Fan-made	Hillary Election Day Health Scare	Just as Clinton touted the importance of universal healthcare for America, a coughing fit forced the end of a live TV interview	647,722.00
Obama	Fan-made	Obama Inspiring Response to "Just Words" Clinton Critique	responding to Hillary Clinton's recent criticism	645,267.00
Paul	Campaign	Ron Paul Progress	Message	629,625.00
McCain	Fan-made	John McCain vs. John McCain	John McCain	538,146.00
McCain	Fan-made	Raw Video: Too Old? McCain Laughs	John McCain answers a question from a high school student	501,956.00
				48,377,489.00

Bringing the Campaign Online

As of March 12, 2008, the number of Americans voting in the primary process surpassed forty-three million. The top campaign videos were watched over forty-eight million times. Barack Obama's website received 0.0415 percent of the 1,319,872,109 global Internet users.[26] In the United States, there are over 215 million Internet users.[27] Not all Internet users seek political information, but clearly the number of people using the Internet for political information is growing. Thus, it is important to assess its impact on candidates, citizens, and the election process itself.

Candidates and the Web

For those who chose to maximize Web technology, the Web proved enormously advantageous. Barack Obama's meteoric rise through the primary process cannot be entirely attributed to Web presence but it cannot be coincidence that his website was always the most trafficked of all candidates, peaking at five times the visitors that other campaign sites received. Moreover, both Obama and Clinton raised enormous sums of money online. Obama set online records in January and February 2008. In January, Obama raised $27 million online. In comparison, Howard Dean "known as the first Internet candidate," according to an article in the *Washington Post*, "raised $27 million online in 2004 during his whole campaign."[28] Obama's prodigious organization in caucus states has been credited for his success, ut that organization was influenced by Web opportunities to sign up and volunteer.

In contrast, the Web provided no identifiable benefit for the established Republican front-runners: McCain, Romney, and Giuliani. They do not appear to have developed much Web presence. The lackluster participation in the Republican primaries might be related to the dearth of effective Web strategies alongside their "real" world strategies (of course, causality is difficult to determine in this type of system), although, as noted in Table 4, Giuliani was the only candidate from either party to link to iTunes, the music-downloading website. A click on the iTunes link connected one to a list of Giuliani speeches that could be downloaded.

The strategic choices made by the campaigns regarding which sites to connect to appear related to the candidates' constituent strategies. The Pew Internet and American Life Project found that 24 percent of Americans claimed to regularly learn something about the campaign from the Internet, up from 13 percent in 2004.[29] However, 42 percent of younger

Americans, from ages eighteen to twenty-nine, regularly learned about the campaign from the Internet. Participation online, particularly in social networking sites, is also age-related. The older one is, the less likely one is to use the Web for social networking. However, for the eighteen-to-twenty-five-year-old demographic, social life functions online. To reach this group, Web presence is a necessity. Fully 27 percent under thirty (including 37 percent under twenty-four) received campaign information from social networking sites. Only 1 percent of older Americans get news in this format.[30] The Obama campaign had the largest Web presence and had the largest percentage of younger voters' support.

Citizens and the Web

For citizens, bringing the campaign interactively online has massive informational benefits. Of course, as with all sources of information, the gathering of knowledge is dependent on the perseverance of the citizen. People must choose to watch the news, listen to the radio, or pay attention to a political advertisement. For those who have Internet access, candidates' presence online makes the gathering of information easier, as availability is no longer time-dependent. Citizens do not have to watch the news at six thirty in order to discover the latest campaign occurrence.

Moreover, citizens who wish to get campaign information directly or participate in a campaign now have easy means to act on that desire. The ordinary Internet user reads e-mail, reads news items, and purchases music and other things online everyday. In 2008, Internet connectivity was important to the campaign. However, that importance seemed to be predominately Democratic; the Democratic websites were visited more frequently than the Republican sites. In addition, within the Democratic dominance, the Obama campaign's website and overall Web presence trumped all others.

YouTube added a different dynamic to the presidential primary campaign, which was not present in previous election cycles. YouTube allows citizens to view video information about a campaign without a partisan filter or a media filter. With YouTube, citizens can avoid navigating through a candidate's website and instead see the most recent ad or event, independent of the campaign and independent of the traditional media. Moreover, YouTube brought the democratizing features of the Internet to the campaign; in a sense, the most popular videos and the viral nature of those videos spawned a narrative within the campaign written by citizens, not the candidates or the media. Future campaigns will assuredly imitate and expand on candidate Obama's Web presence; however, the Internet's ability to provide a less-filtered experience for citizens could change the campaign and election process.

The Political Process and the Web

The value of the Web for candidates is that it is a medium that reaches potential voters and supporters absent a traditional-media filter. Of course, the mechanism is only valuable if people use the medium in a way that advantages the candidate. For Barack Obama, the candidate's website was a valuable resource for connecting with supporters. The fact that 44 percent of his traffic went to a personalized page, my.barack.obama.com, suggests that the site became a consistent portal for transmitting information to the motivated. How influential the website was for more transient support is hard to tell. Viewership on YouTube provides a greater glimpse into citizens interested in the political process but perhaps not interested enough to go to a candidate's website.

Web traffic reports suggest that Mike Huckabee and Ron Paul benefited enormously: the Internet version of word of mouth casts a much larger net than would be possible without the Internet. Moreover, the presence of YouTube and the other social networking sites benefited those with less name recognition and less money. In short, the Internet might be challenging the existence of the so-called invisible primary.

"Invisible primary" refers to the collection of endorsements, the raising of money, and media evaluation of both the polls and the candidates' organizations prior to the casting of any citizen's vote. In the pre-primary period during 2007, media pundits anointed former mayor Rudy Giuliani and Senator Hillary Clinton as the front-runners.[31] The media dismissed the chances of John McCain and speculated about the relevance of the multitude of candidates, from former governor Mitt Romney to Senator Joseph Biden. Obama's Web traffic throughout this period steadily increased, as did his fund-raising—in particular, his fundraising online. Obama's Iowa win surprised the media, perhaps because of the seemingly underground nature of the online campaign presence. Unless individuals used Web-tracking sites, the success or failure of Web presence went virtually unheralded.

YouTube, however, did not go unnoticed in the press. In fact, most mainstream media began including stories about Web traffic and viral videos. Moreover, video interest in the 2008 campaign dates back prior to April 2007. Obama Girl's video first aired in June 2007, six months before the first caucus and primary.

Ultimately, campaign websites offer candidates an opportunity to directly connect with citizens and offer them an opportunity to connect. Citizens can read candidates' stands on issues, they can buy candidate-support paraphernalia, and they can volunteer. Candidates' linkages to other websites where people spend time, like MySpace or YouTube, can only improve opportunities for engagement. Citizens, particularly younger Americans, were clearly taking advantage of the campaign online.

Is this interest in campaign information online a direct result of dissatisfaction with the coverage of politics by traditional media? Perhaps. Evaluations of traditional media by scholars, citizens, and candidates suggest that there is much room for improvement in terms of media coverage of presidential campaigns. These critical media evaluations also invite opportunities for alternative sources of information. However, the vibrancy of the online world has also created its own opportunities. Citizens have grown increasingly familiar with the Internet and reliant on it for information, shopping, and opportunities for social engagement. The eighteen-to-thirty-year-old of 2008 will age and bring their Web savvy to their politics and their mode of political engagement. The Obama campaign clearly demonstrates the benefits of taking the campaign to the voters and encouraging the voters to come to the campaign, online or offline.

Notes

1. S. Farnsworth and S. R. Lichter, *The Nightly News Nightmare: Network Television's Coverage of U.S. Presidential Elections, 1988–2004* (Lanham, Md.: Rowman and Littlefield, 2006).

2. Pew Internet and American Life Project, *Social Networking and Online Videos Take Off: Internet's Broader Role in Campaign 2008* (Washington, D.C.: Pew Research Center for the People and the Press, 2008).

3. R. Klotz, *The Politics of Internet Communication* (Lanham, Md.: Rowman and Littlefield, 2004); A. P. Williams, K. Trammell, M. Postelnicu, K. Landreville, and J. Martin, "Blogging and Hyperlinking: Use of the Web to Enhance Viability During the 2004 U.S. Campaign," *Journalism Studies* 6, no. 2 (2005), 177–86.

4. R. Davis, *The Web of Politics: The Internet's Impact on the American Political System* (New York: Oxford University Press, 1999); J. Tedesco, "Changing the Channel: Use of the Internet for Communication about Politics," in L. L. Kaid, *Handbook of Political Communication Research* (Mahwah, N.J.: Lawrence Erlbaum, 2004), 507–32.

5. J. Trippi, *The Revolution Will Not Be Televised: Democracy, the Internet and the Overthrow of Everything* (New York: HarperCollins, 2004).

6. Williams, et al., "Blogging and Hyperlinking," 185.

7. Kate Kaye, "Clinton Spent Far Less Online Than Obama," *TechPresident*, June 17, 2008, http://techpresident.com/blog-entry/clinton-spent-far-less-online-obama (accessed May 11, 2010).

8. Williams, et al., "Blogging and Hyperlinking."

9. The assessments of the candidate websites arise from a review of the sites between January 1, 2008, and March 10, 2008. Pages under review: www.barackobama.com; www.hillaryclinton.com; www.johnedwards.com; www.mittromney.com; www.johnmccain.com; www.mikehuckabee.com; www.rudy2008.com.

10. Williams, et al., "Blogging and Hyperlinking"; G. Lawson-Borders and R. Kirk, "Blogs in Campaign Communication," *American Behavioral Scientist* 49, no. 4 (2005), 548–59.

11. Alexa.com. http://www.alexa.com/data/details/traffic_details/barackobama.com (accessed March 10, 2008).

12. Giuliani's infrequent traffic highlights two phenomena: 1) Giuliani was the only candidate whose full name was not the website name. Interested individuals might have looked for rudygiuliani.com and then halted in frustration. Rudy2008 was on his bumper stickers but is not the obvious website name. 2) Of course, the lack of traffic could also be explained by his poor showing in the polls and in the state primaries and caucuses.

13. http://www.alexa.com/data/details/daily_page_views/barackobama.com, March 10, 2008.

14. http://www.alexa.com/data/details/daily_reach/barackobama.com, March 10, 2008.

15. http://www.alexa.com/data/details/daily_rank/barackobama.com, March 10, 2008

16. Williams, et al., "Blogging and Hyperlinking."

17. Todd Zeigler, "The Evolution of Barack Obama's Campaign Website," *Bivings Report*, January 7, 2008, http://www.bivingsreport.com/2008/the-evolution-of-barack-obamas-campaign-website (accessed May 10, 2010).

18. Ibid.

19. Ibid.

20. Williams, et al., "Blogging and Hyperlinking."

21. Alexa.com. http://www.alexa.com/data/details/traffic_details/barackobama.com; http://www.alexa.com/data/details/traffic_details/hillaryclinton.com (accessed March 10, 2008).

22. Williams, et al., "Blogging and Hyperlinking"; Lawson-Borders and Kirk, "Blogs in Campaign Communication."

23. As of March 6, 2008.

24. Kaye, "Clinton Spent Far Less."

25. As of March 8, 2008.

26. As of March 6, 2008. On December 18, 2008, 12,404,334 users had viewed the video.

27. Internet World Stats, http://www.internetworldstats.com/stats14.htm (accessed March 10, 2008).

28. Ibid.

29. J. A. Vargas, "Campaigns Experimenting Online to See What Works," *Washington Post*, February 3, 2008.

30. Pew Internet and American Life Project, *Social Networking and Online Videos*.

31. Karen Tumulty; "Is Hillary Still the Front-Runner?" *Time*, Jan. 20, 2007; "Hillary Clinton: Front-Runner and Target: Other Democrats in the Race Take Aim at N.Y. Senator," *CBS News*, Sept. 22, 2007, http://www.cbsnews.com/stories/2007/09/22/politics/main3288426.shtml; "Her latest incarnation: presidential front-runner," Economist, May 17, 2007, http://www.economist.com/world/na/displaystory.cfm?story_id=9196231; "Clinton firmly positioned as Democratic front-runner," CNN, August 9, 2007, http://www.cnn.com/2007/POLITICS/08/09/2008.dems.poll/index.html (accessed April 16, 2010).

Off to the (Horse) Races

Media Coverage of the "Not-So-Invisible"
Invisible Primary of 2007

LORI COX HAN

By all accounts, American voters now live in a perpetual presidential campaign. No sooner have voters made their selection in early November for the next president when speculation begins by political observers and pundits as to who might be running four years hence. Sometimes that speculation begins even before the conclusion of Election Day in November, as the news media attempt to keep people tuned in to the ever-expanding sources of campaign news and analysis. The 2008 presidential campaign provides an excellent example of both the never-ending campaign cycle as well as the dramatic growth in news sources about presidential campaign politics. What used to be a ten-month process from start to finish, give or take, the 2008 campaign lasted nearly two years, with most candidates declaring in the early months of 2007 their intentions to run. Add the increasingly front-loaded primary process, which saw the earliest nominating contests ever held (both the Iowa caucuses and New Hampshire primary were held in early January 2008), along with an issue-intensive campaign, historic candidacies for both Democrats and Republicans, and a 24/7 availability of campaign news in both traditional and newer high-tech media, and American voters experienced an information overload on the way to electing Barack Obama the forty-fourth president of the United States.

While it may seem obvious to even the casual observer of U.S. politics how important news media coverage is for a presidential candidate in the heat of the primary or general election battle, it is the media attention garnered during the pre-nomination phase of the campaign that can play a crucial role in deciding if the candidate even makes it to the first nominating contest. Often referred to as the "invisible primary," the pre-primary period for the 2008 election occurred earlier and lasted longer than in any previous campaign in modern American history. The longer the invisible primary lasts, the more money candidates must raise to remain viable; in addition, the news media have even longer to speculate as to who will win and who will lose in the upcoming primary contests, which can inflate the importance of early public opinion polls and give an advantage to a candidate with more money and name recognition. The invisible primary has traditionally played out behind the scenes as potential candidates explore their options for running and try to gain support among top donors and party officials. However, with the extensive front-loading of the primary and caucus contests for 2008 (more and more states moved up their election dates to compete with the perennial early states, Iowa and New Hampshire, in an attempt to have a louder voice in the nomination process), and with the creation of what was nearly halfway to a national primary on February 5 (with Super Tuesday contests that day in twenty-two states), the invisible primary turned out not to be so invisible after all. By February 2007, which would have been considered early in any other election year, several big-name candidates, like Hillary Rodham Clinton, Barack Obama, Bill Richardson, and John Edwards on the Democratic side, and Mitt Romney, John McCain, and Rudy Giuliani on the Republican side, had already announced their bids for the White House. In what would be a crowded field for each party, the candidates were looking for any advantage in gaining news media coverage and attracting donors.

This chapter will consider two aspects of news media attention during the 2007 invisible primary. First, the role of the news media as the "great mentioner" was considered by analyzing how often candidates' names were mentioned in news coverage in the *New York Times, Washington Post, Los Angeles Times, Wall Street Journal,* and *USA Today* during 2007. By the end of the invisible primary season (that is, right before votes are actually cast in the first contests), a variety of factors contribute to granting a candidate front-runner status or at least placing them within the top tier of viable candidates. News media coverage is an important factor in gaining name recognition and familiarity with voters, and is a crucial tie to a candidate's fund-raising prowess and performance in public opinion polls, both of which make or break a candidate's viability in the primary process. A two-tiered campaign usually emerges during a party's primary process; that is, a few candidates are considered viable early on, while others never break through to that top tier of serious contenders (and as a result, do not receive a tremendous amount of media attention). How is this hierarchy determined? While there is not a specific formula, voters normally take their cues as to which candidate is viable and which is not from news media coverage, so the sheer number of mentions in news stories that a candidate receives can be important. As such, analyzing this aspect of news coverage during 2007 will show how the more newsworthy candidates fared in terms of early news coverage and whether or not that helped to place them among the top-tier candidates.

Second, a more specific analysis will be provided of the four candidates presenting a potential first to U.S. presidential politics—Hillary Rodham Clinton, Barack Obama, Bill Richardson, and Mitt Romney—and the news coverage each received during the invisible primary. The Democrats would have the opportunity to elect the first woman president (Clinton), African American president (Obama), or Latino president (Richardson), while Republicans would have the opportunity to elect the first Mormon president (Romney). While each of these candidates brought impressive accomplishments and résumés to the presidential contest, speculation began early as to whether or not the "first" factor for their respective campaigns would give a decisive edge in breaking ahead of the pack during the invisible primary phase of the campaign. Other candidates also presented firsts—for example, Giuliani had the opportunity to become the first Italian-American president—yet these four candidates presented the most compelling narratives for the news media to cover, as candidates who appeared to be most outside the norm in U.S. presidential elections. Specifically, the issue of gender will be considered for Clinton, the issue of race/ethnicity will be considered for Obama and Richardson, and the issue of religion will be considered for Romney. Content of news coverage in the *New York Times* and *Washington Post* was analyzed to determine if the "first factor" presented the dominant narrative in the coverage for each candidate, as well as whether the "first factor" was framed as a positive, negative, or neutral issue for readers (and by extension voters) to consider.

Media Coverage and the Invisible Primary

What happens during the so-called invisible primary, and why is this so important when selecting presidential nominees? First dubbed the "invisible primary" by journalist Arthur Hadley in 1976, the pre-nomination period is between the end of a presidential election and prior to the first primary of the next when presidential candidates are vetted and when one candidate can emerge as the front-runner to secure the nomination.[1] Two things seem to matter more than anything else during the invisible primary—money and media—particularly as the invisible primary has grown increasingly longer in recent years with the front-loading of primaries. Candidates now announce their intentions to run earlier than ever before, sometimes well over a year prior to the Iowa caucuses (which, on January 3, 2008, were held earlier than any previous nominating contest ever). During this long pre-primary phase of the electoral calendar, candidates attempt to raise large sums of money, hire campaign staffs, shape their ideological and partisan messages, attempt to gain visibility among party elites (and gain high-profile endorsements), and hope to be taken seriously by the news media.[2]

It is during the invisible primary when the often relentless "horse race" coverage of the campaign begins, when "reporters feel obliged to tell us which candidates are leading or trailing well over a year before any primary election votes are cast." In recent campaigns, the news media have not focused much on the effects of front-loading primaries and caucuses (such as the increased reliance on millions of dollars to even remain competitive before any votes are cast), even though they contributed to the trend, since it was "saturation coverage of New Hampshire and Iowa, starting in the early seventies, after all, that spurred the front-loading process." For the most part, voters outside of New Hampshire and Iowa do not actually see much of what the candidates are doing there, because the news media instead focus on the horse race of the pre-primary process as opposed to the actual campaigning and discussion of issues by the candidates.[3] Often, "media buzz" about a candidate can amplify the effects of raising money, hiring staff, and shaping the message of a candidate early on in the process; by February 2007, for example, several Democratic hopefuls had already withdrawn (former Iowa governor Tom Vilsack and former Virginia governor Mark Warner) or decided against entering the race (Senator Russ Feingold of Wisconsin and Senator Evan Bayh of Indiana).[4]

An early study of news coverage of the 2007 invisible primary showed several trends consistent with the usual horse-race coverage as well as other recent trends in campaign coverage. In a study by the Project for Excellence in Journalism, coverage of the presidential race in the first five months of 2007 was the second-most-covered news story in all media behind coverage of the war in Iraq. The increased and early coverage resulted in part from early and heavy fund-raising by the candidates, front-loading the primaries and caucuses, and earlier-than-ever announcements to enter the race, as well as increased interest by readers and viewers leading up to the first wide-open presidential campaign since 1952. In addition, 63 percent of the coverage during this five-month period focused on "political and tactical aspects of the campaign" (the horse race), with 17 percent focused on the backgrounds of the candidates, and 15 percent focused on policy proposals. A majority of the coverage during this time period focused on just five candidates: Clinton, Obama, Giuliani, Romney, and McCain. Another interesting finding reported in the study was that eight in ten Americans surveyed by the Pew Research Center reported wanting more news coverage of the issues in the campaign.[5]

To place the news coverage of the 2007 invisible primary into its proper context, it is important to first understand the current media environment along with the expectation of how journalists are supposed to be covering presidential candidates. Just as in other areas of news reporting, journalists covering presidential campaigns have developed patterns in how news is gathered and reported. Over the years, the news media have been quite consistent in how they cover the presidential race in all its phases, first during the invisible primary, then the primary and caucus season, and finally the general election. While different candidates, campaign strategies, and "big stories" (like scandals and gaffes) have emerged every four years, the American voter can always rely on news coverage to focus on the horse race of the campaign—the journalistic ritual of reporting on which candidate is ahead in the polls, in raising money, and in the delegate count during the primary and caucus season. The news media can also still play a role as kingmaker or the "great mentioner" in helping or hurting a candidate's campaign by the type or amount of coverage provided. Even as primaries and caucuses have become more front-loaded since 1996, the news media are still a tremendous source of momentum for presidential candidates, which can help to propel a campaign along, to survive early contests, and to make a candidate viable for the party nomination. On the campaign trail, news organizations also often report similar stories because they rely on similar sources as part of the news-gathering process (known as pack journalism).[6]

Campaign coverage has also followed overall trends in the news media in recent years. Economic pressures can be critical in the selection of stories, especially for national shows or publications, since mass media companies, like other businesses, must make a profit. Stories and content must appeal to a broad base of viewers or readers, and so stories are aired and published that will have a strong impact, that focus on violence, conflict, disaster, or scandal; and publishers and broadcasters consider in advance the familiarity and proximity of the story to the audience, and whether or not the story is timely and novel.[7] The effect of the Internet on political news has been significant as well, as witnessed during the 2008 campaign season. Various political blogs (such as *Daily Kos* on the left and *Townhall* on the right), vlogging sites (such as YouTube), and social networking sites (such as Facebook and MySpace) now provide extensive and up-to-the-minute political coverage as well as a high-tech way of spreading political information, and these newer sources of information were ever-present throughout the 2008 presidential campaign, garnering a significant amount of news coverage in more traditional sources such as newspapers and television. Other Internet news sites such as *Politico.com* and the *Huffington Post* have also emerged as major players in political and campaign news coverage. According to Michael Scherer, correspondent for *Time* magazine, individual stories as opposed to packaged news sources (like a newspaper or magazine stories) became more influential in the 2008 campaign thanks to the immediacy and availability of online sources:

> This means that the competition on the level of the individual story is more intense than ever before, and there is enormous pressure to distinguish yourself from the pack. Assume, for instance, that 12 news organizations do the same story on the same day about how Hillary Clinton has a tough road ahead of her to get the nomination. Which story is going to get the most links and therefore the most readers? Is it the one that cautiously weighs the pros and cons, and presents a nuanced view of her chances? Or is it the one that says she is toast, and anyone who thinks different is living on another planet? ... This trend towards story-by-story competition, and away from package-by-package competition, is a blessing and a curse. It is forcing better writing, quicker responsiveness, and it is increasing the value of actual news-making and clear-eyed thinking. But it is also increasing pressure on reporters to push the boundaries of provocation.[8]

In addition to the many structural changes occurring within the news industry, another important trend that has emerged is the increase in "soft news." Defined as news having no real connection to substantive policy issues, or as the opposite of "hard news" that includes coverage of breaking events or major issues impacting the daily routines of U.S. citizens, soft news has steadily increased during the past two decades in response to competition within the marketplace. The bottom line is that the new news—soft, entertainment-focused, and market-driven news—is much more profitable than the traditional "who, what, where, when, and why" of traditional political news. Journalism has also become increasingly critical in its tone toward government officials, in an attempt to grab more viewers and readers, to which some scholars point as evidence of weakening the foundation of democracy by diminishing the public's interest in and information about politics.[9]

Various effects of the news media can be particularly evident during coverage of a presidential campaign. For example, agenda setting represents the theory that journalists can influence which stories are treated as important in the news media through the selection process. The news media cannot tell you what to think, but can tell you what to think about. Through prominent coverage, these issues become salient to the public, especially politicians and other elites. Studies have shown that public opinion of important issues often tracks media attention.[10] Priming also has an impact on the audience, which means that the news media have a substantial impact on how Americans view the political system and its participants based on which stories are emphasized; priming by the news media draws attention to some aspects of political life at the expense of others. An example is the ability of the news media to isolate particular issues, events, or themes in the news as criteria for evaluating politicians. For example, when primed by news stories on the economy, the president is then judged on the economic health of the nation. This can be particularly important during a presidential election, as President George H. W. Bush learned in 1992. Following record approval ratings after the first Gulf War in 1991, the media's emphasis on the bad economy in early 1992 just as Bush was beginning his reelection campaign seemed to prime voters to blame Bush and give then-candidate Bill Clinton more support for his economic proposals. Similarly, the strong media focus on terrorism during the 2004 presidential campaign benefited President George W. Bush, who campaigned as the better choice to keep the United States safe from terrorists.[11]

Another effect of news media coverage can include the framing of news, which is when the news media tells us more than what to think about, but how to think about it. The concept of framing has been of particular interest to media scholars in the past two decades as research has attempted to explain not only how the media frame particular issues but how such frames shape public opinion. According to Doris Graber, framing is the act of "reporting the news from a particular perspective so that some aspects of the situation come into close focus and others fade in the background." Journalists can control some aspects of framing through the selection of sources or what Graber refers to as "special pleaders" who share the frame preferences with the journalists. Developments in an ongoing story, such as coverage of a presidential candidate, can also help to determine the frames that are used.[12] David L. Paletz defines framing as "applying a central idea to give meaning to the events reported." A story can have one or more frames, but usually one frame will dominate. Framing is important because "it is through their frames that news stories depict events in particular ways, bring a perspective to bear, emphasize some aspects at the expense of others."[13] Robert Entman has provided what is perhaps the most definitive description of framing: "Framing essentially involves selection and salience. To frame is to select some aspects of a perceived reality and make them more salient in a communicating text, in such a way as to promote a particular problem definition, causal interpretation, moral evaluation, and/or treatment recommendation for the item described. . . . Frames highlight some bits of information about an item that is the subject of a communication, thereby elevating them in salience. . . . [Frames in political news] call attention to some aspects of reality while obscuring other elements, which might lead audiences to have different reactions."[14]

News Story "Mentions" during the Invisible Primary

One of the main goals of a presidential candidate during the invisible primary period is to garner name recognition among voters, and the most effective means of achieving that goal comes through news media coverage. Top-tier candidates (that is, those considered most viable in seeking party nomination and most competitive in earning it) tend to create more media buzz than second-tier candidates (that is, those considered to have little or no chance of winning a particular primary or caucus, let alone the party nomination). Therefore, the sheer amount of coverage or "mentions" devoted to particular candidates should provide an estimate as to how each candidate falls within the pre-primary hierarchy. To determine the number of mentions for each candidate who declared his or her intention to run for party nomination in 2007, a search by candidate name was conducted for five of the nation's leading daily newspapers: the *New York Times,* the *Washington Post, Los Angeles Times,* the *Wall Street Journal,* and *USA Today,* between January 1, 2007 and January 3, 2008 (the latter date representing the first nominating contest in Iowa).[15] These five newspapers are among the largest in terms of circulation.[16] The number of mentions per candidate in Tables 1 and 2 reflect the number of stories per publication in which the candidate's name appeared. All stories, editorials, and columns were counted from the stories generated for each search. The results show, not surprisingly, a stark contrast between the amount of attention paid to top-tier candidates as compared to second-tier candidates for both parties in all five newspapers during the invisible primary period.

For the Democratic candidates (see Table 1), Clinton and Obama dominated in terms of number of mentions in all five newspapers; Clinton topped Obama in all five newspapers with the exception of the *Los Angeles Times.* Clinton had the most mentions in the *New York Times,* although as a high-profile U.S. senator from New York, this result is not surprising. Obama, a U.S. senator from Illinois, also drew significant media attention when he announced his intention to run in early 2007. His first introduction on the national stage came as Obama delivered the keynote address at the 2004 Democratic National Convention, which immediately began media speculation about his future presidential prospects, particularly as the potential first African American president. John Edwards, a former U.S. senator from North Carolina, presidential candidate in 2004, and the 2004 Democratic nominee for vice president, is the only other Democratic candidate based on this analysis that would fall within the top-tier of these five newspapers, as it was long speculated that Edwards would pursue the presidency again in 2008. In addition, these three Democratic candidates dominated the coverage in terms of number of mentions among *all* presidential candidates in both parties, suggesting not only the shifting political winds from the Republican to Democratic party, but also the increased attention paid to a woman candidate and an African American candidate among the front-runners for the Democratic nomination.

The remaining six second-tier candidates can be categorized by those with greater name recognition on the national level as opposed to those not known as well on the national stage. As long-serving U.S. senators with seniority on Capitol Hill, Joe Biden (D-DE) and Chris Dodd

Table 1: Number of Articles with Mention of Democratic Candidate in Newspaper Coverage (1/1/07 – 1/3/08)

	New York Times	Washington Post	Los Angeles Times	Wall Street Journal	USA Today	Total
Hillary Clinton	1,497	1,450	701	705	629	4,982
Barack Obama	1,239	1,332	715	447	352	4,085
John Edwards	786	848	444	319	232	2,629
Joseph Biden	204	319	37	116	224	900
Christopher Dodd	202	362	35	183	161	943
Bill Richardson	183	286	183	89	101	842
Dennis Kucinich	76	121	32	27	64	320
Tom Vilsack	41	59	28	14	16	158
Mike Gravel	38	56	53	10	34	191
Total	4,266	4,833	2,228	1910	1,813	15,050

(D-CT) would receive national news coverage as members of Congress even without announcing a presidential bid. Similarly, New Mexico governor Bill Richardson was also widely known due to his time in the House of Representatives followed by appointments as U.S. ambassador to the United Nations and energy secretary in the Bill Clinton administration; he is also known as one of the most influential Latino politicians in America. The number of mentions in the *Washington Post* for Biden, Dodd, and Richardson also reflect the focus on national politics by the leading newspaper in the nation's capital. Finally, the remaining second-tier candidates—U.S. Representative Dennis Kucinich (D-OH), former Iowa governor Tom Vilsack, and former U.S. senator Mike Gravel (D-AK) received little attention during the invisible primary in these five newspapers, as none emerged as viable candidates in the eyes of the news media and none commanded national attention (despite the fact that Kucinich had also sought the Democratic nomination in 2004). In addition, when compared among the five newspapers, the amount of coverage for all candidates (and the presidential contest in general) shows how the *New York Times* and *Washington Post* provide more in-depth coverage of national politics than the other three newspapers; for comparison purposes, it is also important to note that neither the *Wall Street Journal* (whose primary emphasis is international business and economic news) and *USA Today* do not publish seven days a week.

Table 2: Number of Articles with Mention of Republican Candidate in Newspaper Coverage (1/1/07 – 1/3/08)

	New York Times	Washington Post	Los Angeles Times	Wall Street Journal	USA Today	Total
John McCain	787	868	478	346	270	2,749
Rudy Giuliani	906	694	155	354	259	2,368
Mitt Romney	697	748	423	329	256	2,453
Mike Huckabee	256	361	201	160	114	1,092
Fred Thompson	139	298	187	153	127	904
Sam Brownback	110	174	104	39	57	484
Ron Paul	101	138	80	56	63	438
Tom Tancredo	72	98	79	36	62	347
Duncan Hunter	48	82	76	27	50	283
Tommy Thompson	20	49	21	15	26	131
Jim Gilmore	16	70	13	14	13	126
Alan Keyes	12	13	6	0	6	37
Total	3,164	3,593	1,823	1,529	1,303	11,412

On the Republican side, the five newspapers analyzed also showed a two-tiered approach to how often each candidate was mentioned (see Table 2). Senator John McCain (R-AZ), a high-profile figure on Capitol Hill and a presidential candidate in 2000, was long considered among the potential frontrunners for the Republican nomination in 2008. Former New York mayor Rudy Giuliani, who gained national attention and acclaim for his response to the terrorist attacks in his city on September 11, 2001, had also been regularly discussed in the news media as a possible front-runner. Like with the coverage of Clinton, Giuliani's number of mentions in the New York Times and Wall Street Journal more than likely reflect how each paper covers a hometown politician. Mitt Romney, the former governor of Massachusetts, has a family history in politics (his father, a former presidential candidate, was governor of Michigan) and was also considered to be among the front-runners as early as 2007. Mike Huckabee, the former governor of Arkansas, was initially considered a dark horse for the nomination in early 2007, but gained more media attention as his poll numbers improved leading up to the early state contests (particularly Iowa, which he won) by the end of 2007. Fred Thompson, a former U.S. senator from Tennessee and star of the NBC drama *Law and Order* certainly had a high public profile going in to the campaign. However, Thompson's late announcement in early September 2007 that he was seeking the nomination (after all other candidates, with the exception of Alan Keyes, had already announced their candidacies months earlier) contributed to the lower number of mentions in stories.

The six remaining Republican candidates that made up the second tier, like their Democratic counterparts, suffered from a lack of national prominence and its resulting news media attention. Four of the six were members of Congress—Senator Sam Brownback (R-KS), and Representatives Ron Paul (R-TX), Tim Tancredo (R-CO), and Duncan Hunter (R-CA)—but none had the notoriety or national name recognition as their colleague John McCain. (Ron Paul would gain much more media attention in early 2008 as a grassroots effort emerged to raise money in support of his campaign; many of his supporters were attracted to the libertarian views that distinguished him from his fellow Republican rivals). Jim Gilmore, a former governor from Virginia, became the first Republican to end his presidential bid in July 2007. Alan Keyes, a former State Department appointee during the Ronald Reagan administration, considered a perennial political candidate, did not announce his candidacy until September 14, 2007

The "First Factor" as Narrative in 2007

Over the years, there have been many firsts for the news media to report in U.S. politics. Americans know John F. Kennedy as, among other things, the first Catholic president, while Nancy Pelosi will forever be remembered as the first woman Speaker of the House. Thurgood Marshall and Sandra Day O'Connor represented important firsts on the U.S. Supreme Court as the first African American and female justice, respectively. Americans particularly take note of firsts on the presidential campaign trail. Victoria Woodhull was the first woman to run for president (in 1872), Shirley Chisholm was the first African American to run for president for a major party (Democrat, in 1972), and Jesse Jackson was the first African American male to run for president and was also the first minority candidate to win a presidential primary or caucus (winning five Democratic contests in 1984 and eleven in 1988). Other campaign firsts include Geraldine Ferraro as the first woman to run for vice president on a major-party ticket, as Democrat Walter Mondale's running mate in 1984, and Joe Lieberman as the first Jewish American to run for vice president, as Democrat Al Gore's running mate in 2000. While giving any of these political luminaries the title "first" surely does not take anything away from their substantial list of achievements, it is instead often used as American journalistic shorthand, implying that this is one of their most notable accomplishments. Breaking through a political barrier, whether it is based on gender, race, ethnicity, or religion, is an example of giving voice to the Other in American politics (that is, ones outside the norm of the white, Protestant, male standard for those holding top government positions).

It is the news media that most often give politicians the label of being "first" to reach a particular achievement, as this is an effective way to catch the attention of the reader or viewer, or to assert why someone is deserving of news coverage. As political reporters geared up for covering the 2008 presidential race, the word "first" was popping up quite frequently in discussions and predictions about who the top contenders would be and what Americans could look forward to when selecting their next president. As contenders began throwing their hats into the ring in 2007, the race was billed as the first wide-open nomination process for both Democrats and Republicans since 1952, which was the last time that neither an incumbent president nor his vice president was seeking his party's nomination.[17] Then, as the field of candidates for both parties grew more crowded (a total of nine Democrats and eleven Republicans), discussion centered on the four aforementioned candidates as to the potential historic possibilities of their respective campaigns.

In addition, it is worth noting prevalent trends in how gender, race, ethnicity, and religion tend to be covered by the U.S. news media. As one of the most important agents of political socialization, the mass media—and more specifically the news media—play an important role in how women and minorities are viewed as current or potential political leaders. Theories abound among scholars about how people receive information through the mass media. Some scholars suggest that the media have a powerful impact on society and that people may actually need to be protected from its effects. For example, viewers can be led to believe that reality mirrors the images in the mass media and that women and minorities can develop poor self-esteem due to negative stereotyping by media sources. A contrasting theory, known as the minimal effects approach, suggests that the mass media are weak in their impact on society, since people only expose themselves to media content that goes along with their current views or perceptions.[18] Nevertheless, the mass media perpetrate many negative stereotypes about women and minorities in American society. Stereotyping is the act of using a simplified mental image of an individual or group of people who share certain characteristics or qualities; this allows people to quickly process information and categorize people based on what are often negative characteristics.

News coverage of women in general, but particularly of women professionals and athletes, often relies on stereotyping, and women are drastically underrepresented in news coverage across all news outlets. Even with the steady increase of women in all professions, including politics, law, medicine, higher education, and the corporate world, most news coverage continues to rely on men, and not women, as experts in their respective fields. Women in the news are more likely to be featured in stories about accidents, natural disasters, or domestic violence than in stories about their professional abilities or expertise. A relative lack of news coverage for women politicians can be particularly problematic if they are not portrayed as strong and capable leaders, and as authoritative public policy decision makers, when they *are* covered. This can be a difficult cycle to break, since women in Congress, for example, do not receive as much attention as men, due to lack of seniority and leadership positions (the ascent of Representative Nancy Pelosi to Speaker of the House in 2007 has certainly provided more news media coverage of a woman in a leadership position; however, she still remains the only woman to hold such a position).[19] While breaking the negative stereotypes of women and the portrayal of women as the political Other in the news media is necessary to help facilitate the continued progress of women in government, recent studies have shown that the news media cover male and female candidates differently—female candidates often get less coverage, more negative coverage, and more frivolous coverage (that is, attention to their hair or wardrobes, their personalities, or personal lives).[20]

Similarly, news coverage of racial and ethnic minorities often provides negative stereotypes or inadequate information about and attention to minority communities and issues. The news media industry is still dominated by white men, both within news organizations and in the coverage that is produced. Therefore, the social and cultural norms that are reflected in a majority of news coverage do not represent the views of women or ethnic minorities, since the internal constraints of media organizations and personnel tend to dictate the final news product.[21] During campaigns, news media coverage is often racialized, meaning that the news media either act as racial arbitrators by limiting the emphasis placed on the race of a candidate, or the race of a candidate is highlighted, brought to the forefront by the news media (creating racial dualism in news coverage). One particular study of how the news media has covered African American candidates in congressional campaigns suggests that in news coverage, inter-candidate racial differences are often highlighted, and that coverage "consistently highlights the race of black candidates and their constituents in both same-race and biracial contests." In addition, the news media are often inconsistent in how they cover candidate race and ethnicity, due to the inconsistency of editorial guidelines, which allows reporters to then determine the newsworthiness of a candidate's race during an election.[22]

When it comes to covering religion and its effects on politics, the news media often oversimplify the intersection between the two. One recent study showed that conservative religious voices dominate in news media coverage, with progressive religious voices often left out of the dialogue, particularly when political issues are being discussed: "Religion is often depicted in the news media as a politically divisive force, with two sides roughly paralleling the broader political divide: On one side are cultural conservatives who ground their political values in religious beliefs; and on the other side are secular liberals, who have opted out of debates that center on religion-based values." The study concludes that this type of reporting, where conservative religious leaders are most often quoted, gives the conservative religious viewpoint, and by extension the conservative political viewpoint (for example, the viewpoint of evangelical Christians) a substantial advantage within the deliberative political dialogue.[23] This is a particularly salient point given the increased influence of conservative Christian voters in recent presidential and congressional elections, a trend that began in the late 1970s and reached its peak during the 1990s, with the election of a Republican-controlled Congress in 1994, and then again with the reelection of George W. Bush in 2004.

To determine the extent to which the "first factor" for each of the four potential history-making candidates represented a narrative of each campaign in news coverage, coverage in the *New York Times* and *Washington Post* between January 1, 2007, and January 3, 2008, was content analyzed.[24] The *New York Times* is still widely recognized as the nation's leading newspaper, and is also one of the top national dailies, along with the *Washington Post,* from which the nightly network newscasts take cues in terms of story selection.[25] Each news story filed from the national desk that mentioned any or all of the four candidates (Clinton, Obama, Richardson, and Romney) was included in the analysis. Each paragraph that mentioned a candidate was coded by topic into one of five categories: First Factor, Campaign/Horse race, Personal Background, Domestic/Economic Policy, and Foreign Policy. Within the "First Factor" category, each paragraph was also coded for tone as Positive, Neutral, or Negative (based on whether the information presented about each candidate was framed as an asset or liability in terms of electoral viability). For example, did coverage focus on whether or not men would vote for Clinton, whether or not whites would vote for Obama or Richardson, or whether or not evangelical Christians would vote for Romney? Such a frame would suggest a negative connotation to the unique status of each candidate; they are political Others and outside the norm. Or did the coverage more often frame the "first factor" as a positive attribute for each candidate that set them apart from the rest of the contenders, thereby granting more attention and perhaps momentum to each candidate?

Comparing coverage of the four candidates, Clinton received the most coverage (total number of paragraphs) during the time period studied, while Richardson received a much smaller amount of coverage compared to the other three top-tier candidates. Also, coverage devoted to campaign logistics and the "horse race" dominated for all four candidates, while only a small percentage of coverage was devoted to the "first factor" (particularly for Clinton and Obama). In addition, while coverage of the "first factor" was sparse in both newspapers, the larger percentage in the *New York Times* suggests different reporting styles and editorial guidelines between the two papers (see Tables 3, 5, 7, and 9).

Hillary Rodham Clinton: Not surprisingly, of the four candidates studied, Hillary Clinton received the most coverage. The prospect of Clinton's campaign had been discussed for several years in the press, most notably beginning in 2005 when major news outlets began labeling her as the presumptive Democratic front-runner and the "candidate to beat" in 2008. In addition, while the *New York Times* is the leading national newspaper, it is also the hometown paper for Clinton in her role as a U.S. senator from New York. Also among the four candidates, Clinton received the most campaign horse-race coverage, due in part to her lead in the early national polls throughout most of 2007 and her strong showing in early fund-raising (both polls and the race for money were prominent features for all candidates in the coverage), as well as stories focusing on the role that her husband, former president Bill Clinton, would play or was playing in the campaign. Perhaps surprisingly, just over 1 percent of Clinton's coverage in the *New York Times* and one-half of a percent

Table 3: Coverage of Hillary Rodham Clinton by Topic (1/1/07 – 1/3/08)

	First Factor	Campaign/ Horse race	Personal Background	Domestic/ Economic Policy	Foreign Policy	Total
New York Times	46 (1.1%)	3,228 (78.8%)	369 (9.0%)	306 (7.5%)	145 (3.5%)	4,094
Washington Post	21 (0.5%)	3,525 (86.1%)	237 (5.8%)	174 (4.3%)	136 (3.3%)	4,093
Total	67 (0.8%)	6,753 (82.5%)	606 (7.4%)	480 (5.9%)	281 (3.4%)	8,187

Table 4: Tone of "First Factor" Coverage of Hillary Rodham Clinton

	Positive	Neutral	Negative	Total
New York Times	6 (13.0%)	32 (69.6%)	8 (17.4%)	46
Washington Post	5 (23.8%)	15 (71.4%)	1 (4.8%)	21
Total	11 (16.4%)	47 (70.1%)	9 (13.4%)	67

in the *Washington Post* discussed her campaign within the frame of "the first woman president," with most of that coverage being neutral in tone. Clinton also received less coverage than the other three candidates in the "personal background" category, perhaps due to her years in the national spotlight beginning in 1992, during her husband's successful campaign for the presidency.

Barack Obama: Barack Obama received only three-fourths of the coverage that Clinton received in 2007 in both newspapers, yet his coverage was still extensive thanks to his status as a top-tier candidate and perhaps Clinton's biggest hurdle to winning the nomination, from the moment he announced his candidacy. When combining the two newspapers, 77 percent of the coverage for Obama was in the campaign/horse race category, with just under 12 percent devoted to information about his personal background. Obama also received minimal coverage in the "first factor" category, with little attention paid to whether or not he could attract white voters or build the necessary coalition within the Democratic Party to win the nomination (that type of coverage seemed to come once the primary and caucus voting got underway after January 3, 2008). The

Table 5: Coverage of Barack Obama by Topic (1/1/07 – 1/3/08)

	First Factor	Campaign/ Horse race	Personal Background	Domestic/ Economic Policy	Foreign Policy	Total
New York Times	25 (0.8%)	2,213 (71.6%)	488 (15.8%)	185 (6.0%)	179 (5.8%)	3,090
Washington Post	12 (0.4%)	2,661 (82.1%)	248 (7.6%)	184 (5.7%)	138 (4.3%)	3,243
Total	37 (0.6%)	4,874 (77.0%)	736 (11.6%)	369 (5.8%)	317 (5.0%)	6,333

Table 6: Tone of "First Factor" Coverage of Barack Obama

	Positive	Neutral	Negative	Total
New York Times	4 (16.0%)	20 (80.0%)	1 (4.0%)	25
Washington Post	0 (0.0%)	10 (83.3%)	2 (16.7%)	12
Total	4 (10.8%)	30 (81.1%)	3 (8.1%)	37

bigger question presented in the coverage in both newspapers seemed to focus on whether or not black voters would support Obama or Clinton, since Clinton benefitted early in the primary process from the support Bill Clinton had always enjoyed among African American voters. Much of the coverage of Obama outside of the campaign/horse race category focused on introducing him to readers as a lesser-known quantity than some of the other Democratic contenders.

Bill Richardson: Looking at the coverage in both newspapers, it is clear that Bill Richardson never achieved his goal of breaking into the top tier of the Democratic candidates. He had roughly one-tenth of the coverage of Clinton (just over 8 percent) and Obama (just over 11 percent). However, his campaign as the first Latino running for president did comprise more than 4 percent of his coverage; while still a small amount, he received more coverage in this category than both Clinton and Obama. Coverage of his historic campaign as the first Latino presidential candidate was mostly neutral; his competition with Clinton for the Latino vote (and Clinton's endorsement by Los Angeles mayor Antonio Villaraigosa) led to the only negative comments (with the suggestion that Richardson was not a strong enough candidate to win the Latino vote). Still, Richardson was portrayed as a candidate capable of tapping into the all-important Latino vote in 2008 *if* he eventually emerged as a top-tier candidate. Atten-

Table 7: Coverage of Bill Richardson by Topic (1/1/07 – 1/3/08)

	First Factor	Campaign/ Horse race	Personal Background	Domestic/ Economic Policy	Foreign Policy	Total
New York Times	26 (7.8%)	123 (37.0%)	79 (23.7%)	76 (22.9%)	28 (8.4%)	332
Washington Post	5 (1.3%)	268 (70.9%)	12 (3.2%)	40 (10.6%)	53 (14.0%)	378
Total	31 (4.4%)	391 (55.1%)	91 (12.8%)	116 (16.3%)	81 (11.4%)	710

tion was paid in both newspapers to his impressive résumé (his fourteen years in Congress, his positions as both energy secretary and U.N. ambassador during the Clinton administration, and as a popular two-term governor from New Mexico). He did, however, seem to have credibility in domestic and economic policies, due mostly to his current position as governor (16 percent of his coverage fell into this category). A total of 55 percent of his coverage fell into the campaign/horse race category; this percentage is lower than the other three candidates in the study, due to his second-tier-candidate status. Despite his impressive résumé, Richardson's campaign just did not get much attention. Richardson was often referred to as a "likable" candidate; according to *New York Times* columnist David Brooks, Richardson is "somebody the average person would like to have a beer with . . . he's Budweiser, not microbrew." In that March 4, 2007, column, Brooks suggested that Richardson was the candidate "most likely to rise" as voters grew tired of the "Clinton-Obama psychodrama."[26] The question remains as to whether or not Richardson broke an important barrier for Latino candidates, given that his campaign garnered so little attention. His chances were hurt mostly due to the star power of the other candidates in the Democratic race—a former vice presidential candidate in John Edwards, and the two other historic campaigns of Obama and Clinton.

Mitt Romney: Nearly 70 percent of Mitt Romney's coverage fell into the campaign/horse race category. More than 5 percent of the coverage was devoted to the fact that he would be the first Mormon president if elected, so of the four candidates, he received the most "first factor" coverage. Of that coverage, 49 percent was negative, heavily focusing on distrust and dislike among evangelical Christians of Mormonism. Toward the end of the year, Republican rival Mike Huckabee's comment that "Mormons believe

Table 8: Tone of "First Factor" Coverage of Bill Richardson

	Positive	Neutral	Negative	Total
New York Times	1 (3.8%)	22 (84.6%)	3 (11.5%)	26
Washington Post	1 (20.0%)	4 (80.0%)	0 (0%)	5
Total	2 (6.5%)	26 (83.9%)	3 (9.7%)	31

that Jesus and Satan are brothers" also received attention over a span of several days, which seemed to highlight the reservations among Republican voters about Romney due to his religion. These stories continued to suggest that Romney probably would not, or could not, earn the support of the evangelical voters who have made up a crucial part of the Republican base in recent elections. While the dominant narrative in Romney's coverage, as with the other three candidates, was about the campaign "horse race," there was a regular second-tier narrative on Romney's religion. In this case, in news coverage of his attempt to become the first Mormon elected president, the uniqueness seemed to play against him somewhat.

Table 9: Coverage of Mitt Romney by Topic (1/1/07 – 1/3/08)

	First Factor	Campaign/ Horse race	Personal Background	Domestic/ Economic Policy	Foreign Policy	Total
New York Times	210 (10.0%)	1,233 (58.9%)	359 (17.1%)	232 (11.1%)	61 (2.9%)	2,095
Washington Post	4 (0.2%)	1,462 (82.8%)	128 (7.2%)	135 (7.6%)	37 (2.1%)	1,766
Total	214 (5.5%)	2,695 (69.8%)	487 (12.6%)	367 (9.5%)	98 (2.5%)	3,861

Table 10: Tone of "First Factor" Coverage of Mitt Romney

	Positive	Neutral	Negative	Total
New York Times	17 (8.1%)	90 (42.9%)	103 (49.0%)	210
Washington Post	0 (0%)	2 (50.0%)	2 (50.0%)	4
Total	17 (7.9%)	92 (43.0%)	105 (49.1%)	214

Conclusion

Once the invisible primary ended, and voters began to have their say about the crowded field of candidates for both parties, many different narratives emerged within news media coverage. On the Democratic side, an important narrative following the Iowa caucuses on January 3 became the issue of how the news media was covering gender and race. An Associated Press story on January 14 seemed to sum up the basic question:

> Expressions of sexism and racism emerging from the contest between Hillary Rodham Clinton and Barack Obama have been blatant, subtle and perhaps sometimes imagined, and they are renewing the national debate over what is and isn't acceptable to say in public. Hillary Rodham Clinton's camp has perceived sexism in comments about her appearance and emotions. Supporters of Barack Obama have complained about racial overtones in remarks about his Muslim-sounding middle name, Hussein, and his acknowledged drug use as a young man. Beyond the back-and-forth between a white woman and a black man seeking the Democratic presidential nomination, the situation has created a snapshot of the nation's sensitivity—or lack thereof—to certain kinds of comments. Is it more acceptable, for instance, to make a sexist remark than a racist remark?[27]

This issue would be covered in depth through the end of the Democratic primary fight in June 2008, as both race and gender came to the forefront of the Clinton and Obama campaigns in their epic battle to win the Democratic nomination. However, during the invisible primary of 2007, gender, race, ethnicity, and religion as unique factors for the candidates did not matter much in the overall coverage in the *New York Times* and *Washington Post,* and most of the coverage on the "first factor" was either neutral (just stating facts) or positive in suggesting how race or gender could attract specific voting demographics. The only exception seemed to be religion, and while the coverage of Romney's Mormon faith was still sparse, it took on a negative tone. While the *Times* included more "first factor" coverage than the *Post,* the tone of the coverage was similar in both papers. Comparing coverage of Obama and Clinton (the two "stars" of the Democratic race), Clinton benefitted from being a known quantity and from being a senator from New York, these getting her more coverage, and also from being labeled the front-runner for a good part of

2007 (which blunts the fact that she also had more coverage devoted to campaign logistics and the "horse race").

Perhaps the two most important questions that emerged involving news coverage during the 2008 campaign cycle were whether there was gender bias and whether the press was too soft on Obama. These two questions garnered much attention among political pundits and commentators throughout the primary season in 2008, particularly the issue of whether or not the news media was treating Clinton unfairly due to her gender and whether or not many members of the mainstream press were "in the tank" for Obama (the latter issue continued to be raised throughout the general election campaign).[28] Many other studies will likely follow on these issues and others from media coverage of this historic campaign. The appropriate studies looking for gender bias will probably find that Clinton's campaign did not escape recent trends of stereotyping of women candidates. However, it now seems more acceptable to cover "soft" and "style" issues for all candidates, male or female, than ever before (for example, the attention paid to John Edwards's $400 haircut, or a story in the *New York Times* on the candidates' eating habits on the campaign trail). This fits the trend in recent years for "soft" versus "hard" news.

For anyone looking for evidence that Clinton was treated unfairly because she is a woman, that task will be complicated by the fact that she is also a Clinton. Since American voters have never seen a candidate with such high negatives entering the presidential race, it is difficult to separate the gender factor versus the Clinton factor in her coverage. Also, there is not much that Americans do not already know about the Clintons, and since so many of the "big stories" of Bill Clinton's presidency revolved around negativity (including scandals during his campaign in 1992, followed by the Whitewater investigation, the sexual harassment lawsuit by Paula Jones, the Monica Lewinsky scandal, and the impeachment in 1998–1999), it is difficult to wipe the slate clean of all that the public and journalists, know. Any study of gender bias in Clinton's campaign may have to stand alone in its findings, as Hillary Clinton may not be a good test case to make a clear and clean determination—perhaps any bias is more about Hillary as Hillary (and a partner to Bill) than Hillary as a woman. Obviously the two cannot be separated, but it puts the question into a unique context and perspective.

As for coverage of Obama, did the media wait too long to properly vet Obama (as the Clinton campaign constantly pointed out), or did it just seem unfair in comparison to the long history of covering Hillary Clinton? Obama's introduction to the national stage was as keynote speaker at the Democratic Convention in 2004, for which he received high praise. He really did not make national news again until he announced his candidacy in early 2007, so for almost every candidate, there is a bit of a honeymoon with the press as they introduce themselves to the American electorate. Obama did not really feel the wrath of the press until he became the front-runner, thanks to his lead in pledged delegates, by early March 2008. Negative stories about the Obama campaign came from, among other things, his relationship with his pastor, the Reverend Jeremiah Wright, and Wright's incendiary comments about the United States. When the Clinton campaign announced its "kitchen sink" strategy against Obama in late February 2008, as an attempt to break Obama's momentum as the new front-runner (meaning that they intended to throw every negative charge possible at Obama through the press), Obama's press coverage clearly left its honeymoon stage. And while the issue of race did not resonate much in coverage during 2007, it became a major issue for Obama's campaign in mid-March of 2008 (culminating with Obama's speech on the issue of race in America on March 18).

Many other questions remain about the role of the news media in the 2008 presidential campaign, as this is just an initial look at four candidacies covered by a handful of newspapers, providing a snapshot of the "first factor" in coverage in two of the leading daily newspapers in the United States. There are two ways to look at the findings—first, that a narrative about the "first factor" or the historic significance of each campaign did not dominate news coverage or even come close during 2007, which might suggest that American voters have made some progress in accepting the Other within the political arena (and Obama's election would certainly suggest that). But, second, if that finding is turned on its head, the "horse race" still dominates and shuts out more substantive coverage that might actually work to break down some of the stereotypes that still exist. The ultimate answer as to how gender, race, ethnicity, and religion of presidential candidates are covered by the news media—and in turn how that coverage shapes each candidate's public narrative—and whether the Other still exists in presidential politics, may only come when the next woman, African American, Latino, or Mormon candidate runs for president.

Notes

1. See Arthur T. Hadley, *The Invisible Primary* (Englewood Cliffs, N.J.: Prentice-Hall, 1976).

2. Nelson W. Polsby and Aaron Wildavsky, *Presidential Elections: Strategies and Structures of American Politics,* 11th ed. (Lanham, MD: Rowman & Littlefield, 2004), 92–93.

3. Christopher Hanson, "The Invisible Primary: Now Is the Time for All-Out Coverage," *Columbia Journalism Review,* March/April, 2003.

4. See Linda Feldmann, "Before Any Votes, A 'Money Primary,'" *Christian Science Monitor,* February 26, 2007, 1; Craig Gilbert, "'Invisible Primary' Already Begun," *Milwaukee Journal Sentinel,* March 4, 2007, http://www.jsonline.com/story/index.aspx?id=573038 (accessed February 23, 2008).

5. Project for Excellence in Journalism and the Joan Shorenstein Center, Harvard University, "The Invisible Primary—Invisible No Longer: A First Look at Coverage of the 2008 Presidential Campaign," October 29, 2007, http://www.journalism.org/print/8187 (accessed February 23, 2008).

6. See Jeremy D. Mayer, *American Media Politics in Transition* (Boston: McGraw-Hill, 2008), 266–73; and Stephen J. Wayne, *The Road to the White House 2008,* 8th ed. (Boston: Thomson Wadsworth, 2008), 144–45.

7. Doris Graber, *Mass Media and American Politics,* 6th ed. (Washington, D.C.: CQ Press, 2001), 98–101.

8. Michael Scherer, "The Internet Effect on News," The Swampland, Time.com, March 24, 2008, http://swampland.blogs.time.com/2008/03/24/the_internet_effect_on_news (accessed December 2, 2008).

9. Thomas E. Patterson, "Doing Well and Doing Good: How Soft News and Critical Journalism Are Shrinking the News Audience and Weakening Democracy—and What News Outlets Can Do about It," Joan Shorenstein Center for Press, Politics, and Public Policy, John F. Kennedy School of Government, Harvard University, 2000.

10. David L. Paletz, *The Media in American Politics: Contents and Consequences,* 2nd ed. (New York: Longman, 2001), 157.

11. Shanto Iyengar and Jennifer A. McGrady, *Media Politics: A Citizen's Guide* (New York, W. W. Norton, 2006), 215–16.

12. Doris Graber, *Mass Media and American Politics,* 7th ed. (Washington, D.C.: CQ Press, 2006), 161–62.

13. Paletz, *The Media in American Politics,* 66.

14. Robert M. Entman, "Framing: Toward Clarification of a Fractured Paradigm," *Journal of Communication* 43, n0.3 (Autumn 1993), 51–58.

15. Stories in the *New York Times, Washington Post,* and *USA Today* were accessed via the Lexis-Nexis Academic Universe database, and stories in the *Los Angeles Times* and *Wall Street Journal* were accessed via the ProQuest database.

16. *USA Today* has the largest circulation, followed the *Wall Street Journal,* the *New York Times,* and the *Los Angeles Times.* The *Washington Post* is ranked seventh. Audit Bureau of Circulations figures for six-month period ending March 31, 2008, were taken from the website of BurrellesLuce: http://www.burrellesluce.com/top100/2008_Top_100List.pdf (accessed December 11, 2008).

17. Following his loss in the 1952 New Hampshire primary, President Harry Truman withdrew from the presidential race. His vice president, Alben Barkley, announced his intention to seek the Democratic nomination, but withdrew less than three weeks later when labor leaders stated they would not support his candidacy. Barkley's withdrawal from the race left the presidential contest wide open for both Democrats and Republicans.

18. Paletz, *The Media in American Politics,* 117–21.

19. Maria Braden, *Women Politicians and the Media* (Lexington: University Press of Kentucky, 1996), 18.

20. For a discussion of recent studies about how women candidates are portrayed in the news media, see Gina Serignese Woodall and Kim L. Fridkin, "Shaping Women's Chances: Stereotypes and the Media," in *Rethinking Madam President: Are We Ready for a Woman in the White House?,* eds. Lori Cox Han and Caroline Heldman (Boulder, Colo.: Lynne Rienner Publishers, 2007).

21. Lois Duke Whitaker, "Women and Sex Stereotypes: Cultural Reflections in the Mass Media," in *Women in Politics: Outsiders or Insiders?* 3rd ed. (Upper Saddle River, N.J.: Prentice Hall, 1999), 95.

22. Nayda Terkildsen and David F. Damore, "The Dynamics of Racialized Media Coverage in Congressional Elections," *Journal of Politics* 61, no. 3 (August 1999), 680–99.

23. Media Matters for America, "Left Behind: The Skewed Representation of Religion in Major News Media," May 29, 2007, http://mediamatters.org/leftbehind/online_version (accessed March 22, 2007).

24. Stories in the *New York Times* and *Washington Post* were accessed via the Lexis-Nexis Academic Universe database.

25. See Howard Kurtz, *Reality Show: Inside the Last Great Television News War* (New York: Free Press, 2007).

26. David Brooks, "Neither Clinton, Nor Obama," *New York Times,* March 4, 2007.

27. "Clinton, Obama Fuel Gender, Race Debate," Associated Press, January 14, 2008, MSNBC, http://www.msnbc.msn.com/id/22653232/from/ET/print/1/display-mode/1098 (accessed January 15, 2008).

28. See, for example, Greg Mitchell, "Was the Press Really 'In the Tank' for Obama?" *Editor and Publisher,* November 10, 2008, http://www.editorandpublisher.com/eandp/columns/pressingissues_display.jsp?vnu_content_id=1003889222 (accessed December 20, 2008).

Winning the
White House

The Road to the White House 2000

Lessons Learned for the Future

SHIRLEY ANNE WARSHAW

The candidates for president in 2008 who successfully moved past the early primary states were those who laid the groundwork for their campaigns years earlier. In Barack Obama's case, his quest for the Oval Office began formally more than two years before his election. John McCain, who ran unsuccessfully in 2000, had been planning his campaign for eight years. Other candidates, such as Hillary Clinton, had similarly long planning and fund-raising schedules. While most candidates do not look eight years ahead, as Senators McCain and Clinton had, developing a long-range plan for a presidential campaign is essential.

In George W. Bush's case, the quest for the presidency began eighteen months after the Dole-Kemp ticket lost the 1996 election. With the Republican Party in disarray and looking for a new standard-bearer, Bush began to seriously explore entering the race for the White House. His quest took three years of planning and fund-raising before he entered his first primary in the winter of 2000.

As do all successful candidates for president, George W. Bush pursued the presidency from another elected position: a governor's office. Learning how to raise money and to hire staff, learning how to handle the minefields of negative campaigning, learning how to build an executive office staff and cabinet, and learning how to manage a large bureaucratic organization and to deal with an often contentious legislature are prerequisites for the leap to the Oval Office.

With the exception of Dwight Eisenhower, all modern presidents have served either in a governor's chair or moved from the Senate into the White House. Four of the last five presidents have been governors, with only George H. W. Bush moving into the White House from the vice presidency. Harry Truman, Richard Nixon, John F. Kennedy, and Lyndon Johnson had all been senators. A clear pattern has emerged in the past seventy-five years for presidents to move from statewide elections, for either the governorship or the U.S. Senate, to the White House. If history is to be a lesson, however, mayors do not get elected to the presidency. Republican presidential hopeful Rudy Giuliani, the former mayor of New York City, sought to ignore the lessons of history by arguing that as the mayor of the largest city in America for two terms, he faced the same learning curve in electoral politics and in governance that governors and senators face. Barack Obama's victory in 2008 further deepened the trend of governors and senators moving into the White House.

To a significant extent, Bush was in the right place at the right time for the Republican Party as the 2000 election approached. Without a strong stable of contenders for the nomination within the Senate, the Republican Party leadership explored the governor's offices across the country. Bush had successfully captured the Texas governorship in 1994 from a popular Democratic incumbent in a state that had historically elected Democrats. He slew the giant of Texas politics: the Democratic Party. He had positioned himself to move onto the national stage as a candidate for president.

Barack Obama may also have been at the right place at the right time for the Democratic Party as the 2008 election approached. Obama represented a new political generation for a party whose field was dominated by long-time party leaders, each of whom brought political baggage with them.

In addition to having captured the Texas governorship, Bush was a known quantity in national politics because of his father, former president George H. W. Bush. Although little known himself in the national arena, his father was well known and relatively well thought of. His defeat in 1992 by Bill Clinton was the result of a rare three-way split in the popular vote, after Ross Perot mounted an independent candidacy. With history on his side as a governor, George W. Bush embarked on a quest for the presidency in 1998, halfway into his first term as governor of Texas. He began assembling a campaign staff, creating a fund-raising network, and began building bridges to the Reagan Revolution that would garner him the Republican nomination in 2000.

Barack Obama's successful presidential campaign seized upon many of the lessons learned from previous campaigns, but particularly from George W. Bush's 2000 campaign. Bush built bridges to Democrats using the theme of compassionate conservatism. Similarly, Obama built bridges to Republicans with the theme of change. For both Bush and Obama, campaign themes sought to establish their candidacies as moderate, not extreme, and to emphasize a willingness to work across the aisle. Both articulated a need to end gridlock and to bring a new sense of civility to governance.

The campaign theme of change that was constantly addressed by Obama was a lesson that Karl Rove had carefully moved into the Bush campaign as a lesson learned from the Clinton campaign. As journalists Mark Halperin and John Harris note of the 2008 campaign in their book *Taking the White House: The Way to Win in 2008,* Obama built on the Clinton and Bush experiences of identifying a critical policy area that needed to be publicly changed, and homed in on that during the campaign.[1] For Bush, the policy proposal would reduce government's regulatory role. Obama and Clinton saw a more engaged role for government. In both cases, however, as Halperin and Harris argue, the winning candidate had a very succinct and identifiable role for the government.

The Race for Governor 1994:
Compassionate Conservatism as a Theme

George W. Bush's presidential campaign emerged from the lessons he had learned running for governor in 1994. It was during the this race for the Texas governorship that Bush learned how to create a campaign theme to cross party lines, a theme he would employ again in 2000, a theme that carried him into the White House.

Crafting a theme to break the Democratic Party's lock on the governor's office in 1994 would be the first test of Bush's foray into politics after selling his business interest in the Texas Rangers baseball team. He needed a campaign theme that attracted not only Republicans, but Democrats, in a state that had overwhelmingly propelled Lyndon Baines Johnson into the Senate and then the White House. Although Ronald Reagan had won the state, Texas continued to elect its governors from the ranks of Democrats. Its incumbent governor, Ann Richards, gained national attention as a keynote speaker at the 1988 Democratic Convention in Atlanta, when she said of George H. W. Bush, who was running against Arkansas governor Bill Clinton, "Poor George, he can't help it. He was born with a silver foot in his mouth."[2] Any Republican challenge to Richards in 1994 seemed to be foolhardy, but Bush took the challenge and began to build an electoral coalition in Texas that attempted to unseat her.

Using the campaign theme of compassionate conservatism, Bush cobbled together an alliance of Democrats and Republicans that would oust the incumbent Democratic governor. He rarely used the word "Republican" to define his candidacy, choosing instead to define himself as a conservative (which appealed to Republicans) with a compassionate agenda (which appealed to Democrats). The merging of the words "compassionate" and "conservative" led to the theme of compassionate conservatism, which was designed to appeal to both Republicans and Democrats[3] in a state still wedded to Democrats, albeit conservative Democrats. By identifying himself as a "conservative," Bush hoped to align himself with both traditional Republicans and those Democrats who self-identified as "conservative Democrats."

In order to win, Bush needed to develop a short list of issues that conservative Democrats and his Republican base could coalesce around within his theme of compassionate conservatism. Those issues became immigration, tax reform, and the ubiquitous reference to "compassionate" government. Immigration reform became the heart of his 1994 gubernatorial platform, with a call for stricter enforcement of illegal immigration and a call for Congress to increase funding for border enforcement.[4] By focusing on illegal immigration, Bush harnessed the outrage against illegal immigration that had been building across Texas.

Bill Clinton had used a similar tactic in the 1992 election to woo Republicans, drawn to Clinton's conservative approach to governance, into the Democratic fold. Although Clinton never referred to himself or his policies as conservative, he frequently had used conservative clichés such as references to a smaller federal government and to reforms in the federal welfare system. These had been traditional Republican policies which Clinton was now embracing. Two years later, George W. Bush simply built on the model of co-option that Clinton had created in his presidential race. In his own gubernatorial race, Bush positioned himself as the only candidate that met the needs of both Democrats and Republicans.[5] When the votes were counted, he had successfully built the coalition that he needed for victory.

However, by 1994, the Clinton administration was having problems with the coalition that it had brought together. After two years in office, many of the Republicans and conservative Democrats who had supported Clinton's 1992 election had become dissatisfied. Republicans had successfully tagged the Clinton administration as one of liberal big spending, primarily due to its push for a national health-care system and for its "don't ask, don't tell" policy for the military. Although Clinton campaigned as a "New Democrat," a label he coined and which he used to build Republican support in 1992, many Republicans now viewed the Clinton presidency as one of continued big government and liberal policies. Bush was able to exploit this dissatisfaction in 1994 and draw dissatisfied Democrats under the political umbrella of compassionate conservatism.

The discomfort by southern Democrats, such as those in Texas, with the positions of more liberal Democrats in Washington, D.C., particularly the health-care initiative, bolstered the Bush campaign throughout the election year.[6] By calling himself a conservative, Bush sought to capitalize on the dissatisfaction with the Clinton administration and to enhance his own campaign.[7] Whether or not Bush might have won in any other election year is debatable, but in 1994 he followed the tide of discontent against the Clinton administration and won the election.

The combination of a strong campaign theme, "compassionate conservatism," and a narrow agenda which attracted bipartisan support, Bush scored an upset victory and allowed Ann Richards only a single term in office. The Republican Party had captured the Texas governorship in the 1994 election.

Victory in 1994: Building a Government for Compassionate Conservatism

Bush's first two years in office, however, proved difficult. The Democratic-controlled legislature was not as eager as the voters had been to support his programs. Although Bush had successfully built an electoral coalition of Democrats and Republicans in 1994, he had difficulty transferring that base of support into a governing coalition in the legislature. Democrats, who controlled both chambers, maintained their independence and refused to endorse his legislative agenda.

Not until 1997 when the legislature changed party control was Governor Bush able to significantly impact the policy-making process. His first task with the Republican-controlled legislature was to deal with rising property taxes which, because of the housing boom, were affecting his urban and suburban base in affluent West Texas. Property taxes had doubled in ten years due to the booming economy of the 1990s, as the demand for new school construction, fire, police, water systems, and other public services skyrocketed. Bush tried to push through a $5-billion property tax relief bill, but other taxes increased.[8] The Bush plan proposed that property tax revenue was to be offset by a tax on certain corporations and businesses, called a "business activity levy." Although the tax affected only about 10 percent of the business community, it was perceived as a general tax on goods since businesses would have to increase their prices as a pass-through.[9]

After the business community pressured the legislature, the attempt to create the $5-billion tax relief failed, as did the tax on businesses, but a later attempt successfully provided for a $1-billion property tax relief bill without a concurrent tax increase. The decision to propose as tax relief bill without adding other taxes was made possible by a $2.3-billion tax surplus, generated during previous administrations, in the state's coffers. The success of Bushes tax relief proposal, while modest, provided support for his conservative fiscal agenda. He then turned to the "compassionate" side of compassionate conservatism.

Having mustered some measure of success in satisfying the calls for property tax relief among his affluent Republican constituency, Bush needed to turn his attention to building bridges with his less-affluent Republican and conservative Democratic base. Since he was unable to address immigration, which had been his signature platform proposal in 1995, in any significant way, he needed to find another issue that maintained the umbrella theme of "compassionate" government. He needed a platform in 1997, as he prepared for reelection the next year, which embraced the same theme—and this he found in prison reform.[10] Prison reform had been a constant theme in Texas politics for years, as prison overcrowding became the center of federal litigation.

Texas had been unable to dramatically reduce the number of prisoners or the number of prisons or to reduce overcrowding, and Bush sought to change the way the state dealt with its prison population. He brought in a faith-based group, Prison Fellowship Ministries, that former Watergate conspirator Charles Colson had formed in 1975. Their goal was "for prisoners to become born again and grow as fruitful disciples of Jesus Christ."[11] Prison Fellowship Ministries was paid for by state funds in Texas. Not surprisingly, the faith-based prison ministries became part of the "compassionate" approach to governing which was put forth by Bush in the gubernatorial, and later presidential, campaigns.

The Race for President Begins: 1997

Three years into his first term as the chief executive of Texas, George W. Bush began considering a race for the presidency. An opening to serve as the Republican standard-bearer in the 2000 presidential election emerged with the defeat of the Dole- Kemp ticket in 1996. Bush became a dark-horse contender for the Republican nomination as soon as the lights went out on the November 1996 election. His exposure to the national limelight had been constant throughout his life, growing up as the grandson of a prominent U.S. senator from Connecticut, Prescott Bush, and the son of the U.S. ambassador to China and later president of the United States, George H. W. Bush.

In the spring of 1998, media speculation began to swirl on whether Governor Bush would make a run for the 2000 nomination, as he began to hold a series of private fund-raising and speaking events in California. He denied that the events were connected to a presidential run, saying only that "I'm running for governor of Texas."[12] The trips to California involved fund-raising for his reelection campaign only, he argued. However, he told one group that he had not ruled out a candidacy in 2000, noting that "I think about it."[13]

His reelection as governor in November 1998 with 69 percent of the vote proved that Bush could be a serious contender for the 2000 presidential election. Even before the election, national media were looking at Bush as a possible presidential candidate. Although the Texas media had been speculating about the possibility throughout the 1998 campaign, not until the election appeared to be a landslide victory for Bush did the national media become interested. On October 29, Candy Crowley of CNN posted a story that extolled the strength of Bush as a campaigner. In comparing George W. Bush to his father, Crowley said, "George [W.] Bush is a terrific campaigner, thriving on the limelight, diving into crowds. This George Bush is a retail politician, touching, hugging and autographing his way along the campaign trail."[14] Speculation on a second Bush in the White House had begun in the press but the Bush campaign remained focused on winning reelection in Austin and provided few insights into the conversation on a national campaign. They still had to win the gubernatorial election if they wanted to consider a run for the White House.

The Second Term as Governor: Beginning the Race for President

When George W. Bush was inaugurated on January 20, 1999, on the promenade of the Texas capitol in Austin[15], the first sign of a national campaign emerged. His inaugural address was aimed at Christian conservatives, which bridged the Democratic and Republican parties.[16] He peppered his address with frequent references to God, such as "All of us have worth. We're all made *in the image of God. We're all equal in God's eyes* [emphasis added]," in order to attract their attention. He also reiterated his commitment to compassionate government, to continue his efforts to engage Democrats in his administration.[17] Exactly one year later he would be using many of the same phrases in his presidential inaugural address from the U.S. Capitol in Washington, D.C.

With a legislature in Texas that met only 140 days every other year, Governor Bush had the luxury of not being accountable on a daily basis to political bantering over legislative proposals. A newly installed Republican lieutenant governor, Rick Perry, and a Republican-controlled legislature, eased the transition from full-time governor to full-time presidential candidate. Only a month after being inaugurated to his second term, public speculation emerged as to who would be part of the Bush presidential campaign. The *Austin American-Statesman* began a front-page article on February 28, 1999, "When Gov. George W. Bush turns his attention to trying to become President George W. Bush, he will turn to aides, friends and advisers he has collected on his privileged path from prep school to the political big leagues."[18] Soon after, stories appeared in major newspapers across the country. The campaign for the presidency was underway in full view of the press.

Although the nascent campaign for the presidency indicated that Bush had turned his sights on the White House, in fact he had started the process nearly a year earlier. Gearing up for a national campaign began during the 1998 gubernatorial campaign, in which Bush raised and spent $25 million to his opponent's $3 million.[19] Karl Rove, the political mastermind of both the gubernatorial and presidential campaigns, realized that a landslide victory would catapult Bush into the contender's circle for the 2000 Republican nomination. Part of the $25 million had been raised by out-of-state Republicans looking for a standard-bearer for conservative Republicans.

In California, where he explored the possibility of raising funds, Bush began to test the waters for a national campaign. Los Angeles businessman Bradford Freeman took the lead role in the early fund-raising, introducing Bush to potential donors. Freeman's partner, Ron Spogli, had been a roommate of Bush at Harvard Business School.[20] Another fund-raiser was Craig Stapleton, married to a Bush cousin, who had raised money for George H. W. Bush and been an investor with George W. Bush in the Texas Rangers in 1989.[21] In addition, the inner campaign circle began to be formed, drawing in Joe Allbaugh (chief of staff to the governor), Karl Rove (political consultant), Karen Hughes (communications director), Donald Evans (Midland businessman), Clay Johnson (appointments director), and Harriet Miers (personal lawyer). As would be expected, most of the inner circle surfaced again in key positions in the administration, from the cabinet to the White House staff.

In April 1998, Freeman arranged a fund-raising swing through the Silicon Valley, ostensibly to raise money for the reelection campaign. This gave wealthy California Republicans the opportunity to scrutinize the potential presidential candidate. Freeman, a Stanford University trustee, then arranged a small policy-oriented meeting at the campus home of former secretary of state George Shultz in Palo Alto.[22] Shultz had been on the faculty at Stanford's conservative Hoover Institution since 1989, after he left the Bechtel Corporation, headquartered in San Francisco.

The meeting included about ten Stanford University faculty, including economists Michael Boskin and John Taylor, domestic policy expert Martin Anderson, and Soviet specialist Condoleezza Rice.[23] All had worked in past Republican administrations at senior levels: Boskin, Taylor, and Rice in the George H. W. Bush administration, and Shultz and Anderson in the Reagan administration. Boskin had the closest tie to George W. Bush. A chairman of the Council of Economic Advisors for Bush's father, Boskin had once shared a cottage with George W. Bush in Kennebunkport.[24] Except for Rice, all were part of Stanford's conservative Hoover Institution, and Rice worked closely with many Hoover faculty.[25]

The meeting that Shultz held for Bush and the Hoover faculty that evening was one of many that the Hoover faculty had with presidential hopefuls. As Hoover Fellow Martin Anderson noted in a 1998 interview with the Stanford Review, "Over the years, we've invited most candidates from both parties. When they come, they don't ask for advice."[26] Hoover encouraged its faculty to become engaged in the national political scene. During the 1980 campaign, Ronald Reagan had also met with Hoover faculty. After a 1979 dinner party at the home of Shultz, many joined the Reagan campaign and continued into the Reagan White House. Martin Anderson, the architect of the domestic and economic policies during the 1980 campaign, became the central White House domestic policy advisor.

Having made the initial contact with the Hoover faculty at the Shultz dinner party in April 1998, George W. Bush invited the group to Austin for what became a regular series of policy discussions. For the next two years, Hoover faculty would make a series of visits to Austin to explain policy issues and offer policy positions. Another Reagan administration alumnus, American Enterprise Institute scholar Lawrence Lindsey who had served on the Council of Economic advisors, also became a regular at the Austin policy meetings.[27]

By the spring of 1999, the Stanford faculty and others were regularly visiting Austin. Meetings, which were convened in the formal dining room of the governor's mansion or in the conservatory, lasted about four hours, starting at 8:00 A.M. and ending at noon. They varied in the level of policy discussion, often more specific than Bush might have wanted. For example, in one health policy meeting that Steven Goldsmith presided over, held February 18, 1999, in Austin, there were thirty minutes for introductory remarks and twenty-five minutes for a discussion of the financing system and delivery systems, with such topics covered as trends in patient care, acute to chronic conditions, diffusion of technology, and the rise of pharmaceutical therapy.[28] One comment from a participant was that Bush still "had a lot to learn" about every policy issue at hand. Another participant, Michael Boskin, described Bush as "having a lot of growing to do."[29]

Not surprisingly, as the campaign advisory staff lost the informality of the Austin meetings, the Hoover faculty would continue to play a senior role. Condoleezza Rice became the chief foreign policy advisor, Williamson Evers became the chief advisor on education, and Michael Boskin and John Cogan became senior economic advisors. Edward Lazear, an economist at Stanford's Graduate School of Business, directed positions on labor policy. The faculty at Stanford's Hoover Institution was the ideal tutor for the Texas governor.

They carried the Reagan mantle which Bush sought to continue, they ensured a continuation of the conservative agenda, they built bridges to the Reagan and Bush administrations for additional campaign staff, and they added star power to the fledgling campaign's fund-raising efforts. What better way to bring national attention to a campaign than reaching out to intellectual talent from Stanford University? For conservative Republicans familiar with the Hoover faculty ties to the Reagan and Bush administrations, the message delivered was that there would be continuity in policy direction.[30]

Bush solidified his continuity to the Reagan and Bush years with the choice of Dick Cheney as his vice presidential running mate.[31] Cheney, who served as secretary of defense for George H. W. Bush, had the necessary defense credentials, and as a congressman from Wyoming in the 1980s had created a consistently conservative voting record. Polls in June 2000 showed that Bush had strong support among independents and moderates. He believed that he would be able to shore up this support by bringing another fiscal conservative onto the ticket.[32] Bush avoided putting anyone on the ticket, such as pro-choice Tom Ridge of Pennsylvania, who could upset the support he had with the evangelicals in the party. [33]

The Campaign of 2000

The primary campaign of 2000 run by Bush delivered a clear message to conservatives across the country: the Reagan legacy of fiscal responsibility and less government regulation would continue if Bush was elected. This message had been crafted throughout 1998 and 1999 by the same advisors from Stanford who had crafted the policy for Ronald Reagan.

However, a new message went out which was not crafted by the Stanford faculty, one that focused on "compassionate conservatism." Karl Rove, who orchestrated the 1994 and 1998 gubernatorial elections, created a message which brought together Reagan-Bush fiscal conservatives with Christian conservatives, and which allowed George W. Bush to use his own personal experience with religion as a political tool.

To win the election, Bush would need to marry the message of compassion, which he created himself, with the message of conservatism that was linked to the Reagan and George H. W. Bush years. For conservatives who had supported George H. W. Bush, "compassionate conservatism" meant reducing the size of the federal government as private organizations began to take over social service programs, without government subsidies. These organizations were rewarded by being named one of the "Thousand Points of Light." For these "compassionate" conservatives, government was shrinking. However, George W. Bush rallied Christian conservatives using the phrase to imply that government should partner with private organizations, including private religious organizations, to provide social services. In a campaign speech in June, for example, Bush proposed that government resources "should be devolved, not just to the states, but to charities and neighborhood healers who need them the most."[34] His frequently stated campaign rhetoric included the statement that the First Amendment did not preclude religious organizations from benefiting from federal contracts.

One of the defining moments of the campaign for Christian conservatives came during a debate of Republican candidates in Des Moines, Iowa, on December 14, 1998. When asked by the moderator, John Bachman, "what political philosopher or thinker" they most identified with, Bush answered "Christ, because he changed my heart." When asked by Bachman to elaborate, Bush continued "Well, if you don't know, it's going to be hard to explain. When you turn your heart and your life over to Christ, when you accept Christ as the savior, it changes your heart. It changes your life. And that's what happened to me."[35] Not surprisingly, polls indicated that 40 percent of likely caucus participants identified themselves as evangelicals or "born-again Christians."[36] By winning the evangelicals at the Iowa caucus, Bush began his successful march to winning the nomination in Philadelphia.

By weaving together the Reagan philosophy of small government and fiscal responsibility with the faith-based philosophy of "compassionate conservatism," Bush hoped to build a strong enough coalition to defeat Vice President Al Gore. Not only would the Republican base support him, but a coalition of Catholics and evangelicals who sought to use the resources of government to stop federal funding of abortions, stem cell research, and cloning might also support him. "Compassionate conservatism" became a catch-all phrase that signaled a "pro-life" position but also signaled allowing religious groups to receive federal funds for certain social programs. Bush often wove religious phrases into his speeches and ended them with "God bless you."

As the general election grew closer, the influence of the Stanford faculty lessened. Bush had put forth his domestic and foreign policy positions throughout the election year. His positions had galvanized his Republican base, but Gore's positions had galvanized the Democratic base. For political advisor Karl Rove, in order to win the election Bush needed to move past the speeches on domestic and foreign policy to speeches on how "compassionate conservatism" would work. So Bush gave speech after speech using religious overtones. Rove encouraged evangelical pastors to encourage their flocks to get out the vote for George Bush. By November 2000, the difference between winning and losing in a close election was the degree to which evangelicals would vote in the swing states across the Mason-Dixon Line, in Ohio, and in Florida.

With both the Gore and Bush camps claiming victory on Election Day, a series of state and federal court battles ensued. Not until Gore conceded on December 13, 2000, did Bush finally claim the presidency. Clearly the Rove strategy had garnered the necessary votes for Bush in states such as Arkansas, Tennessee, and West Virginia.

Lessons Learned for 2008

Each of the following points from the successful candidacy of George W. Bush was followed in the 2008 election by Barack Obama. John McCain failed in several points, which proved to be catastrophic to his campaign.

1. *Prepare your candidacy at least two years before the election.* Bradford Freeman's fund-raising in 1998 in the Silicon Valley not only added to Bush's war chest for 2000, but built a new network of backers. Early fund-raising provided much-needed capital for the fledgling campaign, and alerted the financial backers that the candidate was a serious contender who had already developed a sizable war chest. Obama announced his candidacy in February 2007 in Springfield, Illinois, having already enlisted a group of Chicago financiers, led by Penny Pritzker and David Jackson, to build his war chest.[37]

2. *Develop a prestigious bank of advisers.* The connection that Bush made to the Stanford faculty brought not only strong advice from a seasoned group of political professionals, but brought national attention to the campaign. Obama appointed former Senate Majority Leader Tom Daschle as a senior member of his advisory team, and soon added endorsements from key party leaders such as Senator Edward Kennedy, Maria Shriver, Governor Duval Patrick, and Congressman John Lewis. Obama was particularly aggressive in using high-profile economists Lawrence Summers and former Goldman Sacks chairman and secretary of the treasury Robert Rubin as his economic advisors.

3. *Focus on a short list of policy proposals.* Bush narrowed his campaign agenda to a short list of policy proposals, which brought support from his base of fiscal conservatives and the newly empowered Christian conservatives. Fiscal responsibility dominated the concerns of traditional Republican conservatives while Christian conservatives were drawn to a new, religion-engaged social contract with government, called "compassionate government." Obama had a more expansive agenda than did Bush, but folded his proposals into the simple theme of "change," which he called "change we can believe in." This gave the illusion of a short and easily implemented agenda.

4. *Draw parallels to past administrations which the public views favorably.* Bush consistently implied that he would continue the Reagan legacy of a trimmed down bureaucracy and lower taxes. Obama did not compare himself to either Jimmy Carter or Bill Clinton, both of whom had significant problems during their administrations. Rather, he alluded to a comparison with Franklin Delano Roosevelt and the economic policies Roosevelt developed to pull the nation from economic ruin.

5. *Build on past campaign themes.* Bush repeated campaign themes from his two elections to the governorship in Austin, focusing on "compassionate conservatism" and lower taxes. Obama did not use the themes from his recent Senate campaign but chose to focus on his multiple roles as a change agent, as community organizer, state senator, and U.S. senator.

6. *Use the governor's office or the U.S. Senate as the springboard for a national candidacy.* Both offices provide national exposure and opportunities for fund-raising, in addition to executive or legislative experience, which both Bush and Obama built upon.

George W. Bush carefully choreographed his 2000 election for two years, beginning in 1998. He built an intellectual team from Stanford University, many of whom had served in the Reagan and George H. W. Bush administrations. They provided clear tutorials on how to connect to the Reagan legacy of lower taxes, slimmed down government, and strong defense. They also provided clear tutorials on tackling immigration reform, an issue that had been important to Bush, and on social security reform, an issue that remained a major source of angst for conservatives.

The lessons learned from the 2000 Bush campaign for the White House proved invaluable to Barack Obama in the 2008 race. Although the specific agenda items of the two campaigns were quite different, the manner in which Obama sought to capture votes from the opposite party was quite similar. Obama co-opted many of the themes of the Republican Party, including a faith-based orientation of his personal life and a promise for a faith-based orientation for his presidency. He moved directly to a topic, faith-based issues, that the other party was vested in, such as Bush did with immigration reform. Obama also successfully maintained his political base, with his commitment to removing troops from Iraq, as Bush did with his commitment to smaller government.

Perhaps the most striking lesson learned from the Bush campaign was the importance of its constant reference to continuing the Reagan legacy and its inclusion of the Stanford University faculty that guided the Reagan presidency. The Obama campaign was guided by the lessons of the Bush campaign and other successful presidential campaigns, reworking successful tactics to fit the 2008 political environment.

Notes

1. Mark Halperin and John Harris, *The Way to Win: Taking the White House in 2008* (New York: Random House), 160.

2. Joe Holey, "Former Texas Governor Ann Richards Dies," *Washington Post,* September 14, 2006.

3. R. G. Ratcliffe, "Richards Attacks Republican Policy, GOP Fights Back against 'Liberal,'" *Houston Chronicle,* July 10, 1994.

4. Scott Pendleton, "Stetson-Size Agenda for Texas," *Christian Science Monitor,* December 15, 1994.

5. Dave McNeely, "Clinton's Unpopularity Benefiting Republicans," *Austin American-Statesman,* October 9, 1994.

6. Ibid.

7. John Sharp, a Democrat who won reelection as comptroller observed that voters in Texas seemed to prefer "conservative government" after the 1994 election (quoted in "Election '94: GOP Gains in Texas Significant, State Offices Rise from Eight to Thirteen," *Houston Chronicle,* November 10, 1994).

8. Clay Robison, "Gov. Bush Calls for Bipartisan Effort to Cut Property Taxes," *Houston Chronicle,* November 9, 1996.

9. Clay Robison, "Business Tax Levy: Is It a Levy on Income?" *Houston Chronicle,* April 20, 1997.

10. To see the connection between the two, see Marvin Olasky's editorial "Working to Stop Prison's Revolving Door," *Austin American-Statesman*, May 12, 1999. Olasky is one of the ideological founders of "compassionate conservatism."

11. Prison Fellowship Ministries mission statement.

12. R. G. Ratcliffe, "Bush Defends Closing Events to News Media," *Houston Chronicle*, April 21, 1998.

13. R. G. Ratcliffe, "Bush Is Thinking about Presidency: Speech to Movie Industry Heavy With Political Overtone," *Houston Chronicle*, April 24, 1988.

14. Candy Crowley, "Days Away from Re-Election, Will Texas Gov. Run for President Next?" CNN, October 29, 1998.

15. Rick Lyman, "Bush Blends Optimism and Challenge in Texas Inaugural," *New York Times*, January 20, 1999.

16. Inaugural Address of Governor George W. Bush, Austin, Texas, January 20, 1999.

17. Ibid.

18. Ken Herman, "Select Few Earn Spots on Bush's First Team; Small Group of Trusted," *Austin American-Statesman*, February 28, 1999.

19. Carl M. Cannon, Lou DuBose, and Jan Reid, *Boy Genius: Karl Rove, The Architect of George W. Bush's Remarkable Political Triumphs* (New York: Public Affairs, 2003), 114.

20. Bradford Freeman was a partner in the Los Angeles investment firm of Freeman Spogli and Company. Freeman formed the firm in the 1980s with former Los Angeles mayor Richard Riordan, who left the firm in 1988, and Ron Spogli. The firm focuses on leveraged buyouts over $100 million.

21. Ken Herman, "Select Few Earn Spots on Bush's First Team; Small Group of Trusted," *Austin American-Statesman*, February 28, 1999.

22. Burt Solomon, "Issues & Ideas: George W. Bush's New Hooverville," *National Journal*, March 27, 1999.

23. Robert McGrew and Henry Tosner, "Bush Finds Core Advisors at Hoover," *Stanford Review*, October 29, 1999.

24. Ibid.

25. The official White House biography of Condoleezza Rice indicates that she was a Hoover Fellow, with caveat added "by courtesy" (http://www.whitehouse.gov).

26. McGrew and Tosner, "Bush Finds Core Advisors at Hoover."[1]

27. Richard L. Berke with Rick Lyman, "Training for a Presidential Race," *New York Times*, March 15, 1999.

28. Ibid.

29. Ibid. Attached to the Berke and Lyman article is an editor's note at the bottom. It reads as follows,

March 19, 1999, Friday. An article on Monday about the prospect of a Presidential campaign by Gov. George W. Bush of Texas described a series of tutorials aimed at helping him study issues he would face. As published, the article included an opinionated sentence casting doubt on his mastery of those issues. The sentence was sent as a message between editors after the article was written, and the reporters were never aware of it. The comment was typed in a nonprinting computer script, but converted into print through a command error.

30. Whether or not Ronald Reagan would have supported George W. Bush or encouraged his advisors to support him is unknown, but Reagan's diary of May 17, 1986, reveals the following:

A moment I've been dreading. George [Vice President George H. W. Bush] brought his ne'er-do-well son around this morning and asked me to find the kid a job. Not the political one who lives in Florida [future Gov. Jeb Bush], the one who hangs around here all the time looking shiftless. This so-called kid is already almost 40 and has never had a real job. Maybe I'll call Kinsley over at the *New Republic* and see if they'll hire him as a contributing editor or something. That looks like easy work.

31. Among the numerous articles on Cheney's selection as vice president, see Nicolas Lemann, "The Quiet Man," *New Yorker,* May 7, 2001.

32. Frank Bruni, "Bush's List of Possible Running Mates Getting Shorter, but Not Clearer," *New York Times,* June 18, 2000.

33. "Bush Introduces Cheney as Running Mate," *USA Today,* July 25, 2000.

34. Campaign speech, Wayne, Michigan, June 27, 2000. "Governor Bush Heralds Michigan Welfare Reform Success," presidential campaign press materials.

35. Stephen Buttry, "Candidates Focus on Christian Beliefs," *Des Moines Register,* December 15, 1999.

36. Ibid.

37. Lynn Sweet, "The Power of Penny Pritzker," *Chicago Sun-Times,* August 21, 2008.

The Debate about the Debates

Sixty Years of Hopes and Laments for Presidential Colloquies

DAVID GREENBERG

During the vice presidential debate of 2008, Alaska governor Sarah Palin was pressed by her Democratic rival, Delaware senator Joe Biden, and by the moderator, Gwen Ifill, to reply to a question she had just ignored. The chipper Palin—who usually fared best in the campaign when she was under fire—blithely demurred. "I may not answer the questions that either the moderator or you want to hear," she insisted, "but I'm going to talk straight to the American people."[1]

The response in the press to Palin's defiant statement ranged from outrage to ridicule. Almost everyone acted as if there were something beyond the pale about what she had said. And from one perspective, there was. While candidates evade questions all the time in debates, Palin's stark declaration of her evasion was something new, or at least something rare. Her frankness in ducking the question seemed to violate a basic convention of the presidential (and vice presidential) debates—the notion that candidates are there to dutifully report their ticket's positions on prominent policy issues, so as to help voters decide for whom to vote. From this perspective, Palin's remark deserved the response it got, because it encapsulated the oft-cited political axiom coined by the journalist Michael Kinsley: "a gaffe is when a politician tells the truth."[2]

There is, however, another way to view Palin's purported gaffe. If we can put aside the strong feelings bred in the campaign hothouse, her candor may seem oddly refreshing. Precisely because candidates do strain so frequently to avoid answering unwelcome questions—while at the same time to avoid the appearance of ducking—her straightforward declaration that she intended to speak to the audience instead of trying to placate the moderator comes as a dose of welcome frankness. We might even say that in her honesty she was in effect blowing the whistle on the very sham nature of presidential debates—on all the scripted jokes, rehearsed lines of attack, regurgitated talking points, and other conventions that have become standard parts of these verbal duels.

Like several other elements of a presidential campaign—the nominating conventions, the rolling-out of the vice presidential selections, the detail-studded policy speeches—the debates are a ritual whose meaning in our political culture stems from certain assumptions. The main conceit of the debates is that they exist to inform viewers, who presumably watch them with open minds to learn about the candidates and decide how to vote. Grandiose as it may sound, this amounts to assigning the debates a vital role in American democracy. Since effective self-government depends on an informed citizenry, voters are supposed to learn from the debates whatever they still need to know about the candidates in the fall of a presidential election season.

Accordingly, the news media and the public eagerly await these contests every four years. They're often described as the only potential turning points of the fall campaign—the only ones *scheduled,* at least, since external news events can always shake things up—and one of only a few chances for the all-important undecided voters to make up their endlessly wavering minds. In recent elections, the television networks have convened focus groups of these vacillators on whose fleeting impressions the nation hinges, interviewing them on air after each clash to see if they were moved to reach any decisions that might change the campaign's outcome. It's portrayed as one big jury deliberation, and the last few jurors are put under the spotlight as they make up their minds. All this attention stems from the underlying conceit of the debates as a form of rational discourse for sober-minded, independent-thinking, self-governing citizens.

There is a problem, however, with this heroic view of the debates' role. Given the evasions, boilerplate, scripted jokes, and attention to stagecraft that permeate the debates—the games that Sarah Palin brazenly called attention to in admitting she was ducking a question—it's hard for anyone to defend the claims that they fulfill their putative purpose of informing the independent-minded viewer. On the contrary, they seem to fail at this task often enough to earn them unremitting disparagement, frequently from the same pundits who otherwise describe them in such exalted terms. Ever since the first televised debates in 1960 between John F. Kennedy and Richard M. Nixon, critics have complained that the showdowns are not debates at all but well-choreographed joint press conferences—marred, as the *New York Times* editorialized in 1976 (the second time general-election presidential debates were held), by "their show-business nature; their heavy reliance on rehearsal and grooming by professional image-makers; the concern for appearance over substance."[3] Even in 2008, when the debates between Barack Obama and John McCain took place amid a climate of deep fear over the unfolding financial crisis, observers quickly turned cynical about the contests' prefabricated nature. "It didn't matter that the second **debate** was in a so-called 'town-hall meeting' format," wrote a columnist for a Minnesota paper; "the candidates for president said essentially the same things they said at the first **debate**. . . . This is **scripted** presidential campaign politics we're talking about, after all, where nothing is ever said and done without extreme calculation beforehand."[4]

But the tirades about the emptiness of the debates, about their theatricality and extreme calculation, are, like the rhapsodies about their centrality to the democratic process, less than fully satisfying. After all, all modern politics involves image-making and spin, and voters have learned, at least to some extent, to take the measure of politicians even amid all the premeditation that underpins their public performances. It's unrealistic to expect the debates to be grandly edifying, and overwrought to berate them for not rising to such a lofty standard.

Ultimately, then, both the celebrations of the debates as an indispensable fount of insight into the candidates' fitness to govern and the denigrations of their lifelessness and theatricality miss the point. For both rest on flawed assumptions about what the debates are there to do. If, however, we try instead to conceive of the debates' role and purpose differently, we may appreciate the democratic function that they *do* perform: not the provision of vital data to blank-slate voters who are forming considered judgments about the candidates, but rather the stimulation and engagement of broader public interest in politics. This contribution, while more modest than the sweeping claims frequently made on the debates' behalf, nonetheless goes some way toward renewing voters' political commitments and enriching democracy.

1.

The discourse about the high promise of the debates dates to the Kennedy-Nixon contests. Since 1948, when Thomas Dewey and Harold Stassen squared off for an hour in pursuit of the Republican nomination, primary contenders had occasionally jousted over the radio. But for political and legal reasons—mainly the fear that equal-time regulations would force the inclusion of fringe candidates and create a prime-time free-for-all—televised general-election debates remained a dream. Only after the quiz show scandals of the late 1950s did the calculus change. With the networks' reputations bruised, a shot of ennobling public-interest programming seemed like the perfect tonic. Congress suspended the nettlesome equal-time clause of the 1934 Communications Act, and the networks set about conceiving television programs that turned out to be quite like the quiz shows that they sought to displace.

Network spokesmen, however, did not want to be seen as reducing public affairs to the level of Milton Berle. And so they portrayed the debates as something more than commercial enterprises. They were touted as a civic boon, a cure for an ailing democracy. These arguments were not insincere. They came at a time when Americans were grappling with a perceived sense of inauthenticity in politics. For much of the twentieth century, the public had grown anxious that certain forces in modernity were weakening democracy. A series of changes—the astounding growth of the federal government, America's rise to global leadership, and efforts in the Progressive Era to purify politics—combined to make government a more important force in people's lives, but at the same time a more distant one. As Jürgen Habermas put it in one of the few evocative passages in *The Structural Transformation of the Public Sphere,* citizens' "contact with the state [now came to] occur . . . in the rooms and anterooms of the bureaucracy," a decidedly impersonal venue. Meanwhile, new media of mass communication—film, radio, later television—gave audiences an illusion of familiarity with national political figures than print had ever afforded, even as they fed the feeling that politics was playing out in a theatrical display on a faraway stage, remote from their own lives and concerns. The new political culture seemed to downgrade Habermas's celebrated "rational-critical discourse" that he posited was central to the Enlightenment conception of democracy.[5]

The rhetoric surrounding the televised debates suggested that the new medium could restore a form of town-hall democracy in an impersonal age of mass media. Televised debates would bring back an intimacy to politics. The candidates would be in everyone's living rooms for sixty minutes, on four occasions, talking directly to the citizenry. Voters could use their autonomous intelligence in evaluating the two aspirants for the leadership of the free world.

Yet if a restoration was promised, television, that symbol of modern times, was not to be effaced. It was cast as the hero, not the villain, of the civic revival story. CBS president Frank Stanton argued that the televised debates were tailor-made for the mass-media age. In the nineteenth century, he noted, large throngs turned out at campaign events such as torchlight parades and mass rallies; amid alcohol, music, and colorful costumes, they would feed off one another's partisan passions. Writing in 1960, just after the Kennedy-Nixon debates, Stanton dismissed those old-style gatherings as anachronistic, as calculated, in his words, "not to inform, or to create an atmosphere conducive to the appraisal of information, but to whip up attitudes capable of overcoming any temptation to judiciousness." By his own day, he said, America could no longer "afford the blind, uncritical automatic support of one man against another, whatever his insight, his judgment, or his qualities of leadership." The televised debates—a twentieth-century substitute for the nineteenth-century outdoor spectacles—would treat voters as independent of mind, enlightening them about the candidates' stands and enabling them to weigh the issues with the care they deserved. Modern democracy demanded no less.[6]

Briefs like Stanton's set the standards by which the debates would be judged. Usually, alas, they were judged as falling short. Rather than educating voters about the key differences between the candidates, went the critique, the TV extravaganzas stressed shallow qualities such as looks and speaking style, while allowing the presidential aspirants to avoid precisely the kind of substantive back-and-forth that the event was meant to foster. This critique of the debates as plotted and scripted, as valuing image over substance, implied that they weren't meeting their foremost obligation. Voters were instead being treated to a pageant of skilled performances, clever sound bites, packaged statements from stump speeches, and deft equivocations that aimed not to help voters assess the candidates' relative positions on the issues but simply to win them over by strength of charm, wit, polish, misinformation, and spin. Even the rare joke that occasionally delighted the audiences was known to have been devised in advance by a sharp wordsmith, with the candidate responsible merely for finding an opportune moment to deploy it. This criticism of the debates mirrored the hope that they would restore a rational, critical discourse. It embodied the fear that they reinforced an irrational, uncritical discourse.

Exhibit A in the case for the debates' alleged emptiness was the fact of Kennedy's victory. That mythology is so well known that it scarcely bears repeating. With TV sets now in nine of ten American homes, an estimated seventy million people watched Kennedy and Nixon face off on September 26, 1960. Viewers saw a sharp contrast: Kennedy, standing calmly in a dark suit, projected unflappability. Handsome and relaxed, he answered questions crisply, snuffing out any doubts that he might be too callow for the job. Nixon, recovering from a knee infection and a cold, looked terrible. Sweat streaked the pancake makeup applied to his five-o'clock shadow, and his gray suit blended in with the walls. Afterward, the press, is if by unanimous consent, blamed Nixon's appearance for his loss. "Fire the make-up man," Nixon's aide Herb Klein was told. "Everybody in this part of the country thinks Nixon is sick. Three doctors agreed he looked as if he had just suffered a coronary."[7]

There is no doubt that Kennedy looked better. There is also little doubt that debates helped him. Kennedy's pollster Lou Harris, in a memo written after the debate, noted that the senator had opened up a 48 to 43 percent lead in his latest survey, "the first time that either candidate has been able to show the other open water. This is almost wholly the result of the Monday night debate."[8] Other public polls showed a similar trend.

What *is* open to doubt is whether Kennedy's victory owed as much to a purely visual superiority to Nixon as is commonly supposed. No empirical research directly supports the claim. The main piece of evidence buttressing it is the widespread but unsubstantiated notion that radio listeners believed Nixon had won. But the evidence for that assertion is thin. The historian-journalist Theodore White probably deserves the blame for etching it in the accounts of the debates. In his *Making of the President, 1960,* the urtext for chroniclers of the "Great Debates," White wrote, "Those who heard the debates on radio, according to sample surveys"— surveys that White neither specified nor footnoted—"believed that the two candidates came off almost equal" (but not, it should be added, that Nixon won). "Yet every survey of those who watched the debates on television," White added—again, providing no details—suggested that Nixon had done poorly. "It was the picture image that had done it." Even more vaguely, the syndicated columnist Ralph McGill said that a sampling of "a number of people" he spoke to who listened to the debate on radio "unanimously thought Mr. Nixon had the better of it." Earl Mazo of the *New York Herald Tribune* recorded a similar anecdotal impression. But only one formal survey, by a Philadelphia market research firm, supports the claim of Nixon's radio superiority, and its methods have been called into question.[9]

Equally dubious is the idea that the debates gave short shrift to "substance," at least if measured by discussion of the venerated "issues." For all the laments that the candidates postured too much, or that TV focused too much on smiles and stubble, a countervailing line of critique held something like the opposite: not that the debates were utterly vapid but that the rapid-fire, information-rich answers prevented viewers from taking some kind of broader measure of the men. "Not even a trained political observer," noted the journalist Douglass Cater, who moderated one debate, "could keep up with the crossfire of fact and counterfact, of the rapid references to Rockefeller Reports, Lehman amendments, prestige analyses, GNP and a potpourri of other so-called facts. Or was the knack of merely seeming well-informed what counted with the viewer?" Public opinion expert Samuel Lubell agreed, citing voters he interviewed who "tried to make sense of the arguments of the candidates 'but the more we listened, the more confused we got.'"[10]

What matters here isn't whether the debates did or did not exalt mere "image" but the more basic fact that people believed that they did. Perhaps the most lasting articulation of this view came from the historian Daniel Boorstin in his now-classic 1961 work *The Image.* Using the Kennedy-Nixon debates to lament the rise of television and media manipulation in politics, Boorstin argued that "more important than what we think of the presidential candidate is what we think of his 'public image.'" The debates, he said, offered "specious" drama that did nothing to convey "which participant was better qualified for the presidency." They raised the peripheral matters of lighting, make-up, and Nixon's five-o'clock shadow to prominence while "reducing great national issues to trivial dimensions" and squandering "this greatest opportunity in American history to educate the voters." Boorstin elaborated what he saw as the dangers of this new image-conscious culture: nothing less than the demise of representative government. Hearkening back to Lincoln, he said that the maxim "you can't fool all of the people all of the time" was "the foundation-belief of American democracy." It implied, first, that the citizenry can distinguish "between sham and reality," and, second, "that if offered a choice between a simple truth and a contrived image, they will prefer the truth." But in the face artificial pseudo-events like the Great Debates, Boorstin argued, this axiom was void.[11]

2.

It took sixteen years for the stars to align to permit another round of general-election debates. In 1976, Jimmy Carter, as a relatively unknown former governor, needed the debates even more badly than Kennedy had in 1960, to prove that he had presidential stature. And where previous incumbents, Lyndon Johnson and Richard Nixon, had concluded that going head to head could only elevate their rivals, Gerald Ford, having been elected to neither the presidency nor the vice presidency, concluded that he too needed to submit himself to a public vetting.

The 1976 debates are remembered far less well than the 1960 contests. Two episodes above all endure in popular memory. One is the audio failure that occurred near the end of the first match-up, on September 23—resulting in an awkward twenty-seven-minute silence in which the candidates stood still like mannequins. The other is Ford's statement in the second encounter that Eastern Europe was not under Soviet domination. Both moments exposed the problem with thinking about the debates as simply the candidates' unmediated statements and performances during the broadcasts proper. Rather, those performances belonged to a larger context that included how the candidates and the race were portrayed beforehand, how the participating journalists acted during the debate, and the whole post-debate battle for interpretation. "Starting with the Ford-Carter matches," Alan Schroeder, a scholar of presidential debates, has written, "a live debate has come to represent only the centerpiece of the larger media marathon that begins weeks before airtime and ends well after the program fades to black."[12]

In retrospect, the audio failure seems the more remarkable of the two incidents. At 10:51 P.M. eastern time, as Carter was speaking, a technical failure crippled the sound system. In the interim, no one knew what to do. The moderator, Edwin Newman, suggested that the candidates sit down, but they didn't. Nor did they approach each other to chat informally. Both men stood rigidly and silently at their podiums. This spontaneous mutual non-aggression pact became an emperor-has-no-clothes moment. It underscored the fear of spontaneity that had infused the debates. As much as anything, it revived the thread of criticism that had greeted the Kennedy-Nixon contests: that they were not real debates, requiring quick-wittedness and an active intelligence, but joint press conferences, formulaic and rehearsed, short on the substance they were supposed to deliver. The silence, wrote the editors of the *New Republic*, "was *prima facie* evidence, if any were needed, that the debates are not a news event merely available for coverage by the networks; rather they are productions staged for their benefit and even, despite their loud grumbling, to their specifications." As a result, the magazine complained, no real give-and-take occurred; no "inspiring visions" were articulated, only talking points. "From Mr. Ford's first response . . . to Carter's last . . . the candidates delivered what they were programmed to deliver."[13]

Comments like these about the debates were widespread, and they multiplied in the following years. The laments about image superseding substance were fueled, moreover, by a new attention to the debates' backstage maneuverings. Candidates began to hold practice debates, with aides and other supporters playing the roles of the opposing candidates, and the press stared reporting on these preparations with clear delight. Journalists grew excited, too, when in 1983 Laurence Barrett, a *Time* magazine reporter, disclosed in a book that Ronald Reagan's campaign had gotten hold of Jimmy Carter's briefing book before one of their 1980 debates.[14] Though scandalous as a clear-cut violation of the norms of fair play, the subterfuge also caused discomfort for another reason: like the proliferating reports about debate preparation, "Debategate" pointed up the practiced nature of the performances and further dispelled any illusion of spontaneity surrounding them.

As viewers figured out that the debates didn't begin when the program itself came on TV, they also realized that the debates didn't end with the candidates' closing statements either. The fallout from Ford's remarks about Eastern Europe showed the importance of the post-debate instant analysis and spin. As a substantive matter, the president's comments hadn't been terribly confusing or controversial. In context, his intent was clear enough—a desire not to write off Eastern Europeans' aspirations for freedom from Soviet influence. According to polling, most viewers didn't consider the comments to be a gaffe. Some surveys that night showed a plurality of respondents believing that Ford had outperformed Carter. The incident mattered, however, as an illustration of how the debates burst the time limits of the actual broadcast. Despite the public's indifference to Ford's comments, television and newspaper pundits seized on them is if he had made a horrendous blunder. At his press conference the next day, the first eleven questions dealt with the remark. Carter harped on it in his own appearances. Soon polls showed that the public had adopted the journalists' view. "I thought that Ford had won. But the papers say it was Carter. So it must be Carter," one voter was quoted as saying—ironically no doubt, but not without reinforcing the importance of post-debate commentary.[15]

Post-debate spin was largely new in 1976. In 1960, neither party had tried hard to shape verdicts about the debates. Both camps simply said their men had done well, in a restrained tone. "Some Kennedy aides, asking not to be quoted, said they felt their candidate had scored more points and over-all had made the best impression," the *New York Times* noted.[16] Kennedy did use unflattering clips of Nixon sweating and scowling in a television advertisement, but that move was aimed at taking advantage of an already-clear public verdict, not at influencing the verdict.

By 1976, the candidates' handlers had grown cannier. After the first vice-presidential debate that year, between Bob Dole and Walter Mondale, the Republican ticket conscripted three Dole supporters—Texas governor John Connally, Vice President Nelson Rockefeller, and Dole's wife, Elizabeth,—to praise the senator's performance. Each appeared on all three TV networks. The practice grew apace. By 1988, journalists were referring to "Spin Alley," a corridor of the debate site where staffers argued shamelessly why their man had prevailed, whether they believed it or not.[17] The candid acknowledgment of "Spin Alley" dispensed with the pretense that the debate analysts were offering objective or even sincere analysis. Reporters knew they were getting a partisan take. Yet they quoted their sources anyway and happily passed it all on to their audiences with the stark disclaimer that it was all "spin" for the home viewer to sort out. Not only the journalists and the spinners but the audiences too were presumed to agree that what mattered as much as the debate performances was the subsequent effort to shape perceptions of the outcome and of the candidates.

Given this incessant attention to the staging and spinning of the debates, laments about their hyper-scripted character spread. In 1988, *New York Times* columnist A. M. Rosenthal raged about the vapidity of the vice presidential match between Democrat Lloyd Bentsen and Republican Dan Quayle. "It was not a debate," Rosenthal insisted. "It was not even a good news conference. It was a staged, manipulated, choreographed performance, stilted and artificial. At the end the most important question remained unanswered." Like so many others, Rosenthal (who, it should be said, has been described as writing like Peter Finch's anchorman in *Network*, "as if he were shouting from the fire escape") saw the debate as emblematic of media-age politics. The entire campaign, Rosenthal said, took place not "between two sets of candidates but opposing teams of political packagers, script writers, handlers, spinners, and sound-bite artists." Two years later, no less a personage than Walter Cronkite, in delivering (fittingly) the first annual Theodore White Lecture at Harvard's Kennedy School of Government, made a similar pronouncement. "The debates are part of the unconscionable fraud that our political campaigns have become," he said. "Substance is to be avoided if possible . Image is to be maximized."[18]

In September 2008, the same arguments returned once again. It was an unusual environment in which the debates occurred: Lehman Brothers, one of America's leading financial houses, had just failed; other leading banks teetered on the edge of bankruptcy; and Wall Street and Main Street alike feared that the entire economy might be on the brink of collapse. In that environment, John McCain, trailing in the polls, undertook a bizarre gambit to seize control of the race, stating that he was suspending his campaign even as the debates loomed just days off. Eventually he had to resume his campaign, and in the process he forsook his image as strong and level-headed in a crisis—one of few distinct advantages he had held over Obama to that point. Obama then remained cool and collected in the debates, cementing his lead—but it was clearly the crisis, and not the debates, that gave the Democrat his widening lead.

One might have expected the debates to generate more serious discussion of how the candidates would deal with the unfolding financial crisis. But both candidates retreated, for the most part, to sound bites and nostrums. "Both McCain and Barack Obama appeared equally eager to move past the central issue of the day and on to—anything else," wrote columnist Gail Collins of the *New York Times*. "Neither seems capable of saying anything about the credit crisis except that it's important to protect Main Street from Wall Street."[19] Editorialists around the country were similarly cynical, with many drawing invidious contrasts with the Lincoln-Douglas debates in 1858. "How far we have come—fallen— from the quality of debates a century and a half ago between Abraham Lincoln and Stephen A. Douglas, when those Senate candidates faced each other in seven verbal clashes lasting three hours each," a Cox newspaper editorial argued. "The Lincoln-Douglas encounters were transcribed in their entirety by news reporters and printed, often in full, in the major newspapers of the day. . . . The modern debate has become little more than a stage for candidates to recite their campaign's talking points, while trying to avoid directly answering the questions posed by moderators."[20] "I wish there were some way to add some spice to these things. Lincoln/Douglas comes to mind," wrote a contributor to the Macon, Georgia, *Telegram*. "We all want to hear the truth, but perhaps we should make them not prepare. Send 'em out there with nothing but original thoughts."[21]

Such invocations of the legendary Illinois senate debates of 1858 have long been part of the standard criticism of modern presidential face-offs. The *New York Times* editorial cited above, deriding the "show-business nature" of the 1976 debates, also contained one of many such contrasts to 1858, insisting, "The 1976 presidential debates resemble the Lincoln-Douglas debates, to which they are inevitably compared, as much as a town meeting resembles—well, a television spectacular."[22] Journalists, moreover, have had no corner on the glib Lincoln-Douglas comparisons. In *Amusing Ourselves to Death,* the late, unamused media critic Neil Postman railed against the Kennedy-Nixon Great Debates as a pale imitation of Lincoln-Douglas. Their advent, he said, marked a passage from "the Age of Exposition" to "the Age of Show Business." The hours-long, touring contests between Abraham Lincoln and Stephen Douglas in the fall of 1858 exhibited a "a kind of oratory that may be described as literary," with "a semantic, paraphrasable, propositional content," Postman continued, while the four Nixon-Kennedy clashes were empty charades made for television, which "speaks in only one persistent voice—the voice of entertainment."[23]

Please, Mr. Postman. Scholars should know better than to traffic in such nostalgia. The Lincoln-Douglas contests provided plenty of entertainment, too, along with double-talk, cheap shots, pandering, and no small concern with appearances. As the media scholar Michael Schudson has written, "There is much to learn from the Lincoln-Douglas debates about the politics of the 1850s, but there are no lessons to 'apply' to our own time, certainly not in the form of a rebuke to a purportedly diminished political culture."[24] Although differences between the two sets of debates are undeniable, to judge the change from 1858 to the present as simply a decline is to make a moral judgment, not a historical one.

3.

Even as it became a cliché to lament the debates' failure to carry out their appointed democratic function, however, there remained a concurrent strain of commentary that regarded the debates as a useful exercise in public education. Though not dominant, this strain of commentary wasn't hard to find, either.

In *The Making of the President, 1960,* Theodore White had spoken of television as having the properties of an X-ray, magically revealing a politician's inner self.[25] Though ridiculous as a scientific proposition, this was a felicitous metaphor, and one convenient for those who wished not to take too dim a view of the modern political TV dramas like the debates. The X-ray view of TV was a sort of update of nineteenth-century ideas of the daguerreotype, which was believed to disclose its subject's soul— and, indeed, the continuing myth that photographs capture "reality" as words cannot. These notions imagine the camera, whether photographic or television, as a transparent medium—a medium that doesn't mediate. Implicit, too, was a trust in the judgment of ordinary citizens, a reluctance to part with the Enlightenment faith in human reason. At the end of the day, went this argument, people could put aside the spin and stagecraft and arrive at sound conclusions.

Remarkably, this determination to vindicate the TV debates often coexisted snugly alongside the sharp criticisms. In the same 1976 editorial in which it spent six paragraphs excoriating the Ford-Carter debates, the *New York Times* concluded, without a shred of evidence, "Character, integrity, compassion, intelligence—or lack of them—do have a way of showing through." In the same vein, Joe Duffey, an adviser that year to Jimmy Carter, told the *Times* in a separate news article: "Character is what I think is finally displayed. It's either there or it isn't, and television is a great revealer."[26] This idea would persist.

In 1980, Daniel Henninger, writing in the *Wall Street Journal,* deepened the argument on behalf of the debates' intrinsic value. He praised the opportunity to see Carter and Ronald Reagan relatively unfiltered, speaking live and without a script (or at least not a literal script). "Television, in formats like Tuesday's debate, is nicely suited to passing democratic judgment in this country," Henninger noted. "It provides unimpeded and thorough access to the ideas and opinions of men and women in public life." Compared to the evening news, in which "images rush by [and] the on-camera reporter intrudes, pressing his opinion, flattening mine," the debates did indeed provide a rare opportunity to take the measure of two men; you could ignore the pre- and post-debate hullaballoo and fall back on your own impressions of the candidates going head to head.

From a slightly different angle, the political analyst Jeff Greenfield also sang the praises of debates when he wrote of the 1988 match-ups between George Bush Sr. and Michael Dukakis. Greenfield also praised the contests as revealing, though he departed from Henninger in that he saluted the role of the questioning journalists as a beneficial ingredient in the mix. "The much-maligned format produced the most significant glimpses we have had into the thinking and character of the candidates since the general-election campaign began on Labor Day," he wrote. Suggesting that the journalist-interrogators made the format more illuminating than a true Lincoln-Douglas encounter would have been, Greenfield said that the candidates' responses to questions about criminal penalties for abortionists and Dukakis's bloodless demeanor gave viewers useful data for forming judgments. In contrast, letting the candidates say whatever they pleased would have given us "programmatic formulations of speechwriters such as Peggy Noonan and Robert Shrum."[27]

As noted, the pro-debate argument—that the contests elicit some important qualities in the candidates—is not wholly wishful. Sustained, relatively unimpeded viewing of the candidates certainly can help viewers form impressions different from what they get from other forms of political communication. Some viewers certainly glean from them some information that they find useful. On the other hand, many viewers do so because they don't follow political affairs as intensively as journalists or news buffs, and as a result the debates reveal to them some elementary information about a candidate—that he supports universal health care or a balanced budget—for the first time. These viewers don't mind that the candidates are spouting phrases they've used umpteen times before; the phrases are new to them. It shouldn't be surprising that voters claim to find the debates helpful in deciding how to vote.

But that doesn't, of itself, mean the debates are fulfilling Frank Stanton's professed vision. First, while the debates may serve as a convenient source of easily discoverable news, this hardly justifies their existence. Newspaper and magazine articles, TV news segments, and countless other journalistic forms provide the same information, and much more; it's just that many debate viewers don't pay attention to those sources. In 2008, after the second encounter between Obama and McCain, reporters for National Public Radio's *Morning Edition* interviewed undecided voters. "After watching these debates, I've become more undecided," said a woman named Martinique Chavez. "I think that I need to wait till another debate and see and learn more of the facts." But Chavez did not have to "wait" for anything to learn more facts. She could have easily turned to a huge trove of newspaper and magazine articles, or the candidates' comprehensive websites, for far more detail than she could ever get in ninety minutes of TV.[28]

Nor does the fact that the debates sometimes sway dithering voters justify the conclusion that these voters are acting as democratic theory prescribes. On the contrary, if they're ignorant about the candidates going in, they're more likely to be seduced by clever or disingenuous statements in the debates—or by a winning smile, poised delivery, or snappy one-liner hatched weeks earlier. Anyone who watched the focus groups convened by the networks to watch the 2000 debates between George Bush and Al Gore had to come away at least a bit dismayed about the public's capacity for critical thinking. On CBS, a viewer named Sandra Harsh said she was influenced by what she saw. "I was very impressed with Bush's specifics, his points of—of his program, what he planned to do," she said. "I like—I liked the line about trusting people, not the federal government. I liked his format for national health care. I—I think he showed himself as the superior candidate."[29] Not to harsh on Sandra, but if viewers who turned on the debate that night had never before heard Bush recite his mantra about trusting the people, not the government, or came away thinking that he would implement a national health-care plan, it should give us pause about the debates' value in helping undecideds decide.

It's comforting to think that the debates disclose telling qualities about a candidate, whether it be Dukakis's sangfroid in 1988, Bush's indifference to people's struggles when the camera caught him looking at his watch in 1992, or Al Gore's superciliousness when he was roasted for high-decibel sighing in 2000. And surely it's proper for voters to consider personal qualities, even superficial ones, of the candidates alongside their records and their stands. All viewers have subjective criteria of what kind of politicians they like and dislike, and watching the candidates in a debate can help us gauge our own comfort level with them as television presences. Much of the commentary in 2008 held that Obama "won" because in holding his own, he conveyed to undecided voters that despite his lack of past achievement, he could lead the country in a crisis.

All that said, whether the *specific personal traits on view in the debates* should matter *to the same degree that they're exhibited* in a single performance or commented upon by the talking heads is totally speculative and highly dubious. Ultimately, the idea that debates give people the information they need to make a sound choice—whether about issues or about personal qualities—has to be seen as the expression of a wish. It may be true sometimes, but we don't have positive grounds for believing it to be true, and we have reason to doubt it as well.

4.

If debates aren't a great democratic service to the autonomous modern citizen, coolly assessing the candidates on the issues, and they aren't just the poor progeny of Lincoln-Douglas—empty spectacles that have no public value—then how are we to view them?

One possibility is to modify the assumptions we take to them—specifically the idea that their value resides in the information they supply.

The communications scholar James Carey once proposed a distinction between what he called a "transmission view" of communication and a "ritual view." The transmission view is the one with which most of us usually operate. It holds that the purpose of communication—of which presidential debates are of course one form—is to impart information. The ritual view, in contrast, is, according to Carey, "a minor thread in our national thought." On this view, he says, communication is "directed not toward the extension of messages in space but toward the maintenance of society in time; not the act of imparting information but the representation of shared beliefs."[30]

It may make sense to conceive of the debates as rituals rather than as transmitters of information. They are, after all, rites like holidays or parades, which gain meaning from the way they figure in our daily experiences. They may not educate, but they evoke feelings, bolster sentiments, and provoke action. Debates bring pleasure to following campaigns. They bind us together socially with our compatriots. They can even trigger political involvement. On this view, Frank Stanton—and all of us—have had it backwards. The debates matter not because they differ from the rallies and torchlight parades of bygone times but because they *resemble* them.

Thinking of debates as a ritual more than as a source of information helps explain certain riddles. Why, for example, have presidential candidates since 1976 never declined to participate? One possibility is the fear that the naysayer would be called a coward, and it is true that in the fall of 1992 George Bush Sr. was drawn into televised arguments on the campaign trail with a man dressed as a large fowl who taunted "Chicken George" for shrinking from debates with Bill Clinton. But a candidate ahead in the polls could easily choose to weather such taunts if the advantages seemed great enough, or to demonstrate courage in another way. The harder obstacle to overcome is that declining to spar would now be seen as neglecting a civic duty—like failing to put your hand on your heart at the playing of the national anthem or not showing up for the president's State of the Union address. Debates draw strength from their status as important rituals.

Or consider another riddle: If the debates exist to inform the undecided, why do so many viewers tune in who already have their minds made up? The transmission model makes these viewers superfluous. Yet for many such people, watching the debates is a beloved pastime. Admittedly, I'm something of a political junkie, but I often find myself over at a friend's apartment watching the encounters with a small group, all of us cheering on our candidate (usually the same for all of us). The act of participating in such a shared experience renews our political commitment and excitement. And this is an old tradition. There were debate-watching parties in Democratic and Republican clubs back in September of 1960; Jackie Kennedy hosted one in Hyannisport, where Archibald Cox, Arthur Schlesinger, and assorted politicians, family members and journalists gathered over coffee and pastries to watch the tanned and polished JFK on a rented sixteen-inch portable TV set.

Even for those who are genuinely undecided, the debates may perform this kind of a ritual function too. Starting in 1992, the National Communication Association and the Commission on Presidential Debates set up a project called Debate Watch to bring together citizens in local communities to watch and discuss the contests. Although the results are too inconclusive to allow for confident generalizations, they seem to suggest that joining in these colloquies spurred people to vote on Election Day. At the least, they appeared, as one scholar of the project noted, to "engage voters in the ideas, perspectives, and concerns of others in their communities." According to the *New York Times*, "participants lauded the sheer experience of post-debate discussion as much as the debates, bonding like jurists with other panel members and compounding their appetite for politics." Diana Carlin, a scholar involved with the effort, declared, "This is creating a sort of civic discourse that I don't think takes place in this country"—a claim that might be hyperbolic but nonetheless hints at some ground-level value derived from the contests.[31]

Evidence that the debates achieved this less lofty but more realistic goal dates back to 1960. "The TV medium in the past has been legitimately criticized for injecting too much show business into areas where it is not appropriate," wrote the *New York Times* television critic Jack Gould after the first Kennedy-Nixon debate. "But last night the networks demonstrated the civic usefulness of the broadcasting media." A few days later he built on his observation. "Overnight, as it were," he wrote, "there was born a new interest in the campaign that earlier had been productive only of coast-to-coast somnolence." Even Teddy White agreed that the debate managed to "generalize this tribal sense of participation . . . for the salient fact of the great TV debates is not what the two candidates said, nor how they behaved, but how many of the candidates' fellow Americans gave up their evening hours to ponder the choice between the two."[32]

The choreography and sound bites that constitute the presidential debates should be recognized as an unreliable and inadequate method for casual voters to get the facts about the nominees. But the experience of watching debates, perhaps in groups, or in discussing them "the next morning," as Gould wrote, "in kitchen, office, supermarket and commuter train" has value.[33] In an age of desiccated politics, when too many citizens feel adrift and overburdened in trying to judge complex policy issues for themselves, this experience serves, in some quiet way, to thicken our commitments to political life.

Notes

1. "Transcript of Palin, Biden debate," CNN, October 3, 2008, http://www.cnn.com/2008/Politics/10/02/Debate.transcript (accessed December 1, 2008).

2. Michael Kinsley, "A Gaffe Is When a Politician Tells the Truth," *New Republic*, June 18, 1984, reprinted in Michael Kinsley, *The Curse of the Giant Muffins: And Other Washington Maladies* (New York: Summit Books, 1987), 272–75.

3. "Lights—Camera—Candidates!" *New York Times*, September 24, 1976.

4. Mike Christopherson, "No Matter the Format or Location, Debates Are Predictable," *Crookston (Minn.) Daily Times*, October 19, 2008.

5. Jürgen Habermas, *The Structural Transformation of the Public Sphere* (Cambridge MIT Press, 1981), 211.

6. Frank Stanton, "A CBS View," in Sidney Kraus, ed., *The Great Debates: Kennedy vs. Nixon, 1960* (Bloomington: Indiana University Press, 1977 [1962]), 65–72.

7. Fawn M. Brodie, *Richard M. Nixon: The Shaping of His Character* (New York: W. W. Norton, 1981), 427.

8. Louis Harris, Memorandum. Robert F. Kennedy Papers, Political Files, Box 45. John F. Kennedy Library, Boston.

9. Theodore H. White, *The Making of the President, 1960*, 348; Ralph McGill, "TV vs. Radio in the Great Debate," *Washington Evening Star*, October 1, 1960, quoted in Alan Schroeder, *Presidential Debates* (New York: Columbia University Press, 2000), 176; Michael Schudson, "Trout or Hamburger: The Politics of Telemythology," in *The Power of News* (Cambridge, Mass.: Harvard University Press, 1995); David L. Vancil and Sue D. Pendell, "The Myth of Viewer-Listener Disagreement in the First Kennedy-Nixon Debate," *Central States Speech Journal* 38 (1987), 16–27; *Broadcasting* 59 (November 7, 1960), 27–29.

10. Douglass Cater, "Notes from Backstage," in Kraus, p. 130; Samuel Lubell, "Personalities vs. Issues," in Kraus, ed., *The Great Debates,* 152.

11. Daniel Boorstin, *The Image* (New York: Atheneum, 1961), 36, 41–43, 204.

12. Schroeder, *Presidential Debates,* 173–74.

13. "Packaged Politics," *New Republic,* October 9, 1976, 7–8.

14. Laurence I. Barrett, *Gambling with History: Ronald Reagan in the White House* (New York: Doubleday, 1983); Phil Gailey, "Baker and Stockman Report Receiving '80 Carter Material," *New York Times,* June 24, 1983.

15. Larry J. Sabato, *Feeding Frenzy* (New York: Free Press, 1991), 127–29; quoted in Doris Graber, *Processing the News* (New York: Longman, 1984), 264, and in Thomas E. Patterson, *Out of Order* (New York: Knopf, 1993), 57.

16. Schroeder, *Presidential Debates,* 181.

17. The first printed references I've found to this term were in Steven Komarow, "Protocol Takes a Powder as Senators Beat Up on Colleagues," Associated Press, October 6, 1988; and Christine Chinlund, "Spin Doctors Swing into Operation," *Boston Globe,* October 14, 1988.

18. A. M. Rosenthal, "The Bentsen-Quayle Whatever," *New York Times,* October 7, 1988; James Wolcott, "Hear Me Purr," *New Yorker,* May 20, 1996, 57; Cronkite quoted in Tom Wicker, "Improving the Debates," *New York Times,* June 22, 1991.

19. Gail Collins, "McCain: Bearish on Debates," *New York Times,* September 27, 2008.

20. "Should We Keep Having Debates?" *Fairfield (Ohio) Echo,* October 21, 2008.

21. Sonny Harmon, "Modern Debates Don't Match Up to Lincoln-Douglas," *Macon (Ga.) Telegraph,* October 15, 2008.

22. "Lights—Camera—Candidates!" *New York Times,* September 24, 1976, 24.

23. Neil Postman, *Amusing Ourselves to Death* (New York: Viking, 1985), 44–49, 79.

24. Michael Schudson, *The Good Citizen: A History of American Civic Life* (New York: Free Press, 1998), 143.

25. White, *The Making of the President, 1960,* 347.

26. "Lights—Camera—Candidates!" *New York Times,* September 24, 1976; James M. Naughton, "The Debates: A Marketplace in the Global Village," *New York Times,* September 26, 1976.

27. Daniel Henninger, "The Great Debate and Electronic Democracy," *Wall Street Journal,* October 30, 1980; Jeff Greenfield, "There's No Debate: The Format Works," *New York Times,* October 13, 1988.

28. "Undecided Voters Watch Debate in Albuquerque," *Morning Edition* (National Public Radio), October 8, 2008. Accessed via Lexis/Nexis database, October 14, 2008.

29. Phil Jones, transcript, "Focus Group Gives Their [*sic*] Views of the Presidential Debate," CBS News Transcripts, October 17, 2000, accessed via Lexis/Nexis database, February 29, 2008.

30. James W. Carey, *Communication as Culture: Essays on Media and Society* (Boston: Unwin Hyman), 4–15, 18.

31. Francis X. Clines, "'Ask Not . . . ' ' . . . Military-Industrial Complex . . . ' ' . . . but Fear Itself . . . ,'" *New York Times,* September 23, 1996; Barbara A. Pickering, "The American Democracy Project at Work: Engaging Citizens in Argumentation," *Argumentation and Advocacy* 42 (Spring 2006), 220, 222; Christina Nifong, "Efforts to Engage Voters via Political 'Tupperware Parties,'" *Christian Science Monitor,* October 16, 1996.

32. Jack Gould, "TV: The Great Debate," *New York Times,* September 27, 1960; Jack Gould, "The 'Debate' in Retrospect," *New York Times,* October 2, 1960; White, *The Making of the President, 1960,* 352.

33. Gould, "The 'Debate' in Retrospect."

Swing States and Electoral College Strategy

JOHN C. FORTIER AND TIMOTHY J. RYAN

For all the strategic speculation about targeting "independent" voters or some other supposedly crucial demographic group, the core of a presidential campaign strategy is simple: secure the 270 electoral votes that constitute a majority in the electoral college. Every other strategic component is important only insofar as it contributes to this sole determining factor. The practice exercised by virtually every state of allocating all its electoral votes to the popular-vote winner, no matter how small the margin of victory, leads candidates to tailor their strategies narrowly. They focus on winning a subset of competitive "swing states" where the outcome is substantially in doubt.

We develop an objective system with which to scrutinize trends in the identities of these so-called swing states. We measure the speed with which states shift in their partisan leanings, and thus their susceptibility to be courted by one campaign or another, a measure that should be of interest both to political strategists and those interested in institutional reform. Along the way we take into account factors that tend to obscure underlying trends, such as the comparative strengths of various campaigns and an ever-fluctuating political climate.

Contrary to some scholarly work,[1] we find that states follow relatively predictable partisan patterns from one presidential election to the next. Once one takes into account a small number of confounding factors, such as chaotic voting patterns in the South before 1984 and the boost that candidates receive within home states, a relatively predictable pattern of partisan voting emerges. This does not mean that individual states have not evolved over time, but the changes have been generally gradual, and consistent trends can be identified. Very rare is the dramatic shift in one direction or another that is not explained by a "favorite son" candidate or some similarly apparent exogenous factor.

We apply a method of filtering out some of the factors that typically obscure the consistency of election results to recent election outcomes. We are able to use this information to make some educated guesses about which states will become more and less competitive in coming years. We find reason to caution political strategists against efforts to dramatically swing states away from their historic leanings.

We begin with a discussion of the importance of the Electoral College and presidential campaign strategies for citizen engagement and political inclusiveness. We also consider some of the factors that make the development of predictive models of presidential elections difficult. In the next section, we lay out a method for calculating states' partisan leanings relative to the national presidential election results, an approach that we believe lends to a meaningful interpretation of historical trends. From this, we examine which states might have been more competitive but for the existence of unpredictable exogenous factors, and which are likely to be competitive in the future. We then consider individual states, explaining the implications that past trends might have for future elections. We close with recommendations for how Electoral College strategists might approach coming elections.

Swing States: Effects and Determinants

A proper examination of the Electoral College must begin with a consideration of the "swing" states that, to a large extent, define the conduct of campaigns. What factors contribute to a state's level of competitiveness? How stable are state voting patterns? What secondary effects does the narrow focus of presidential campaigns have on other important variables, such as citizen engagement and habitual voting? Some factors, such as a candidate receiving a "boost" in his home state, are repeated so often that they have become part of seldom-questioned conventional wisdom; to what extent do these ring true?

Perhaps no American political institution has received and endured more ire than the Electoral College. Controversial from the very start, when an ill-conceived election process necessitated the ratification of the Twelfth Amendment in 1804, the College has demonstrated resiliency and resistance to change, time and time again. Of particular concern to skeptics are the possibility of the College electing a "minority president" who received less than half of the popular votes cast, as occurred in 1824, 1876, 1888, and 2000; the advantage that the College gives to small states, which are represented by more electors per person than larger states; and the practice whereby nearly every state awards all its electoral votes to the candidate with a plurality of the popular vote, no matter how small the margin of victory. It is the last of these characteristics that provides one of the impetuses for our current effort, as it leads candidates to tailor their campaigns for a small number of states where the popular vote winner appears to be in serious question. Our goal is not to weigh in on the normative desirability of this arrangement, but rather to comment dispassionately on its effects.

A review of previous research demonstrates that swing states are very much different from non-swing states in the way they are treated by campaigns. Thomas E. Patterson characterizes the situation succinctly: "The Electoral College works to the advantage of a mere handful of competitive states, which change from one election to the next. These states drive the candidates' strategies in the final phase of a closely contested campaign ... The only states that truly count in a close election are those that either candidate could win. In 1960, 1968, 1976, 1980, and 2000, the candidates poured nearly every available resource into the toss-up states."[2] This description is borne out in statistics. Swing states are recipients, for instance, of far more personal attention from candidates. The median "battleground" state, as classified by David Hill and Seth C. McKee, received more than fifteen times as much media attention and approximately ten times as many candidate visits as the median non-battleground state in 2000.[3] George Edwards also notes that although the vast majority of candidate speeches did not address the unique interests of an individual state, the few that did tended to be directed toward large swing states rather than small states. In 2000, George W. Bush did not give a single speech that highlighted the interests of a small state.[4]

The large discrepancy was similarly apparent in 2004, when, during the peak campaign season of late September to early November, the three competitive states of Florida, Ohio, and Pennsylvania received fully 62 percent of campaign spending on television advertisements, compared to less than 10 percent for thirty-nine other states combined. These same three crucial states also received 45 percent of candidate visits during the peak season.[5] Florida, for one, was visited twenty-two times by President Bush and twenty-one times by Democratic presidential nominee John Kerry during the 2004 campaign. By contrast, twelve states received no visit from a presidential candidate.[6] The same attention difference was evident in the pattern of television advertising from state to state. Battleground states received far more attention than their less competitive counterparts. In 2004, Florida media markets showed nearly 25,000 advertisements on behalf of the major-party candidates. However, not a single political ad aired in any California media market, even though California has the largest state population.[7] The implications of this imbalance for policy decisions are not apparent, but it is very clear that the importance of swing states is not lost on campaigns.

There is much reason to believe that the extra attention that swing states receive from campaigns bears on the engagement and political behavior of the electorate. Political scientists have long speculated that campaigns are one of the chief mechanisms through which citizens initially become involved in politics and civic affairs.[8] Indeed, the ability of campaigns to contribute to political learning has been observed in a modern context.[9] As such, it is natural to expect the citizens of swing states, the focus of the most salient and energetic campaigns in American politics, to become more politically engaged.

In fact this seems to be the case. Data from the National Election Study indicate that low-income voters, the income group least likely to be engaged in political affairs, become more engaged when they live in a swing state and are contacted by a political campaign.[10] As such, one could expect campaigns to increase the diversity of the electorate in swing states. Such changes have the potential to endure, as some evidence suggests that political behavior like voting is, to a degree, habit forming.[11] Further research is necessary to parse out exactly how pronounced these possible effects are; an examination of whether swing states enjoy a financial windfall from the in-office presidential administration seeking to gain favor would be especially interesting.

A related question is to what degree the identities of swing states change. The concerns of those who fear that the winner-take-all arrangement will unfairly make a small number of states recipient of all the agreeable benefits enumerated above should be ameliorated to a large extent if the swing states are relatively unstable, making the benefits scattered wide and with particular long-term advantage to no one. Is the identity of swing states relatively constant? Or does is it characterized by surprising, unpredictable variation? Or does some sort of middle ground, a slow, relatively steady evolution, provide the best description? Indeed we find this to be the case.

Surprisingly, little scholarly work seeks to answer this question. We are aware of only one recent study that directly measures the predictability and rate of change of swing states.[12] Bonnie J. Johnson finds some evidence that, when examining a long time frame, the identities of swing states have become less predictable in recent years.[13] This analysis is based on an aggregate examination of the frequency, over the course of the past 184 years, with which a given state has been competitive. Johnson does not examine how much states change from one election to the next. How predictive are one cycle's election returns of the next cycles? We approach the question from a very different perspective, examining only the past sixty-eight years and focusing on individual states and the degree to which their partisan leanings change in the short term.

The approach we outline may be welcomed by academics concerned with using broad indicators, such as economic growth, incumbent fatigue, and any number of other national factors, to predict election results. These efforts typically attempt to predict the national vote shares for each party,[14] a measure which, of course, has only incidental bearing on which candidate will be elected, given the absolute precedence of the Electoral College.

Needless to say, swing state volatility should also be of immense importance to candidates and strategists seeking to win an election. Should they allocate their limited resources more or less in keeping with the previous cycle's allotment, or are drastic alterations necessary to respond to a changing landscape and different competition? How much credence should be given to election prognostication based on the motivation or lack of interest of demographic groups, the issues supposedly of interest to "independent" voters, or any number of other supposedly crucial factors, compared to the shortcut of simply extrapolating from past election results and historical trends? The flexibility or inflexibility of states' partisan leanings bears heavily on this calculus. It is practical questions like these for which we hope to provide at least partial answers.

One element that may have confounded other attempts to distill useful information from past election results is the existence of a few factors that seemingly cause wild deviations from states' past results. Chief among these is simply the relative strengths of the two major-party candidates. It seems clear that an unbalanced match-up can lead to obvious sway in election returns. We would be surprised to hear an account of Ronald Reagan's overwhelming victories in 1980 and 1984 that did not, in some way, point to his personal charm and likeability as well as the comparative weaknesses and liabilities of his two opponents.

Another factor affecting election returns is the advantage that candidates enjoy in their home states and regions. Although one can point to examples of candidates failing to win their home states—Al Gore's shortfall in Tennessee is the most recent example—a number of scholarly studies find a home-state or regional advantage when one examines more nuanced data describing margins of victory, rather than the binary win-loss outcome.[15] This advantage appears to exist, albeit to a lesser extent, for vice presidential candidates, as well.[16] It is not surprising, therefore, that candidates tend to choose running mates so as to maximize this advantage.[17]

Finally, it seems that substantial third-party candidates can palpably sway election returns. Regional candidates, such as the segregationist candidates that experienced success in southern states in the middle part of the twentieth century, wreak havoc on predictive models of elections, as do more recent national third-party candidates such as John Anderson and Ross Perot. Such candidacies can "steal" votes from the major parties, and also turn out new voters.[18]

Fortunately, it is easy to account for the effects of these generally agreed upon variables. Once one begins to scrutinize election results independently of these confounding factors, a picture begins to emerge that characterizes the evolution of swing states as much more incremental than is generally described. It is this effort that we take up in the next section.

Putting State Results in Context

At the heart of this essay is an analysis of state-level presidential election returns relative to the national returns. National-level results provide a "catch-all" measure of the various macro-level factors that favor one party or another. In a single measure, they paint a picture of how the candidates' strengths, unpredictable current events, and any number of additional factors have affected overall election results. Identifying all the myriad factors that allowed, for instance, Ronald Reagan to win approximately 60 percent of the popular vote in 1984 is impossible, but it is not important to do so. We can see that some confluence of events occurred to give the Republican candidate an advantage of 10 percent over perfect fifty-fifty parity.

This approach provides a useful tool with which to examine state-level results because, all things being equal, we would expect individual states to track the national results. Much as a rising tide raises ships moored to a dock, we would expect, all things being equal, that if the Republican candidate won the national popular vote by ten percentage points, his margin of victory in each state would be approximately ten points greater than in a typical election. If a state were to deviate from this trend, we would take such deviation as evidence of a change in the state's partisan leanings.

A hypothetical example is illustrative. If Massachusetts, which has given the Democratic candidate an average of 62 percent of the popular vote in the past five elections, were to *still* give the Democratic candidate 62 percent in a year where the Republican won 55 percent of the popular vote, we would take this as evidence that Massachusetts had trended five percentage points in the Democratic direction, as it resisted the sway of a five-percentage-point Republican victory.

Thus, we take a state's deviation from a sort of normalcy to be

$$D = (S_v - S_{avg}) - (N_v - 50\%)$$

where S_v is a party's percentage of the popular vote within the given state, S_{avg} is the party's *average* percentage of the popular vote in the state's previous five elections, N_v is the party's national percentage of the popular vote, and D is the state's deviation. In order to keep the model simple and avoid the complication of third parties, we focus solely on the *two-party* vote. For the sake of uniformity, we focus on Democratic percentages. Because third parties are not included in our analysis, the Republican figures are simply a mirror image, for instance, a deviation of -5 instead of 5 percentage points.

A similar, but not identical, approach has been employed in past attempts to analyze candidates' home-state advantages.[19] The most significant difference in the current approach is that, where past efforts have used a five-cycle rolling average to place a single election's national popular vote in context, we simply use the number 50 percent, thereby comparing election results to long-term parity.

The method described above also permits us to derive some other fruitful measures. First, we derive a state's average partisan lean. We calculate the average degree to which each state differs from national results for the previous five cycles. For instance, for the five elections between 1988 and 2004, Democratic candidates fared an average of 11.8 percentage points better in Massachusetts than they did in the national popular vote. Therefore, for 2004, we conceptualize the "base" vote share for a Democratic candidate as 61.8 percent.

Second, we calculate each state's trend toward the Democratic Party compared to the previous election. For instance, Massachusetts trended *away* from the Democratic party by .5 percentage points in 2004 because Al Gore's Massachusetts returns exceeded his national returns by 14.5 percentage points, while John Kerry's Massachusetts returns exceeded his national returns by only 14.0 percentage points.

Finally, we calculate the average trend toward the Democratic Party based on the previous five cycles. For instance, in 2004, Massachusetts exhibited an average trend toward the Democratic Party of 1.2 percentage points because the Democratic candidate increased his Massachusetts margin of victory—vis-à-vis the national returns—by an average of 1.2 points per cycle for every cycle since 1988. It is this average trend that we eventually use as one tool with which to speculate as to which states will be competitive in future elections.

We admit this model to be crude in some regards. It assumes, first, that the two parties are in long-term national parity, or else the effort to place national results in context will be skewed. Second, it assumes that success in the national popular vote is attributable to local advantages that are evenly spread, such that a national advantage of, for instance, five percentage points is roughly indicative of a five-point advantage within each of the states. Our effort to place election results in a meaningful context will be skewed to the extent that vote advantages are concentrated in specific states or regions. Finally, our prognostication of future trends assumes that the trends we identify are more or less constant. If, instead, state leanings follow more of a "random walk," where past trends have little bearing on future results, our predictions will have little advantage over blind guessing.

To test the predictive usefulness of our measure, we gauge how well it applies to known election results. We use our determination of each state's "base" partisan leaning—as stated above, for each state, this is the average degree to which Democrats exceeded their national results in that state over the past five election cycles—as well as the apparent "trend" effect, the average movement toward one party or the other, relative to the national results.

For example, we determine Mississippi's "base" partisan leaning after the 2000 election to be -6.9 percent Democratic because, for the five elections between 1984 and 2000, Democrats fared an average of 6.9 percentage points worse in Mississippi than they did in their national returns. Moreover, we find Mississippi's average trend toward the Democratic Party after the 2000 election to be -2.7 percentage points per cycle (in other words, 2.7 percentage points toward the Republican Party) because the vote share for Democratic candidates in Mississippi *relative to their national vote share* has been decreasing by an average of 2.7 percentage points per cycle. To predict Mississippi's results for the 2000 election, we assume that this trend will continue and therefore add -2.7 percent to the "base" leaning of -6.9 percent and predict that the Democratic candidate's vote share will be 9.6 percent below his share of the national vote. In fact, John Kerry's share of the vote in Mississippi was only 8.7 percentage points below his national share, and so our prediction missed by 0.9 points.

We apply this algorithm to the state-level results of every presidential election since 1960 (a model that incorporates results going back to 1940, in order to compile state partisan leanings derived from five previous election results). With no adjustments made, this method shows an average error of 4.55 percentage points.

However, even a cursory look at the election results finds two factors that confound the predictive model. First and most prominent, the South has had very volatile presidential election results. Second, as noted above, presidential candidates—and, to a lesser degree, perhaps vice presidential candidates—tend to sway election results substantially in their home states and regions.

The South

Throughout much of the period we examine, the South's political leanings were in flux. This once solidly Democratic region sat uncomfortably within the Democratic Party, with its members often in fierce disagreement with more progressive Democrats in the Northeast and Midwest. In Congress, the Democratic caucus was often split.[20] Over time southern states began to migrate to the Republican Party, first at the presidential level, and then at the state and local levels as well. A slow evolution of partisan leanings would have been consistent with the thesis of this paper, namely that sudden interruptions of partisan leanings are rare. But the story of the South in presidential elections is much more complicated than a simple evolution.

The case of Alabama is telling. Alabama was one of the most politically volatile states from 1944 to 1980. Sometimes this volatility was evident in Alabama's voting for Republican nominees like Barry Goldwater. Other times, Alabama cast its votes for segregation-focused Dixiecrats. It supported Strom Thurmond in 1948 and, to add further complication, in 1968 it supported its favorite son, American Independence Party candidate George Wallace. Alabama also sometimes voted for the Democratic nominee, FDR in 1944 and Adlai Stevenson in 1952 and 1956. In 1964, Alabama voted for Barry Goldwater, but recorded no votes for incumbent President Lyndon Johnson. The votes that did not go for Goldwater were cast for an unpledged Democratic slate of electors. Four years after Nixon's big victory in Alabama in 1972, the state swung dramatically in the Democratic direction to vote for a Democratic nominee from the South, Jimmy Carter. And while Alabama went for Reagan in 1980, the close result still showed some of this "Carter effect," as, within Alabama, Carter significantly exceeded his national vote share. Since 1980, Alabama has been reliably Republican.

Alabama palpably exhibits many confounding factors typical in the region. It is perhaps one of the more extreme cases, but each of the southern states experienced not only a migration toward the Republican Party, but also violent hiccups along the way associated with third-party candidates, a strong pull for Carter, and in some states even a pull for fellow southerner Bill Clinton.

Because the South contributes analytical difficulties not typical of other regions, we measure the predictive usefulness of our context-focused model excluding the South. The error in predicting the differential between state and national election results drops to 3.5 percentage points—far from perfect, but a relatively accurate predictor given the statistical simplicity of the approach.

We note above that some anomalies in the prediction of future election results stem from a candidate's effect on his or her home state. In developing a state model to determine swing states, Carl Klarner found that presidential candidates between 1948 and 2006 received about 4 percent more of the vote in their home states, a statistically significant figure.[21] There is also an unevenness to this effect that makes it more difficult to exclude from analysis than the southern region effect. For instance, it is unclear to what extent candidates are advantaged in their home *states* versus their home *regions*. Likely, the advantage will depend on the individual characteristics of the candidate and the localities in question. Also, in some cases it is unclear which state a candidate is from. Dwight Eisenhower was originally from Kansas, but had ties to New York, where he was president of Columbia University, and Pennsylvania while conducting his presidential campaign. Richard Nixon served as a senator from California, but lived in New York after his tenure as vice president. We do not systematically remove candidates' home states from the analysis, but are careful to account for these possible factors in discussion.

In spite of all these drawbacks, the picture painted by our analysis comports very well with much of the prevailing wisdom about the evolution of states over time. We now move on to our findings.

Swing States Old and New

It is our intention to look at swing states from a different perspective. We do not define swing states simply as those states that had close elections. Rather, we aim to identify states that could have been or could plausibly become competitive in an election with the two parties roughly at national parity. Specifically, we define swing states as states where the partisan lean—again, the average degree to which Democrats exceeded their national results over the previous five election cycles—is within 2.5 percentage points of parity. If the national results are close and if states roughly track national results, these states could potentially be within reach of either party.

The 2004 election provides an illustrative example. Democrats won 48.8 percent of the national two-party popular vote. We therefore consider states where the Democratic vote share was between 46.3 percent and 51.3 percent—a 2.5-percentage-point margin around the national share—to be swing states, as we would expect them to be competitive in an election of parity. In 2004, these were Colorado, Florida, Iowa, Missouri, Nevada, New Hampshire, New Mexico, Ohio, Pennsylvania, and Wisconsin.

Of course, the results of the 2004 election allow us to update the figures used to represent each state's average partisan lean. Not yet accounting for the trend that states exhibit toward one party or the other, we are able to identify thirteen states as potentially competitive in 2008.

Of these thirteen, there are three that arguably might not belong in the category. Arkansas is, by this simple measure, one of the most competitive states on the electoral map. However, it seems clear that Arkansas was affected significantly by Bill Clinton's two campaigns in 1992 and 1996. Looking more closely at the data, in 1984 and 1988, Arkansas voted less Democratic than the national popular vote by 2.1 percent and 3.3 percent respectively. Going further back is also problematic because in 1976 and 1980, Arkansas, like every state in the South, was affected by Jimmy Carter's run for president. In 1976 and 1980, Arkansas voted more Democratic than the national average by 14 percent and 5 percent respectively. In the three elections before 1976, Arkansas voted below the national average for Democrats.

State (EV)	Avg. Lean towards Democrats, 1988-2004
Arkansas (6)	0.2%
Colorado (9)	-2.4%
Iowa (7)	2.2%
Louisiana (9)	-2.1%
Michigan (17)	1.8%
Missouri (11)	-0.1%
New Hampshire (4)	-2.0%
New Mexico (5)	0.6%
Ohio (20)	-1.4%
Oregon (7)	2.5%
Pennsylvania (21)	1.9%
West Virginia (5)	1.1%
Wisconsin (10)	1.5%

A fairer assessment of the voting tendency of Arkansas could be reached by excluding the 1992 and 1996 elections and calculating the average for 1984, 1988, 2000, and 2004. The performance of Arkansas in those years is relatively consistent, ranging from 2.1 percentage points less than the national Democratic vote to 3.7 percentage points more. The average is just over 3 percent, which would put Arkansas just outside the swing state category.

The categorization of Louisiana as a swing state also merits some discussion. Louisiana's pattern in recent elections is similar to that of Arkansas. Louisiana had been voting Republican before the Carter years, appears to have had a substantial Democratic bump during the Carter elections, voted Republican again in 1984 and 1988, and then was perhaps affected by Bill Clinton in 1992 and 1996, as Clinton's advantage in his own state seems to extend, albeit to a lesser degree, to some other southern states.

Arkansas Dem. Victory over Nat'l Avg.	
2004	-3.7%
2000	-3.1%
1996	4.6%
1992	6.5%
1988	-3.3%
1984	-2.1%

Louisiana Dem. Victory over Nat'l Avg.	
2004	-6.1%
2000	-4.2%
1996	1.8%
1992	-0.8%
1988	-1.3%
1984	-2.2%

The results here are not as clear as in Arkansas. In 1996, Clinton earned a higher Democratic share in Louisiana than the national average. In 1992, Louisiana tilted slightly Republican, but to a smaller degree than in 1984, 1988, 2000, and 2004. Using the five-cycle measure of partisan lean, Louisiana falls 2.1 percentage points below the national Democratic average—still within the swing state category, but on the edge.

West Virginia is the most problematic case and is discussed in greater depth below. It is one of the rare states which voted consistently in one direction and then suddenly in one election switched to the other party and remained there. Using the five-cycle measure of partisan lean, West Virginia appears to be extremely competitive, favoring Democrats by 1.1 percentage points. However, West Virginia suddenly changed from a strongly Democratic state in six straight elections to a solidly Republican state in 2000 and 2004. The 2008 results will help to determine whether this surprising shift is attributable to some special characteristics of President Bush. Outside of the South, which merits special treatment for reasons listed above, we find no other instances in which a state switched its lean to such a great magnitude, only to reverse itself a short time later. It seems likely that the 2000 and 2004 performance in West Virginia will be echoed in 2008.

Finally, in an attempt to refine our predictions, we incorporate a measure of the shifts in partisan identification each state experiences over time. We determine the average trend movement that each state has made toward one party or the other—vis-à-vis the national results—over the previous five cycles. With this addition, the familiar states of Florida and Nevada fall under the swing state definition. Louisiana disappears from the list.

Clearly the landscape is extremely competitive. Examining the states that appear safe for one party or the other, the Democrats hold 200 electoral votes and the Republicans hold 202. The battle will be fought over the middle 136 votes outlined above; with 69 of these, the presidency seems within reach.

We now turn to a state-by-state discussion of the swing states.

State (EV)	5-year Avg. State D Victory over Nat'l Avg.	Avg. 5-cycle trend toward D	Predicted differential from Nat'l Vote in 2008
Republican Likely (36 EV)			
Florida (27)	-3.0%	1.0%	-2.0%
Colorado (9)	-2.4%	0.8%	-1.6%
Republican Leaning (25 EV)			
Nevada (5)	-3.0%	1.6%	-1.4%
Ohio (20)	-1.4%	0.1%	-1.3%
Toss-ups (30 EV)			
Missouri (11)	-0.1%	-0.3%	-0.4%
New Hampshire (4)	-2.0%	2.3%	0.3%
Wisconsin (10)	1.5%	-0.6%	0.9%
New Mexico (5)	0.6%	0.4%	1.0%
Democratic Leaning (28 EV)			
Iowa (7)	2.2%	-0.9%	1.3%
Pennsylvania (21)	1.9%	-0.6%	1.3%
Democratic Likely (17 EV)			
Michigan (17)	1.8%	0.7%	2.5%
Special Cases			
Arkansas (6)	0.2%	-0.3%	-0.1%
Louisiana (9)	-2.1%	-0.8%	-2.9%
West Virginia (5)	1.1%	-1.8%	-0.7%

Analysis of the Swing States

"TOSS-UP" STATES

Missouri—According to our analysis, Missouri is the most competitive of all the states. In 2004, Missouri was at the outside edge of Republican leaners, with John Kerry losing by 2.4 percentage points more than he did the national vote. But over the past five election cycles, Missouri has been very competitive, sometimes exceeding the Democratic national popular vote, sometimes falling short. Though Kerry's vote in Missouri fell short of his nationwide popular-vote percentage, Bill Clinton's win there in 1992 exceeded the percentage of his national popular-vote victory. If Missouri has a slight lean, it is toward the Republican side, and on average it has been moving slightly in the Republican direction.

New Hampshire—Over the past five cycles, New Hampshire has shifted faster than any other state, trending 2.3 percentage points in the Democratic direction each election. In the 1980s, New Hampshire was a solidly Republican state, but projecting the trend forward, it is now a true swing state. George W. Bush took New Hampshire in 2000 with 48.1 percent of the popular vote, narrowly surpassing his national total. But in 2004, John Kerry put the state in the Democratic column, exceeding his national popular vote total by 1.9 percentage points.

New Mexico—The Democratic vote share in New Mexico was within 0.5 percent of the popular vote in 2000 and 2004, and so it stands out as a classic swing state. Under our analysis, the continuing closeness of New Mexico actually points to a slight shift in the Democratic direction. The fact that New Mexico was not moved by George W. Bush's larger margin of victory in 2004 indicates a slight Democratic shift. New Mexico has a modest trend toward Democrats over the past five election cycles.

Wisconsin—Wisconsin had close elections in 2000 and 2004, and like New Mexico the fact that it remained close while Republicans gained in the national popular vote points to a slight shift favoring Democrats. However, the picture over the past five election cycles is of a very close swing state that has moved from being Democratic to more competitive. In 2004, John Kerry won the state, but by a very narrow margin of 0.4 percent. Wisconsin has a slight average trend toward Republicans of 0.6 percent per election.

Swing States That Lean Slightly Democratic

Iowa —Iowa had close elections in both 2000 and 2004. George W. Bush won it by 0.7 percent in 2004 after losing the state in 2000, but it still appears to be a slightly Democratic-leaning swing state because on average for the past five elections, Democrats have exceeded their national popular vote by 2.2 percentage points per cycle. It is trending 0.9 percentage points in the Republican direction per cycle.

Pennsylvania —Pennsylvania has been a swing state in most elections since World War II. In the past five election cycles, Democrats have averaged 1.9 percentage points above their national vote. John Kerry won the state by fewer than 3 points in 2004. But Pennsylvania's trend has been toward Republicans by 0.6 percent each election. Pennsylvania and Michigan are often spoken of together as two "Rust Belt" swing states that lean Democratic but which are potentially winnable by Republicans. We find Michigan to be ever so slightly more Democratic, and trending very slightly in the Democratic direction, while Pennsylvania is a bit more Republican and has a slight trend in the Republican direction.

Swing States That Lean Slightly Republican

Nevada—In the 1980s, Nevada voted very substantially Republican in presidential elections. In the 2004 election, it nearly mirrored the national popular vote, only voting 0.1 percent less than the national Democratic number. As the fastest-growing state for the nineteen years up until 2006,[22] it is unsurprising that Nevada's voting patterns have changed. It has a large Hispanic population, which will likely play some role in Nevada's movement toward the Democratic Party.[23]

Ohio—George W. Bush's 2004 victory in Ohio, one of the closest and most pivotal states in recent general elections, won him a second term in the White House. Ohio has been a slightly Republican-leaning swing state for some time. Ohio's Democratic vote share was barely higher than the national vote share in 2004. Overall, Ohio shows little trend toward one party or the other.

Swing States That Lean Democratic

Michigan —Michigan has consistently been a Democratic-leaning competitive state. The last Republican to win the state was George H. W. Bush in 1988, yet John Kerry's margin of victory there in 2004 was fewer than 4 points. Additionally, Michigan appears to have a very slight trend in the Democratic direction. For 2008, we project it to be a borderline swing state. Were even a slight Democratic trend to continue in future election cycles, it would fall outside the swing state category.

Swing States That Lean Repulican

Colorado—Colorado has been a fairly reliable Republican state in recent elections. But it has trended significantly in the Democratic direction so that it now has the potential to be competitive. The states of the Southwest in general have trended more Democratic. One significant factor is the Hispanic vote in these states. Ruy Teixeira and John Judis, among others, have pointed to the rise in Hispanic population and the possible accompanying increase in Democratic votes.[24]

Florida—The epicenter of controversy in the 2000 election, Florida remained competitive in 2004, with George W. Bush claiming a 5-point victory there. No demographic shifts suggest a major change in Florida's voting patterns in 2008.

Other Non-Swing States of Interest

Several other states that fall outside our swing state category are worth considering. Some were once swing states but have been moving substantially toward one party over time and have become less competitive. Some could become swing states in the future. And a few are not trending toward either party, but are close enough to the swing category to merit comment and the sustained attention of campaign strategists.

Some of the categorizations that pundits make have become outdated. There are a number of states, such as New Jersey and Delaware, that are occasionally referred to as competitive, but have in fact moved safely into the Democratic column, and their continued trend in this direction makes them poor targets for a Republican nominee.

Of course, some states mirror these changes. Once swing states, they continue to migrate and become more and more Republican. Consider Arkansas, Louisiana, and Tennessee. These states, discussed above, do not have the most pronounced trends toward Republicans, but especially when one accounts for the effects of the Bill Clinton campaigns, each of these states shows a longer-term trend toward Republicans.

Two previously uncompetitive states are becoming more competitive. Arizona appears to be a Republican state moving in the Democratic direction and Minnesota appears to be a Democratic state moving in the

Republican direction. Arizona is further from swing state status than Minnesota. On average over the past five election cycles, Republicans have exceeded their national vote share by 4.5 percentage points in Arizona. It is also moving more slowly in the Democratic direction than Minnesota is in the Republican direction. On average, Arizona's trend has been 0.8 percentage points in the Democratic direction per election cycle. Minnesota has on average voted 4.1 percentage points more Democratic than the national average. Its trend is 1.3 percentage points in the direction of the Republican Party. Adding the trend to the five-cycle partisan lean places Minnesota just outside the swing state category for 2008.

Three states are not far outside the swing state category, but have shown essentially no trend over the past five election cycles: Oregon, Washington and Virginia. For many years in the 1950s through the early 1980s, Oregon was a swing state. It then began to creep in the Democratic direction. In 2000, the election result in Oregon was extremely close, with a similarly close national popular vote. We would consider Oregon a swing state for 2008 if we were not accounting for its movement over time. But the slight average trend of 0.1 percentage point per cycle pushes it just outside the swing category. Essentially, Oregon is a borderline Democratic swing state that is not trending in either direction.

The voting history of Washington State looks very much like that of Oregon but it has always been a point or two more Democratic. Today its five-cycle measure of partisan lean is 3.8 percentage points more Democratic than the national average, which is 1.3 points more Democratic than Oregon. Washington does have a small average trend of 0.5 points in the Democratic direction.

Looking at recent history, one could view Virginia as a red (Republican) state that may be turning purple. In 2004, Virginia voted more Democratic than one might have anticipated. It also elected a Democratic senator in 2006 and has elected two consecutive Democratic governors; now Democrats seemed poised to contend strongly for the retiring John Warner's seat in 2008. Still, we find no evidence of such a shift over the past five election cycles. After 2004, Virginia was a fairly solid Republican state with voters casting Republican ballots at 5.1 percentage points higher than the national Republican vote. Virginia also showed almost no trend in the Democratic direction, only 0.1 point per cycle. We remain unconvinced that Virginia will rank among the most competitive states in 2008.

West Virginia is perhaps the most anomalous state in our study, and one whose voting pattern contradicts our characterization of state-level partisan change as generally incremental. We have found a pattern of relative stability in state voting patterns. When the South and home states of presidential candidates are exempted, there are few dramatic shifts in a state's voting pattern from election to election. And even in the relatively few cases of a substantial cycle-to-cycle shift, there are very few cases like West Virginia, which seems to have shifted from being safely in one party to safely in the other. The West Virginia of 2000 is the Holy Grail for Electoral College strategists. Such latently vulnerable states would be the most valuable of resources.

This appears to be what happened in West Virginia in 2000. If George W. Bush had won Florida without controversy, the memorable phenomenon from the election would have been the sudden conversion of this seemingly Democratic state, which provided the five electoral votes that pushed Bush over the 270-electoral vote margin needed for victory.

Bush strategist Karl Rove saw an opportunity in West Virginia that few others did. Even though the state had been reliably Democratic, he saw a place that in many ways exhibited a southern culture potentially sympathetic to conservative moral values, appeals against gun control, and protectionism. The state had never been organized at the presidential level. James C. Moore and Wayne Slater recount Karl Rove's perceptive decision to target West Virginia.[25] In hindsight, this explanation makes sense, but at the time the prevailing wisdom expected the blue-collar economic concerns of coal miners to keep the state comfortably in the Democratic column.

The most significant trends in the Electoral College map that we see are the movement of the upper-midwestern states of Wisconsin and Iowa, as well as Pennsylvania toward Republicans. Democrats see the southwestern states of Arizona, New Mexico, Colorado and Nevada moving in their direction. The latter three are already in the swing state category, and it is possible that if trends continue in Arizona, it may approach swing state status in the next few elections. Democrats also see Florida and New Hampshire moving in their direction. Again, both are swing states, and our model predicts they will be more competitive in 2008. New Hampshire in particular has trended substantially towards Democrats.

Our model also shows that the interest in Virginia as a swing state may be misplaced, as it is neither particularly competitive over the past five election cycles, nor is there a trend in the Democratic direction. It is true that in 2004 Virginia leaned more to the Democratic side than the model would have anticipated and that Democrats won key gubernatorial and senatorial elections, but our model still shows a relatively safe Republican state without much of a trend in either direction.

Finally, a broad look at the states that can reasonably be considered "safe" by one party or the other lends much credence to the notion that the two major U.S. political parties have become markedly polarized.[26] All twenty-four states that lean toward one party or the other by five percentage points or more appear to be trending away from competitiveness. In other words, the twenty-four safest states appear to be becoming safer still. This is visually evident in the charts presented in the appendix.

Practical Recommendations

There are also some trends in partisan leaning of the states that will be of interest to the Electoral College strategist. There are only a few states that appear to be becoming more competitive. Minnesota is one. Arizona is another, but has substantially farther to go.

The trends of states currently considered to be swing states are also of interest. Nevada, Colorado, New Mexico, Florida and New Hampshire appear to be becoming more Democratic, while Iowa, Wisconsin, and Pennsylvania seem to be trending Republican.

Hardly earth-shattering, the simplest piece of advice to offer to both parties is to focus on the swing states. There are enough electoral votes in this category that winning a majority of them, when added to safe Republican or Democratic states, will be enough to get to 270 electoral votes. Of these swing states, Missouri is the most competitive, and it is one of the closest of the moderately large states. Florida, Ohio, and Pennsylvania are the biggest three swing states and all potentially up for grabs. Michigan is also a large state worth contesting, but it is toward the edge of the swing state category.

Practical Advice to Republicans

• Republicans should ignore states with significant Democratic leanings. We doubt the existence of more West Virginias out there. Similarly, past swing states like New Jersey, Delaware, and California are no longer likely to go to the Republican column in a presidential election. They have moved out of the swing state category and continue to move in a Democratic direction.

• Republicans should continue to emphasize the upper Midwest swing states of Wisconsin and Iowa, which are trending slightly toward the GOP.

It should also consider emphasizing Minnesota, which is just outside the swing state category in our model, but is trending Republican.

• When choosing between Michigan and Pennsylvania, the Keystone State is the more logical choice. It has more electoral votes; is Democratic in leaning, though less so than Michigan; and is trending slowly toward Republicans, while Michigan is trending slowly toward Democrats.

• Republicans could contest Oregon, which falls just outside the swing state category, but has no strong trend in the Democratic direction. Washington State, on the other hand, is too far out of the swing state category, and has a small trend in the Democratic direction.

Practical Advice to Democrats

Democrats should target three swing states in the Southwest: Colorado, New Mexico, and Nevada. All have been trending Democratic. Arizona has also exhibited a Democratic trend, but is far enough out of the swing state category to be considered a good prospect in a close election.

• Democrats should target New Hampshire, a swing state that has moved dramatically in the Democratic direction over the past five election cycles.

• Arkansas and Louisiana lean Republican and are not as close in presidential races as they may seem, particularly because their election results were boosted by Bill Clinton's home-state advantage and potential regional effects on these states. They are not necessarily out of reach, but they are harder to win than the simple election results suggest. Tennessee is even more difficult and should not be considered a competitive state.

• Despite the hype, Virginia does not provide a good opportunity for Democrats to win. It is still relatively far from being a swing state and has not trended toward Democrats over the past five election cycles.

• Florida is by far the most compelling target in the South for Democrats, perhaps the only southern target they should consider. Our model predicts that Florida will still lean slightly Republican relative to the national vote, but it is trending toward Democrats.

Conclusion

The electoral map is better characterized by gradual evolution than dramatic change. Landslide elections such as those that occurred in 1972 or 1984 can sway large numbers of states to vote contrary to their predisposition, but when compared with national results, state returns are generally consistent with the recent past. In a hotly contested election, a small, relatively stable group of genuinely contested states emerges. It is these states that will be the recipients of campaign attention and media spending, and it is in these states that campaigns will most effectively expend their resources.

Post-election Postscript

We developed a model to identify the partisan leaning of states in presidential elections. The underlying premise of the model is that the popular vote within each state tends to follow the national popular vote. If a Democrat, for example, wins the national popular vote with 52 percent of the two-party vote (or 2 percent above 50 percent), then our simplest model predicts that an individual state will also vote 2 percentage points more in the Democratic direction than average than in a fifty-fifty election. Our more complicated model added a trend factor, which incorporated the direction and the magnitude of the movement of a state toward or away from the Democratic Party.

In this postscript to the election, we look at what states were predicted to be swing states if the election had been fifty-fifty. Next, we look at which states were in reach for Obama and McCain, assuming the final national outcome was as it ended up a 7.3-percentage-point win for Obama in the two-party vote. Finally, we look at how the model held up: which states were surprising in their margins? We also look at a question that we examined in earlier elections: were there any states that exhibited sudden ideological swings, as West Virginia did in 2000, and will they make a distinct break from past voting patterns going forward to future elections?

Results are mixed. Our more complicated model with the trends included predicted that there would be fourteen swing states in a fifty-fifty election: Alaska, Colorado, Florida, Iowa, Louisiana, Michigan, Missouri, Nevada, New Hampshire, New Mexico, Ohio, Pennsylvania, Wisconsin, and West Virginia. Of those fourteen, we believed that Alaska, Louisiana, and West Virginia did not belong in the swing state category because of distortions of home state, regional distortion, and, in the case of West Virginia, an anomalous change of voting patterns.

It is not surprising that Barack Obama won ten of the eleven states that we left in our swing state category. By our definition, these were states that our model predicted would vote within 2.5 percent of the national Democratic popular vote. As Obama took 53.6 percent of the national two-party votes, states in this category should have shifted into Obama's column. The only exception was Missouri, which John McCain won by less than 1 percent of the vote. Even though he came close to winning Missouri, Obama underperformed in that state relative to his national performance.

Some states moved just as predicted with the popular vote: Ohio, Florida, Iowa, and Pennsylvania. Obama took 3.6 percentage points over 50 percent of the two-party vote nationally, and these states exceeded their predicted vote by roughly the same amount.

Some states moved more than expected; the three southwestern states of Nevada, New Mexico, and Colorado stand out, with Obama exceeding his predicted vote share in Nevada by 4.1 percentage points.

Swing States with Obama Winning 53.6 Percent of the Two-Party Vote

Another way that the method of identifying swing states can be useful is to employ it to identify which states would be competitive if the national vote was shifted in one direction or the other. After the fact, we know that Obama won the election with 53.6 percent of the two-party vote. We can then shift our model's prediction for each of the states by 3.6 percentage points in the Democratic direction, and we can identify which states would be swing states (or likely to be closely contested states given the overall Democratic shift in the electorate). Using our definition of swing states as states that are between -2.5 percent and +2.5 percent of the predicted Democratic vote, a 53.6 percent Obama win generates a new list of swing states: Arizona, Colorado, Florida, Louisiana, Nevada, North Carolina, Ohio, Tennessee, and Virginia. On this list three states stand out as problematic. Arizona is John McCain's home state, and we found that Obama underperformed by 4.2 percentage points over the expected result. We have not found a consistent home-state advantage, but we have frequently noted clear home-state advantages in a number of cases, and it would be a reasonable assumption that McCain's home-state advantage prevented Arizona from being very close. Our model predicted that Obama would have received 49.9 percent of the two-party vote in Arizona, given the size of his win in the national popular vote. Louisiana and Tennessee, we have noted, seem to have been affected by a mini southern swing toward Bill Clinton, and/or by proximity to the Clinton's home state and the fact that Tennessee was Al Gore's home state.

Leaving these three states out, the other six swing states all went for Obama. Two states are especially worthy of comment. Our model did not anticipate that Virginia would be a close state in a fifty-fifty election. It did predict that in an election victory of Obama's size, Virginia would be in play. But our model did understate Virginia's Democratic performance. Even with 53.6 percent of the national popular vote, our model predicted that Virginia would give 48.7 percent of its vote to the Democratic candidate, close enough for Obama to contest in this election, but still leaning Republican. In reality, Obama won 53.18 percent of the popular vote, 4.5 percentage points more in the Democratic direction than would be anticipated.

North Carolina, which was for many one of the biggest surprises of the election, was only slightly surprising according to our model. We would have predicted that North Carolina would have a 47.8 percent Democratic vote; instead Obama eked out a victory with 50.17 percent of the two-party vote.

The Big Surprise: Indiana

Obama did better than anticipated in the southwestern states of Colorado, New Mexico, and Nevada. He also somewhat over-performed in North Carolina and, more significantly, in Virginia. All of these states were won by George W. Bush in 2004 and all but New Mexico were won by Bush in 2000. So these states were surprising in the sense that Republican states went to the Democrat. They were also mildly surprising in that they moved more in the Democratic direction than our model anticipated, with a Democrat taking 53.6 percent of the national two-party vote. But while these states voted more strongly Democratic than the model would predict, the magnitude of the change was not so dramatic.

Discussing our model in the early part of this paper, we noted that states rarely radically change their voting patterns from one party to the other. The iconic but extremely rare case we identified along these lines is West Virginia before and after 2000. In this case, a historically Democratic state moved significantly into the Republican column. Two subsequent elections have borne out that this change is lasting, not the product of particular forces in the 2000 election. The magnitude of the West Virginia change from what the model predicted in 2000 is large; the model anticipated West Virginia voting 54.7 percent Democratic, but it actually cast 46.8 percent of the vote for Democrats, a difference of about eight percentage points; the state voted about 4 percent less Democratic than the nation as a whole. In 2004, John Kerry received 43.5 percent of the two-party vote in West Virginia, while taking 48.8 percent nationally; the state voted over 5 percent less Democratic than the nation as a whole. In 2008, West Virginia cast 43.3 percent of its vote for Obama, almost ten percentage points lower than the nation's Democratic vote.

Is the Indiana of 2008 the West Virginia of 2000? Indiana did not show up as a swing state in our model even when one factored in a 53.6 percent Obama win. The predicted result for Indiana with Obama winning the national vote with 53.6 percent was for Obama to lose Indiana with 44.7 percent of the vote. Instead, Obama won a narrow victory in Indiana, with 50.52 percent of the vote. This deviation of almost 6 percentage points from the model approached the nearly 8 percent deviation of West Virginia in 2000. A few caveats: West Virginia moved from several points Democratic-leaning to several points Republican-leaning in an almost even election between Al Gore and George W. Bush. Even if Indiana's shift is lasting, it would not be a swing state in a fifty-fifty election, but only one in which there is a noticeable Democratic advantage. Indiana would be the state that a Democrat leading in the polls strives for, not a state to contest in a toss-up election. Second, Indiana bears watching in future elections. Perhaps the geographical proximity to Illinois helped Barack Obama win there, and it is possible that future Democratic presidential candidates may not perform as strongly there as did Obama. But overall, Indiana's move was the most striking of states and may indicate a future of voting patterns that are more Democratic than past performance had indicated.

Other Anomalous Results

Other states which deviate from the model fall into several categories. We saw several states that likely exhibited strong home-state tendencies. One of the largest deviations came in Hawaii, one of the home states of Barack Obama. Hawaii voted a full 11.5 percentage points more Democratic than our model would have expected in an election where the Democrat gets 53.6 percent of the vote. The effect in Illinois was not as great as in Hawaii, but Illinois still voted 3.3 percent more Democratic than expected. Delaware, home of vice presidential nominee Joe Biden, voted 4.5 percentage points more Democratic than expected. On the Republican side, we already indicated that Arizona voted more Republican (or 4.6 percentage points less Democratic) than anticipated and might have been quite competitive in a 53.6 percent Democratic national victory had a Republican nominee from another state been running at the top of the ticket. Alaska, Sarah Palin's home state, voted 1.6 percent less Democratic than predicted.

The Appalachian states were another region that voted out of character, voting less Democratic than anticipated. Kentucky voted 10.3 percentage points less Democratic, Alabama 4.4 percent less. We have already mentioned Arkansas, Louisiana, Tennessee, and West Virginia.

The explanation for these results may lie in the history of Bill Clinton doing well in this region in 1992 and 1996. If these states might not typically consider Democrats in the presidential election, Bill Clinton's particular appeal and his regional proximity might have artificially inflated the Democratic baseline in these states relative to subsequent years.

In addition, we should consider the possibility that Obama appealed less to voters in these states. Certainly in the primaries, these are the type of states that Hillary Clinton did quite well against Barack Obama.

Overall, however, the model still shows a great consistency of state results. In general, states move with the national average. And even this simple model can be useful in identifying which states will most likely be swing states in future elections and will most likely receive the attention of future campaigns.

Appendix

The vertical lines on the charts below represent each state's "partisan lean," the average differential relative to national vote share of the Democratic Party for the previous five cycles. The charts also show how each state would vote in 2008, relative to the national vote, if its average trend for the previous five cycles were to continue. This information is represented by the thicker horizontal lines. For example, after the 2004 election, the Democratic candidate received a vote share in Alabama an average of 8.2 points below the national average for the previous five cycles. Over the same period of time, Alabama also trended away from the Democratic Party at an average rate of 1.9 points per cycle. If this trend were to continue for 2008, Alabama's Democratic vote share, relative to the national Democratic vote share, would decrease from -8.2 percent to -10.1 percent.

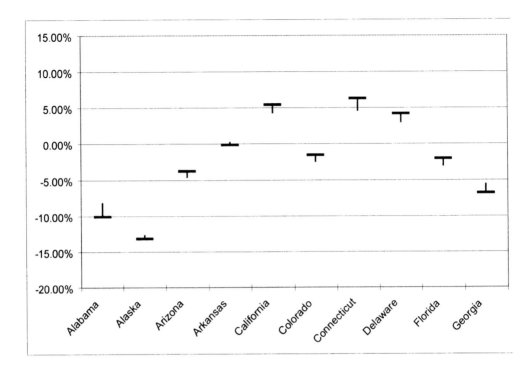

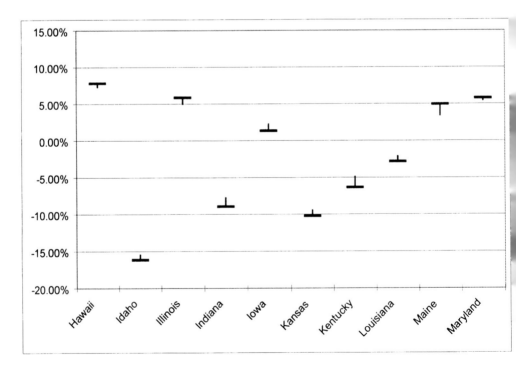

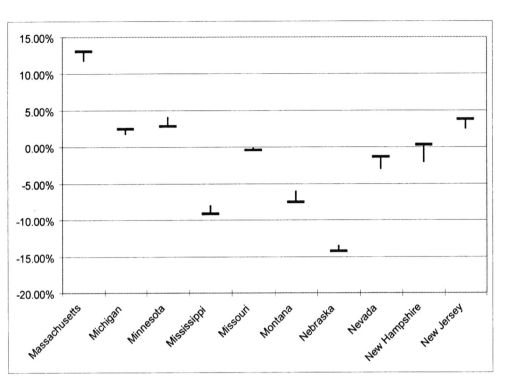

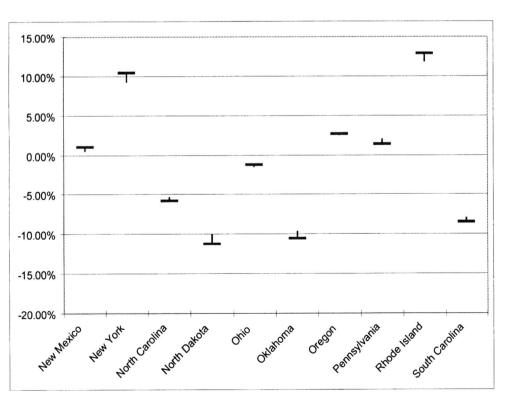

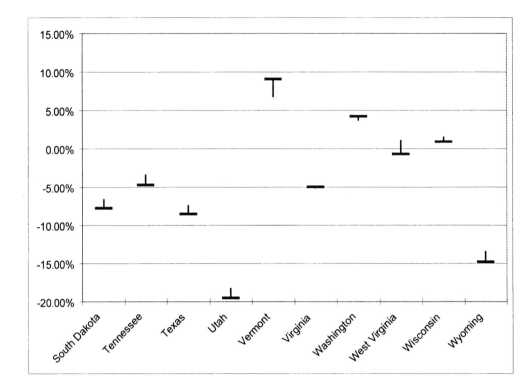

Notes

We would like to thank Jennifer Marsico for her superior research and editing work. Thanks also to Jamie Hester, who suggested many helpful revisions.

1. Bonnie J. Johnson, "Identities of Competitive States in U.S. Presidential Elections: Electoral College Bias or Candidate-Centered Politics," *Publius: The Journal of Federalism* 35, no. 2 (Spring 2005), 337–55.

2. Thomas E. Patterson, *The Vanishing Voter: Public Involvement in an Age of Uncertainty* (New York: Knopf, 2002), 139, 141.

3. David Hill and Seth C. McKee, "The Electoral College, Mobilization, and Turnout in the 2000 Presidential Election," *American Politics Research* 33, no. 5 (September 2005), 700–725.

4. George C. Edwards III, *Why the Electoral College is Bad for America* (New Haven: Yale University Press, 2004), 101–3.

5. "Who Picks the President?" *FairVote Presidential Elections Reform Program,* http://www.fairvote.org/media/research/who_picks_president.pdf (accessed March 25, 2008).

6. Daron R. Shaw, *The Race to 270: The Electoral College and the Campaign Strategies of 2000 and 2004* (Chicago: University of Chicago Press, 2006), 187–97.

7. Ibid., 177–86.

8. Angus Campbell, "Surge and Decline: A Study of Electoral Change," in Philip E. Converse, Warren E. Miller, and Donald E. Stokes, eds., *Elections and the Political Order* (New York: Wiley, 1966), 40–62. Also see V. O. Key Jr., *Southern Politics in State and Nation* (New York: Alfred A. Knopf, 1949).

9. Shanto Iyengar and Adam F. Simon, "New Perspective and Evidence on Political Communication and Campaign Effects," *Annual Review of Psychology* 51 (2000), 149–69. For international observations, see Kevin Arceneaux, "Do Campaigns Help Voters Learn? A Cross-National Analysis," *British Journal of Political Science* 47, no. 1 (January 2002), 159–73.

10. James G. Gimpel, Karen M. Kaufmann, and Shanna Pearson-Merkowitz, "Battleground States versus Blackout States: The Behavioral Implications of Modern Presidential Campaigns," *Journal of Politics* 69, no. 3 (August 2007), 786–97. But in contrast, see Jennifer Wolak, "The Consequences of Presidential Battleground Strategies for Citizen Engagement," *Political Research Quarterly* 59, no. 3 (September 2006), 353–61.

11. Alan S. Gerber, Donald P. Green, and Ron Shachar, "Voting May Be Habit Forming: Evidence from a Randomized Field Experiment," *American Journal of Political Science* 47, no. 3 (July 2003), 540–50.

12. Johnson, "Identities of Competitive States in U.S. Presidential Elections."

13. Ibid.

14. Larry M. Bartels and John Zaller, "Presidential Vote Models: A Recount," *PS: Political Science and Politics* 34, no. 1 (March 2001), 8–20.

15. Michael Lewis-Beck and Tom W. Rice, "Localism in Presidential Elections: The Home State Advantage," *American Journal of Political Science* 27, no. 3 (August 1983), 548–56; Steven Rosenstone, *Forecasting Presidential Elections* (New Haven: Yale University Press, 1983). For a study that agrees with qualification, see James C. Garand, "Localism and Regionalism in Presidential Elections: Is There a Home State or Regional Advantage?" *Western Political Quarterly* 41, no. 1 (March 1988), 85–103.

16. Garand, "Localism and Regionalism in Presidential Elections."

17. Lee Sigelman and Paul J. Wahlbeck, "The 'Veepstates': Strategic Choice in Presidential Running Mate," *American Political Science Review* 91, no. 4 (December 1997), 855–64.

18. Dean Lacy and Barry C. Burden, "The Vote-Stealing and Turnout Effects of Ross Perot in the 1992 U.S. Presidential Election," *American Journal of Political Science* 43, no. 1 (January 1999), 233–55.

19. Lewis-Beck and Rice, "Localism in Presidential Elections; Garand, "Localism and Regionalism in Presidential Elections."

20. Nelson W. Polsby, *How Congress Evolves: Social Bases of Institutional Change* (New York: Oxford University Press, 2004).

21. Carl Klarner, "Forecasting the 2008 U.S. House, Senate, and Presidential Elections at the District and State Level," *PS,* October 2008, 726.

22. "Growth States: Arizona Overtakes Nevada," *CNN Money,* December 25, 2006, http://money.cnn.com/2006/12/22/real_estate/fastest_growing_states/index.htm (accessed March 29, 2008).

23. Regarding the partisan effects of demographic change, see John Judis and Ruy Teixeira, *The Emerging Democratic Majority* (New York: Scribner, 2002).

24. Ibid.

25. James Moore and Wayne Slater, *Bush's Brain: How Karl Rove Made George W. Bush Presidential* (Hoboken, N.J.: John Wiley & Sons, 2003).

26. See Pietro S. Nivola and David W. Brady, eds., *Red and Blue Nation? Characteristics and Causes of America's Polarized Politics* (Washington, D.C.: Brookings Institution Press, 2006).

Governing
in the
White House

Separation Anxiety

Unified and Divided Government in Layered Context

DAVID A. CROCKETT

Fifty years ago, Richard Neustadt argued that the Constitution created not a government of separated powers, but "a government of separated institutions *sharing* powers."[1] This observation has since assumed the status of conventional wisdom, repeated as fact in numerous analyses of American politics as well as most undergraduate textbooks. Embedded in this phrase is the basic recognition that divided government is a fact of political life. Unlike parliamentary democracies, where the election results for the legislature determine the makeup and leadership of the executive branch, the separated system in the United States allows for the possibility that the elective branches of government will be separated not only in a formal and constitutional sense, but also in a partisan sense. Competing parties frequently claim control of different institutions in the same election.

This constitutional fact has created tremendous professional anxiety in some circles, best articulated in James Sundquist's summary critique of the dangers of divided government. Dating the beginning of the era of divided government at either 1954 or 1968, Sundquist is concerned primarily with government ineffectiveness. Divided government prevents the political branches from pursuing a unifying and integrated policy agenda. It leads to confrontation marked by at best bickering, and at worst open political warfare as the two branches seek to deny each other victories, all the while incapacitating the government from dealing with pressing problems. Finally, because different parties control different institutions, divided government prevents citizens from holding accountable these political leaders through a coherent vote.[2] Later analyses have not been as grim. In his classic examination of divided government, David Mayhew argues that "unified as opposed to divided control has not made an important difference" when it comes to investigations of the executive branch and the enactment of important legislation.[3] Morris Fiorina in turn argues that "there is little evidence that divided government alone can account for the perceived failings of the federal government."[4] And Charles Jones rejects the party government paradigm, arguing that a separationist model with varying patterns of inter-branch relations is both the historical reality and preferred norm.[5] Of course, from a political perspective these analyses are hardly comforting—every president prefers a Congress allied with his goals, and concerns about partisan strength in Congress are part of the normal political calculus.

Too often, however, examinations of divided government proceed from a narrow perspective that does not do justice to the complexities of the constitutional system. Sundquist, for example, bases his critique of divided government on two questionable premises: first, that party government—unified government—is essential if we are to overcome the problems of efficiency presented by the separation of powers system; second, that the president performs an important leadership function, in his capacity as head of his party, serving as the "prime mover of the entire governmental system."[6] This perspective views separation of powers as a barrier to efficient governance and the president as the central actor responsible for the conduct of the system. This distinctly presidency-centered approach can be linked to Neustadt, who chose "to view the Presidency from over the President's shoulder."[7] Neustadt's interest is in "what a President can do to make his own will felt within his own Administration; what he can do, as one man among many, to carry his own choices through that maze of personalities and institutions called the government of the United States."[8] A properly functioning political system, then, is one where the president is successful in pursuing his agenda through the skillful leadership of Congress, and the primary focus of scholarly analysis targets the political and strategic challenges presidents face when presented with unified or divided government. Jones is more circumspect, insisting that "ours is not a presidential system" and criticizing the notion that a "good president" is one who "makes government work."[9] Yet even Jones accepts Neustadt's basic paradigm for the American constitutional order—that it is a system of separated institutions sharing powers.[10] The resulting picture is of a government whose actors compete for power, and the central question concerning unified or divided government is whether this competition leads to positive or negative consequences. What is often missing is a sense for the different constitutional roles the political branches play in our system and the larger historical context that frames the political drama.

What is needed to come to a more complete understanding of the phenomenon of divided government—it may or may not be a problem—is a more nuanced perspective on the place of the presidency in the constitutional order. The presidency is a multilayered office that involves constitutional, historical, institutional, organizational, and operational levels, each of which engages the political question of separated institutions from different sets of rules and concerns. This essay analyzes the problems and possibilities associated with the question of unified and divided government by confronting each of these presidential layers, determining where and how much divided government matters, and where it is irrelevant. Doing so allows us to understand the various ways unified and divided governments impact the presidency in the constitutional order, and to place this central feature of American constitutional government in broader perspective.

Use of the phrase "multilayered" is intentional, for the presidency can be understood architecturally, as a building whose different levels represent different political phenomena. Like physical buildings, political institutions are planned and constructed, presenting us with multiple layers that require analysis to understand the whole. The architectural model recognizes that the presidency is a designed structure. As a layered phenomenon it is like a pyramid whose levels each constitute a specific aspect of the office, each with its own set of questions, rules, assumptions, and goals. Just as a building has some levels that are more foundational than others, so the presidency has analytical layers that are more foundational, and which influence or constrain other layers. This does not mean that some layers are less important than others, but it does imply a logical ordering of layers, and they are best viewed in relation to each other and as being informed by each other.[11] This perspective also acknowledges that designs can be modified and renovated, a fact we clearly see with changes in the presidential selection process and the rise of political parties. It is through the lens of this model that we need to examine the phenomenon of unified and divided government.

The Constitutional Layer

Divided government is a constitutional reality that has occurred frequently in American history. Table 1 illustrates this frequency from the founding

The Presidential Pyramid

Operational:
Tactical and
Strategic

Organizational: Structural
and Temporal

Institutional: Intra-branch
and Inter-branch

Historical: Cyclical and Secular

Constitutional: Explicit, Implicit, and Prerogative

Table 1: Historical Frequency of Divided Government, 1789–2010

Unified Government	Divided Government
134 of 222 years – 60%	88 of 222 years – 40%

to the present. In the 222 years from 1789 through 2010, the American government has experienced more unified government than divided—but a rate of 40 percent certainly indicates that divided government is a frequent enough occurrence to merit study. This is especially so in the era since 1952, when the frequency of divided government has been much higher—thirty-six out of fifty-eight years, a rate of 62 percent. The question is whether this is a phenomenon that should evoke concern.

Turning first to the constitutional layer, it should be clear that it is the most foundational layer because the presidency is a product of the Constitution, which gives the office its authority and spells out its duties. More important, the Constitution spells out the functions of all three branches of government. Contrary to Neustadt's assertion that we live in a system of separated institutions sharing powers, it is more accurate to say we live in a system of separation of functions, for the Framers made a principled distinction between different types of power, referring explicitly to "all legislative powers," "the executive power," and "the judicial power." In turn, the structure of each branch is designed to make more likely the achievement of several core objectives of republican government, including responsiveness to the popular will, protection of rights and liberties, security, and steady administration of the law. Jeffrey Tulis outlines the connection between structure and function for each branch. Congress is a plural institution designed to represent the people and enact policies in response to the popular will through a complex deliberative process. The Supreme Court is a small body of learned experts with job security, designed to interpret the law and protect rights and liberties from unjust action. Finally, the presidency is a unitary institution designed to ensure the security and stability of the nation by acting energetically to set goals, respond to crises, and provide for the steady administration of the law.[12] Tulis makes clear that the three branches of government are structured differently in order to make more likely the fulfillment of these objectives. Although these basic functions remain separated, the Framers' goal to constrain power and prevent tyranny also means that the three branches share concerns in each area, and their interaction incorporates some overlapping powers. Still, their priority of concerns differs. It is important to highlight that, contra Sundquist, efficiency in policy making is not the preeminent or sole concern of the constitutional system, nor is the presidency the central actor in each of these functions. The separation of powers system is designed to provide for greater effectiveness in governance by regulating the inherent tension that exists among these essential functions.

Any analysis of the president's place in this dynamic must also take account of the different duties he must perform. Scholars have long noted that the president wears two different hats, that of leader and clerk.[13] As a leader the president sets the agenda, reacts to crises, and focuses on the security of the nation. As a clerk the president is responsible for the steady administration of the law. Although more ink tends to be spilled on the president's leadership role, both are important constitutional functions. The president as leader occupies a position of independence and equality with respect to Congress; as clerk he occupies a more subordinate role, charged as he is with administering laws passed by Congress.[14] As leader the president sets the agenda for Congress through his annual messages and the recommendation of legislation. He responds swiftly to foreign and domestic threats to security and stability, and he has wide latitude in the management of foreign policy. His oath of office gives him the explicit duty to "preserve, protect, and defend the Constitution of the United States." As clerk the president uses his resources to, in the words of Article II, "take care that the laws be faithfully executed." Alexander Hamilton highlighted the qualities we hope to get from a position occupied by one, marked by the quality of energy. He argued that the function of the presidency consists of "the execution of the laws and the employment of the common strength, either for this purpose or for the common defense."[15] Such energy is "essential to the protection of the community against foreign attacks; it is not less essential to the steady administration of the laws; to the protection of property ... to the security of liberty against the enterprises and assaults of ambition, of faction, and of anarchy." Qualities such as "decision, activity, secrecy, and dispatch" constitute "the bulwark of the national security."[16]

This functional understanding of American political institutions should be the starting point for any analysis of a specific phenomenon such as divided government. From a strictly constitutional perspective divided government is irrelevant. The institutions were created divided, but the functions are nonpartisan. The Framers separated the different functions of government precisely to ensure the overall effectiveness of these institutions in meeting their different objectives. James Madison, in his extended argument about separation of powers in Federalist Nos.

47–51, argues that these functions are rightly separated, given to branches uniquely constructed to meet these objectives. Just as we would not want to see presidents decreeing statutes unilaterally, neither should we expect effective leadership in a crisis from Congress, an institution structurally incapable of providing it. The interplay and conflict between the branches makes it more likely that the tensions that exist among the various objectives and functions can be resolved in ways that do not sacrifice any of them. It is true that the president's powers are rarely, if ever, plenary. In the area of agenda setting, for example, nothing compels Congress to act on or fulfill the president's agenda. Congress is free to pursue it, alter it, revamp it, or ignore it. There is no guarantee that the president will enjoy policy success, nor should presidential success be the standard of effectiveness. In fact, there may very well be times when we want the president to fail in his pursuits. Mayhew[17] and Jones[18] demonstrate that significant legislation gets passed under a wide variety of institutional combinations. We should not forget, however, functions of the presidency other than lawmaking partner, and any analysis of the dynamics of unified and divided government must proceed with a clear understanding of the different roles the presidency performs in the constitutional order. The president's basic duties under the Constitution remain valid regardless of the institutional dynamic, and any anxiety that focuses purely on policy production is misplaced.

The Historical Layer

The second layer we should examine is the historical layer. Although the Constitution created the presidency and armed it with the tools to perform its unique functions, individual presidents are also captives of their place in history. All presidents share the same duties and functions, but all presidents are not created equal. Different times call for different types of leadership, some more energetic than others. One of the more influential examinations of historical contingency and context is Stephen Skowronek's analysis of the president in political time.[19] Skowronek argues that American history can be understood as a series of regime cycles in which one party and its governing philosophy dominate American politics for a specific era, redefining the terms of political debate. Presidents of reconstruction, such as Abraham Lincoln and Franklin Roosevelt, are followed by their partisan affiliates, who work to manage the regimes the reconstructors established and adapt the party's agenda to future issues.

Opposition presidents try to preempt that agenda. Over time the regime collapses as the governing party fails to account for emerging issues and divisions, and a new era begins.

While the constitutional presidency is nonpartisan in the pursuit of leadership and clerkship, the historical presidency becomes a partisan animal. It is here that we see political leaders at all levels organizing as parties in an effort to take control of the government and determine public policy. Because partisan fortunes vary, it makes a difference whether a president holds the office when his party is rising in strength and influence or declining. It matters greatly whether the president is pursuing the politics of repudiation and reconstruction, affirmation and articulation, or opposition and preemption. The dynamics of political time may affect a president's ability to put greater focus on the leadership role of agenda setting.

What does political time tell us about the question of divided government? What opportunities and constraints does it present to the president? Table 2 places each president in American history prior to Barack Obama into his partisan and institutional dynamic. Presidents in the left column were members of the dominant party in their specific era, while those in the right came from opposition parties. The top half of the table lists presidents from both camps who enjoyed unified government; the bottom half lists those who faced divided government. The table constitutes a summary depiction of all presidents, according to whether they were affiliated with or opposed to the governing party, and whether they faced unified or divided government.

Some interesting observations arise from these data that demonstrate the greater constraints opposition-party presidents face. Although Americans grant their presidents unified government 60 percent of the time throughout history, the vast majority of that time unified government is enjoyed by the governing party. Where governing party presidents often enjoy numerous years of unified government in succession, most opposition presidents—Woodrow Wilson is the only exception—enjoy unified government for only their first two years. Both parties have faced their share of divided government, but the numbers here also tell an interesting story. Many governing-party presidents face divided government for only brief periods of time, while it is typical for opposition presidents to live with divided government for larger proportions of their terms. Governing-party presidents enjoy unified government more than twice as often as they do divided government; the situation for opposition

Table 2: Presidents in Historical Context, 1789–2008

	President Affiliated with Governing Party	*President Opposed to Governing Party*
Unified Government	Washington 1789–1793 Adams 1797–1801 Jefferson–Monroe 1801–1823 Jackson 1829–1833 Jackson–Van Buren 1835–1841 Polk 1845–1847 Pierce 1853–1855 Buchanan 1857–1859 Lincoln 1861–1865 Grant 1869–1875 Garfield/Arthur 1881–1883 Harrison 1889–1891 McKinley–Taft 1897–1911 Harding–Hoover 1921–1931 Roosevelt–Truman 1933–1946 Truman 1949–1952 Kennedy–Johnson 1961–1968 Carter 1977–1980 Bush 2003–2006 118 years – 54%	Harrison–Tyler 1841–1843 Cleveland 1893–1895 Wilson 1913–1919 Eisenhower 1953–1954 Clinton 1993–1994 14 years – 6%
Divided Government	Washington 1793–1797 Monroe 1823–1825 Quincy Adams 1825–1829 Jackson 1833–1835 Polk 1847–1849 Pierce 1855–1857 Buchanan 1859–1861 Grant–Hayes 1875–1881 Arthur 1883–1885 Harrison 1891–1893 Taft 1911–1913 Hoover 1931–1933 Truman 1947–1948 Reagan–Bush 1981–1992 Bush 2001–2002, 2007–2008 50 years – 23%	Tyler 1843–1845 Taylor–Fillmore 1849–1853 Johnson 1865–1869 Cleveland 1885–1889 Cleveland 1895–1897 Wilson 1919–1921 Eisenhower 1955–1960 Nixon-Ford 1969–1976 Clinton 1995–2000 38 years – 17%

presidents is the reverse. Table 3 repackages this dynamic to highlight how often opposition presidents face divided government compared to their governing-party colleagues. The governing party has controlled the presidency for 168 years of the 220 since Washington's inauguration. The opposition party has controlled the office for fifty-two years. Of its 168 years, the governing party has enjoyed unified government 70 percent of the time, while enduring divided government for 30 percent of the time. The opposition party is the near-mirror image of the governing party, enjoying unified government for only 27 percent of the time, and facing divided government for 73 percent of the time. Clearly, looking through the lens of political time, opposition-party presidents are far more likely to face divided government than governing party presidents.

Of course, one of the dominant stories in political science for many years has focused on the prevalence of divided government in the current era. Table 4 breaks down the institutional and historical question by era. The columns identify the different eras in political time, while the rows provide the raw numbers and percentages for governing- and opposition-party presidents facing unified and divided government. We see both continuity and change in these data. Although there is no opposition president during the patrician era, the first four eras reflect very similar dynamics that are consistent with the overall numbers listed in the final column. Throughout these periods the governing-party presidents enjoyed unified government at rates just the opposite of their opposition-party counterparts. The real change comes with the Reagan era, and there it is only with the governing party. The opposition party in the Reagan era experiences an institutional dynamic quite similar to earlier incarnations of opposition control. The governing party, however, for the only time in American history, experiences more divided government than the opposition party. Clearly there is little unusual about divided government and opposition-party presidents in the current era; it has become a much bigger constraint for governing-party presidents. Throughout history opposition presidents have faced significant problems with political capital, restricting their freedom of action. Those constraints became more gen-

Table 3: Divided Government as Institutional Constraint, 1789–2008

	President of Governing Party	President of Opposition Party
Unified Government	118 of 168 years – 70%	14 of 52 years – 27%
Divided Government	50 of 168 years – 30%	38 of 52 years – 73%

eral in the contemporary era. The question that remains to be explored is whether these historical constraints impact the ability of the president to perform his constitutional roles.

In addition to historical cycles, secular developments in the party structure can also affect a president's ability to achieve legislative success. What defines the specific era matters greatly to a president. For example, we know that partisan polarization has increased significantly in Congress since 1980, as more liberals aligned with the Democratic Party and conservatives with the Republican Party. The result is that there are fewer moderates in Congress now, making it more difficult for any president to construct the necessary bipartisan majorities to pass legislation. The center has nearly disappeared on Capitol Hill, and this ideological polarization is a fact of political life whether a president faces unified or divided government. Evidence suggests that the impact of polarization in causing legislative stalemate is even greater than that of divided government.[20]

The Institutional Layer

The third layer we should examine is the institutional layer. Although this constitutional office experiences a cyclical pattern of constraints and opportunities, it is also true that the institution of the presidency has evolved over time. At the institutional level we take account of the secular development and growth of the office. This is one of the most popular lines of analysis in the field of presidency studies, for the "modern presidency" construct has dominated political science since Neustadt's paradigm-estab-

Table 4: Divided Government by Partisan Regime

Partisan Dynamic	Patrician (1789–1829) N years %	Jacksonian (1829–1861) N years %	Republican (1861–1933) N years %	New Deal (1933–1980) N years %	Reagan (1981–2008) N years %	Total (1789–2008) N years %
Governing/ Unified	30 of 40 75	16 of 24 67	38 of 52 73	30 of 32 94	4 of 20 20	118 of 168 70
Governing/ Divided	10 of 40 25	8 of 24 33	14 of 52 27	2 of 32 6	16 of 20 80	50 of 168 30
Opposition/ Unified	0 of 0 0	2 of 8 25	8 of 20 40	2 of 16 13	2 of 8 25	14 of 52 27
Opposition/ Divided	0 of 0 0	6 of 8 75	12 of 20 60	14 of 16 88	6 of 8 75	38 of 52 73

lishing work. It is easy to exaggerate the impact of this level, however. Tulis argues that significant developments in the office of the presidency do not constitute a metamorphosis in the institution,[21] and David Nichols's work demonstrates that many aspects of the modern presidency were present in some form at the creation.[22] There is, as Erwin Hargrove and Michael Nelson suggest, a genetic code in the very structure of the constitutional office that has provided for its subsequent development.[23]

Nevertheless, development has taken place, and the typical marker point for when the modern institutional presidency began is the administration of Franklin Roosevelt. Sidney Milkis provides the most comprehensive argument for the consequences of Roosevelt's achievement, focusing on the passage of the Reorganization Act of 1939 and subsequent creation of the Executive Office of the President (EOP).[24] Roosevelt's embrace of the administrative state, centered in the Oval Office, has given presidents stronger tools to pursue policy development and execution in the White House. They do not alter the president's constitutional duties and functions—leadership and clerkship remain his purview—but they provide him with greater resources, as well as potentially greater problems.[25]

What this means is that the modern president facing divided government has a more powerful tool kit at his disposal than earlier presidents. While the stereotype of nineteenth-century presidents is that they were relegated to stopping congressional action through the veto, the modern president can respond to congressional recalcitrance by pursuing an administrative strategy, an approach embraced by Richard Nixon and further developed by his successors. He can use these tools to construct a policy agenda, and even push that agenda unilaterally. With a staff of hundreds at his disposal, the president as a unitary officer has a distinct advantage when dealing with Congress, by nature a fragmented entity that has a perennial collective action problem. In addition to crafting the policy debate to favor his agenda, the president has a tremendous ability to determine how to interpret and execute the law.[26] Creative use of executive orders enables him to make policy that effectively binds his successor—although research indicates that presidents do not compensate for divided government through greater use of executive orders.[27] Evolving use of presidential signing statements provides another potential avenue for influencing the policy execution process.[28]

The secular developments of institutions can cut both ways, however. Just as the presidency has acquired greater resources in the modern era, so have parties in Congress responded in their own fashion. Whereas the question of partisan control of institutions determines whether a president faces unified or divided government, this metric is based on simple majority control of each house of Congress. The evolution of the use of the filibuster in the Senate has allowed minority parties during periods of unified government to create a scenario of de facto divided government. Once a rare and exceptional occurrence, the filibuster has become a routine part of the Senate minority party's legislative strategy. In many cases in the contemporary era, presidents have to construct majorities that exceed 60 percent in order to get important measures passed. While such majorities have occurred at various points throughout history, they have not been the norm in recent years. In fact, since the 60 percent rule for cloture votes went into effect in 1975, the average strength of the majority party in the Senate has been 55. Until Al Franken joined the Senate in 2009, only during the 94th and 95th congresses did the majority party in the Senate hit the 60 percent mark, and these were the first two post-Watergate Congresses. Thus, with supermajorities required for most measures in the Senate, one can reasonably argue that all presidents for the past thirty years have faced a type of divided government—not a prospect likely to change any time soon. The willingness of minority parties to employ this tactic means presidents face a government that is all divided, all the time.

The Organizational Layer

The fourth layer we should examine is the organizational layer. As much as any president must confront his place in political and secular time in the pursuit of his constitutional duties and functions, so does he face a specific short-term organizational context. In the midst of any specific task, it is important to ask key questions. Is a presidency in its first or second term? Is it facing its initial honeymoon period, a reelection battle, or lame-duck status? What, precisely, is the president's party's strength in Congress? Much of the focus of short-term popular and journalistic analysis targets this arena of action, which is natural, for Publius himself recognized that there is a natural rhythm to a presidential term.[29] It makes a difference whether a president faces a foreign policy crisis just as his presidency gets off the ground or when he is more seasoned, as Kennedy discovered with the Bay of Pigs invasion. When it comes to establishing and pushing a policy agenda, it matters whether a president has most of his term ahead of him or faces an election year. Different functions of the presidency may be impacted by lame-duck status in different ways. In fact, it is here that the immediate concern over unified and divided government—the specific short-term level of partisan strength at any specific point in a presidency—resonates the strongest. This may, for example, determine how likely it is that a president will employ a veto strategy to obstruct Congress rather than pursue a positive program, or how likely the threat of impeachment is from Congress.

It is important to understand, however, that these considerations, particularly that of divided government, are best understood in light of the more foundational layers discussed earlier. The immediate question of what is necessary for specific measures to be passed should be super-imposed on considerations of constitutional functions, historical contingencies, and institutional tools and constraints. We know that divided government does not render the federal policy-making process impotent, for the two elective branches find ways to work together to accomplish a variety of goals, even if those accomplishments do not satisfy everyone's standard of efficiency.[30] But often simple numerical measurements of short-term victories and defeats miss the deeper and more important story. For example, one standard measurement of presidential success is the support score he earns when it comes to getting legislation passed in Congress. The resulting scorecard—the percentage of bills passed on which the president took a position—presumably tells us how effective a president is in pursuing his agenda.

Table 5 illustrates the problem of taking these numbers at face value. I have gathered all the presidential support scores calculated by the *Congressional Quarterly Weekly* since the beginning of that journal's data collection, 1953, and reconfigured it in a table that incorporates regime cycles (a Level 2 analysis) and divided government (a Level 4 analysis). The top half of the table lists presidents who enjoyed unified government, while the bottom half lists those who faced divided government. The right side lists presidents who were opposed to the reigning party in the New Deal or Reagan eras, and the left side lists presidents who were affiliated with the governing party. The average scores for each quadrant indicate that the question of unified or divided government is more important than affiliation or opposition to the specific regime when it comes to success in Congress. The average scores for presidents who enjoyed unified government—whether affiliated or opposed—are more than twenty points higher than the average scores of those who experienced divided government.

Table 5: Presidential Support Scores in Historical Context, 1953–2008

	President Affiliated with Governing Party	*President Opposed to Governing Party*
Unified Government	Kennedy 1961 – 81.4 Kennedy 1962 – 85.4 Kennedy 1963 – 87.1 Johnson 1964 – 87.9 Johnson 1965 – 93.1 Johnson 1966 – 78.9 Johnson 1967 – 78.8 Johnson 1968 – 74.5 Carter 1977 – 75.4 Carter 1978 – 78.3 Carter 1979 – 76.8 Carter 1980 – 75.1 Bush 2003 – 78.7 Bush 2004 – 72.6 Bush 2005 – 78.0 Bush 2006 – 80.9 Average score: 80.2	Eisenhower 1953 – 89.2 Eisenhower 1954 – 78.3 Clinton 1993 – 86.4 Clinton 1994 – 86.4 Average score: 85.1
Divided Government	Reagan 1981 – 82.4 Reagan 1982 – 72.4 Reagan 1983 – 67.1 Reagan 1984 – 65.8 Reagan 1985 – 59.9 Reagan 1986 – 56.1 Reagan 1987 – 43.5 Reagan 1988 – 47.4 Bush 1989 – 62.6 Bush 1990 – 46.8 Bush 1991 – 54.2 Bush 1992 – 43.0 Bush 2001 – 86.7 Bush 2002 – 87.8 Bush 2007 – 38.3 Bush 2008 – 47.8 Average score: 60.1	Eisenhower 1955 – 75.3 Eisenhower 1956 – 69.7 Eisenhower 1957 – 68.4 Eisenhower 1958 – 75.7 Eisenhower 1959 – 52.0 Eisenhower 1960 – 65.1 Nixon 1969 – 73.9 Nixon 1970 – 76.9 Nixon 1971 – 74.8 Nixon 1972 – 66.3 Nixon 1973 – 50.6 Nixon 1974 – 59.6 Ford 1975 – 61.0 Ford 1976 – 53.8 Clinton 1995 – 36.2 Clinton 1996 – 55.1 Clinton 1997 – 53.6 Clinton 1998 – 50.6 Clinton 1999 – 37.8 Clinton 2000 – 55.0 Average score: 60.6

A simple look at the names in these quadrants demonstrates the shallow nature of numerical analysis free of historical and constitutional context. Few people would argue that the first two years of Clinton's presidency, when he experienced unified government and high support scores, was anything but rocky, laying the foundation for the sweeping Republican victory in 1994. Despite the trauma of impeachment, it was Clinton's second, divided-government phase—with support scores considerably lower, including two of the three worst years on record—that secured his political success. Similarly, while Jimmy Carter enjoyed unified government and support scores higher on average than those of divided-government-afflicted Ronald Reagan, it was Reagan who had the more consequential presidency. On the other hand, the scores earned by George W. Bush in 2001 and 2002, most of which was under divided government, are considerably higher than those earned in 2007 and 2008, also under divided government. The existence of divided government is insufficient to explain many important aspects of these presidencies. This dynamic must be understood against the deeper backdrop of the first three layers.

The Operational Layer

The final layer we should examine is the operational layer. This layer is of greatest concern to individual presidents, for it concerns strategic questions about personal success. For better or worse, presidents are ambitious politicians who desire glory and reputation. They want to succeed, and work hard to achieve their goals. The Framers recognized this dynamic, and one of the more famous passages from *The Federalist Papers* describes how "personal motives" will make the separation of powers system work by playing ambition against itself.[31] Indeed, much of the scholarship in presidency studies constitutes advice to the president on how to succeed. Political analysts from Aristotle to Machiavelli to Neustadt presume to give such advice to the ruler. From this perspective, concerns about the constraints and opportunities presented by unified or divided government are natural and expected.

It is important to recognize, however, from the layered perspective presented here, that personal success for the president is not as important as system success. The presidency exists to serve leadership and clerkship functions in the constitutional order, but that should not come at the expense of the deliberation and responsiveness peculiar to Congress or the concern with liberty and rights that is the dominant focus of the courts.

As stated earlier, the separation of powers system exists in part to regulate the natural tension that exists among these various functions, and it is quite possible that we should desire a president *not* to succeed in some specific endeavor. When evaluating dynamics such as divided government, the focus on presidential success needs to be properly contextualized. Factoring in the short-term political context and the contemporary state of the institution, we must always account for the president's placement in political time, centering our analysis on the functional roles of the presidency in the constitutional order. Personal success is normatively subordinate to the more foundational layers. As we proceed to bring this analysis to its major point—putting these layers together in an effort to understand where divided government is important and where it is not— we must remember the architectural quality of this institution. Making personal success our sole or preeminent concern is akin to building the proverbial house on a foundation of sand.

Bringing It All Together

Perhaps the easiest way to understand the relative opportunities and constraints placed on the presidency by the unified-divided government dynamic is to examine specific examples in light of the layered perspective outlined above. It is important to resist the notion that all institutional dynamics are created equal. It makes a difference whether unified or divided government presents itself early or late in a regime cycle, and whether it is experienced by a governing or opposition party. It also makes a difference which function the president is pursuing within this context—leadership or clerkship. In this section I separate the core functions of the presidency and explore to what extent unified and divided governments impact the operation of that function, given the larger context represented by the various layers discussed above. This exploration takes the form of comparisons of various presidents who represent different contexts. It is a first pass through this topic, which itself merits deeper study. I then conclude with some comments about President Barack Obama's opportunities and constraints.

Leadership: Security. The first constitutional function to consider is the leadership function of ensuring the security of the nation. This function encompasses two separate roles, that of foreign policy leader and crisis manager. In this arena the president works to ensure the nation's security, set the foreign policy agenda, serve as commander in chief of the military, and respond to crises, whether foreign or domestic, man-made or natural. The relevance of political time and divided government in the pursuit of this function is murky and ambiguous at best. When it comes to legitimate crises, in fact, it would seem that the constitutional layer trumps other levels of concern. As a unitary office best equipped structurally and politically to respond energetically to crises, the presidency naturally draws support from other political actors and the general public when engaged in this function, despite other contextual considerations. The clearest recent example of this phenomenon is the wide support experienced by George W. Bush following the terrorist strikes of September 11, 2001. Bush was a late-phase regime manager who came to power in a controversial election, quickly facing divided government in the Senate, yet he was able to sustain popular and political support for actions ranging from war in Afghanistan to a preemptive invasion of Iraq. While it is true that support for the war in Iraq declined considerably with time, that decline was in part due to the fact that the sense of crisis faded as the situation came to be seen as normal. Similarly, this same regime affiliate, when enjoying unified government in 2005, failed to manage adequately the natural disaster crisis of Hurricane Katrina, leading to a loss of popular support from which Bush never fully recovered. In these examples, it would seem that competence and practical wisdom affect presidential effectiveness far more than unified or divided government or placement in political time.

Other examples supporting this conclusion include Bill Clinton's bombing of Yugoslavia—here an opposition president faced divided government in the immediate wake of impeachment; George H. W. Bush and the invasion of Panama and expulsion of Iraq from Kuwait—here a regime affiliate faced divided government; Ronald Reagan's invasion of Grenada—here a regime builder faced divided government in the House; Gerald Ford's rescue mission of the merchant ship *Mayaguez*—here an unelected opposition president faced a particularly strong divided government; and Richard Nixon and the response to the Yom Kippur War—here an opposition president in an impeachment crisis faced divided government. Unified government examples of crisis management include John Kennedy, the regime affiliate who worked through both the Bay of Pigs affair and the Cuban Missile Crisis, and Jimmy Carter, the late-regime affiliate who handled the Iranian hostage crisis—another crisis that turned sour once it became the new norm. It would seem that the very nature of this core constitutional function—ensuring the security of the nation, often in the capacity of commander in chief—grants presidents in a variety of political contexts wide latitude to demonstrate their effectiveness, and that effectiveness is the principal determinant of success.

Matters are not as clear when the security question is less obvious. Although the president typically takes the lead in managing foreign policy, this is an area that crosses over into agenda setting, which can evoke greater congressional resistance. The paradigm case of foreign policy failure remains Woodrow Wilson's futile effort to gain Senate ratification of the Treaty of Versailles. Context mattered significantly here, for Wilson was an opposition president who faced divided government in a political battle that required a supermajority vote in the Senate—about as constrained a context as one can imagine. Decades later Bill Clinton suffered a similar defeat when the Senate rejected the Comprehensive Test Ban Treaty—the first defeat of a major international security pact since Versailles. It is no accident that Clinton shared Wilson's political context, both in his status as an opposition leader and in facing divided government. This is not to suggest that governing-party presidents enjoy conflict-free foreign policy power. Franklin Roosevelt, a regime builder who enjoyed unified government, had to tread carefully where isolationist sentiments were concerned, never completely getting his way until the bombing of Pearl Harbor. Similarly, Ronald Reagan, a regime builder who faced divided government, experienced numerous confrontations with Congress over his anticommunist efforts in Nicaragua. Again, however, these are ambiguous examples. Although Roosevelt enjoyed unified government for his entire presidency, he also faced a sizable opponent in the cross-partisan conservative coalition, and Reagan was the weakest of the regime builders by virtue of never claiming complete control of the House. By contrast, Harry Truman, a regime affiliate facing divided government, engineered the Marshall Plan, one of the more consequential achievements of American foreign policy.

Finally, it must be acknowledged that modern presidents, by virtue of the institutionalization of the office, have stronger tools to pursue foreign policy objectives even in the face of constrained circumstances. Reagan's weakest point in his presidency was following the Iran-Contra scandal, when he was a lame duck facing Democratic majorities in both chambers of Congress, but it was during this phase that he forged consequential agreements with the Soviet Union that reduced tensions between the two regimes. Jimmy Carter, Bill Clinton, and George W. Bush—at different points in political time, facing different organizational dynamics—all pursued personal diplomacy seeking Middle East peace, with varying levels of success. Finally, in perhaps the most famous example of an individually driven reversal of foreign policy, Richard Nixon transformed U.S.-China relations, despite being an opposition president who never enjoyed unified government. It would appear that divided government can, at times, constrain the president in his capacity as foreign policy agenda setter, but the latitude he enjoys to act independently in this arena is considerable.

Leadership: Agenda Setting. The second constitutional function to consider is the leadership function of agenda setting. This function allows the president to clarify goals and set and pursue a policy agenda, aided by such constitutional tools as the State of the Union address and the ability to recommend legislation, statutory tools such as the submission of the president's budget, and rhetorical tools such as the use of the bully pulpit. Because such agenda setting typically involves the passage of legislation, which requires acts of Congress, it is in this arena that factors such as political time and divided government are most relevant. In a very obvious way, it matters to a president interested in enacting policy goals whether he enjoys majorities in Congress. However, it is also clear that the dynamics of political time, a more foundational concern, trump those of divided government.

In previous eras a favorable setting in political time usually coincided with unified government. Regime builders like Lincoln and Roosevelt enjoyed strong partisan majorities as they rewrote the terms of political debate, and their regime affiliates rarely endured divided government longer than two years at a stretch (see Table 2). Opposition presidents, as discussed earlier, typically faced extended periods of divided government. This historical trend changed when divided government became the new norm (see Table 4). While the patterns of unified and divided government for opposition presidents remain consistent with the historical norm, governing-party presidents have been forced to face the constraints of divided government. Has that fact had a major impact on governing-party presidents' abilities to set the national agenda? In some ways the answer is yes. Ronald Reagan's budget battles with Congress in the 1980s testify to his frustration at facing a House led by Tip O'Neill. Again, however, simple comparisons demonstrate how narrow this analysis is. Both Dwight Eisenhower and Bill Clinton enjoyed unified government for the first two years of their presidencies, with congressional support scores generally higher than those earned by Reagan (see Table 5), but no reasonable analysis would suggest that Eisenhower and Clinton reshaped politics in their image. Eisenhower recognized the foolishness of waging a frontal assault on the New Deal system, so he governed as someone who accepted the new reality and simply tried to make it more efficient. Clinton attempted to govern largely as an old-fashioned liberal, with universal health care as his signature issue, only to see the most important elements in his core agenda fail as he lost control of Congress for the duration of his presidency. Reagan, by contrast, never had unified control of Congress, but his status as a regime builder allowed him to overcome the limitations of divided government and redirect the political argument in new trajectories. A similar argument could be made comparing any of these three presidents with Jimmy Carter, who never experienced divided government, but whose status as a late-regime affiliate in the throes of a great repudiation demonstrates the limited advantage unified government gives a president when other factors do not favor him.

None of this is to argue that divided government is irrelevant to a president's ability to set the agenda. We can see this with George W. Bush, a regime manager in the Reagan era who faced several alternations of unified and divided government. When Bush enjoyed unified government in early 2001, tenuous though it was, he succeeded in engineering a significant tax-cut package, certainly something that represented a core governing-party concern. His second major tax cut had to wait until he regained control of Congress after the 2002 midterm election. The prospects of extending those tax cuts past their expiration date and making them permanent were problematic at best under divided government. On the other hand, unified government does not guarantee even a recently reelected regime affiliate victory in his core agenda items, as Bush discovered in his attempt to enact substantive reform of the social security system in 2005. Some agenda items may be too big even for unified government, absent the politics of reconstruction. It is also important to understand that the dynamics of political time constrain most presidents when it comes to setting the policy agenda. It is a conceit to think that all new presidents have an equal opportunity, if facing unified government, to enact their policy agendas. In fact, if there is anything to regime cycles, it seems only a few presidents—the reconstructors—have the opportunity to reset and redefine the political universe, and they tend to do so in their first term. Their regime affiliates are not completely free agents; they are constrained to follow in the path of the regime founder, working to adapt the reigning governing philosophy to changing conditions and emerging issues as time passes. Similarly, opposition presidents are also forced to govern in the shadow of the previous regime builder. Most presidents, in fact, have only a marginal ability to set the long-term agenda in any significant way. This judgment includes even the regime founders, for the longer they serve the more they are constrained by their own early epoch-making decisions. Franklin Roosevelt stands as the very paradigm of the regime-building president who always enjoyed unified government, but his domestic program ran aground in his second term, he failed to persuade his own Congress to follow his lead in his court-packing plan, and he failed to purge uncooperative partisan allies. Charles Jones said it best: we have a "tendency to overstate the role of the president as an agenda setter."[32]

There is one sense, however, in which a president facing divided government, even in a constrained context in political time, can be successful, and that is through adjusting his agenda to meet the demands of the times. It is a negative type of agenda setting, but it can be very effective. Clinton, for example, adjusted to his new divided government context in 1995 by making effective use of the veto power to resist specific proposals of the Republican-controlled Congress, while also carefully selecting certain items, such as welfare reform and balanced budgets, to embrace. Discarding his more traditional liberal agenda, Clinton engaged in more tempered pursuits—blocking some aspects of the Republican agenda, using veto threats to gain victories here and there, and achieving small wins where possible. Similarly, George W. Bush was forced late in his presidency to use the veto power to defend earlier victories and adjust his priorities by pursuing only the most important items, usually those concerning the war on terror.

In all of these cases, it is important to remember that the specific function we are concerned with is leadership through agenda setting. Nothing about political time or unified and divided government actually impairs the president's ability to set the policy agenda. As discussed earlier, this is a constitutional function of the president—but Congress is not obligated to fulfill that agenda. As the deliberative branch of government Congress is free to do what it wants with the president's agenda, and failure of the president's agenda should not be interpreted as failure of the constitutional system.

Clerkship: Steady Administration. The final constitutional function to consider is the clerkship function of steady administration of the laws. In this arena the president works to execute the laws of the land passed by Congress. He is responsible to staff the top level of the bureaucracy and take care that the laws are faithfully executed. At face value, this should make questions of political time and unified or divided government irrelevant. It does not matter what sort of Congress has passed the laws or where the president sits in political time, the president is constitutionally bound to execute the law.

Of course, things are not so simple. One of the principal changes in national politics since divided government became the norm has been increasing antagonism between the presidency and Congress. Sundquist notes this in his own critique of the dangers of divided government.[33] Much of this, however, appears to be an artifact of ideological divisions. As with crisis management, many aspects of presidential clerkship seem to be questions more of competence and wisdom than partisan division. Just as Hurricane Katrina was a test of the president's crisis management abilities, so it was also a test of administration—the ability of the government and its president-appointed leaders to perform its job. Management competence should not be affected by partisan divisions or political time. It is certainly true that divided government may impair a president's ability to staff his administration with personnel of his choice, as George H. W. Bush discovered when secretary of defense designate John Tower was rejected by a Democratic Senate. Hamilton is very clear, however, in Federalist No. 76, that the Senate cannot impose an appointee on the president,[34] and Bush replaced Tower with Dick Cheney—hardly a partisan victory for the Democratic Congress. Also, confirmation problems are not limited to divided government. Bill Clinton, facing a Senate controlled by his party, had difficulty with several early appointments. The fact is that presidents get most of their executive branch selections confirmed because the Senate tends to agree with the notion that a newly elected president ought to be able to pick his leadership team.

Having said that, some scholars have argued that the contemporary era, which happens to coincide with the development of divided government as the norm, has witnessed an acceleration of "politics by other means."[35] If institutional conflict and resort to investigations is typical of divided government, then they will be more prevalent in an era in which divided government is the norm. Evidence suggests, however, that divided government does not lead to higher levels of high-publicity investigations.[36] Congressional oversight can be a thorn in the side of any president. At the same time, the tools of the modern administrative state enable presidents to employ an administrative strategy when pursuing their goals, and presidents have significant latitude in interpreting the law and affecting its implementation. Tools and strategies first developed by Richard

Nixon—an opposition president facing divided government—have now been adopted and refined by presidents of all political contexts who face divided government. George W. Bush made efforts to claim even greater discretionary power over the execution of the law through his vigorous use of signing statements—a tool that was used by the administration when facing both unified and divided government. The tactic generated more heat than fire, and it remains to be seen whether signing statements will have a substantive effect on the actual execution of the law, but the threat to act (or not) remains. The one area where political time and divided government have a clear influence on the broader issue of congressional oversight is impeachment. There have been three serious impeachment efforts in American history, and all three involved opposition presidents facing divided government. Scandals in governing-party presidencies have never led to the constitutional "death sentence," even during periods of divided government. Again, the larger historical context drives these political calculations more so than short-term organizational dynamics.

President Obama in Layered Context

In summary, it appears that divided government by itself has only a marginal impact on presidential effectiveness. This judgment, of course, is not based on a paradigm of presidential power that sees the president as the prime mover of the American constitutional system. Each branch has its own priority of concerns, and political effectiveness in the United States depends on each branch being self-conscious of its roles and functions, and being willing to engage the separation of powers system to regulate the inevitable conflicts that arise. The presence of divided government does not affect the president's functions equally. He has much greater room to maneuver when acting as a crisis manager than as agenda setter. He is more constrained when making foreign policy, but there are plenty of examples of presidents enjoying significant success in this arena, acting on their own discretion. The president is most constrained when setting the policy agenda for the nation, though even here it must be stressed that the constraint is not with setting the agenda but with getting that agenda enacted. Both in this area and executing the law in his clerkship capacity, the impact of divided government is ambiguous and unpredictable, leaving a lot of room for varying expectations. The question of unified or divided government remains a secondary political consideration to more foundational issues of constitutional function, historical context, and institutional resources, and can be best understood only when taking into account those other factors.

This observation raises the final question of what President Obama can expect, for Obama's victory in 2008, coupled with strong Democratic majorities in both houses of Congress, raises some interesting questions for the forty-fourth president. Serving as president in the twenty-first century, Obama has all of the institutional tools that have accrued in the presidency since FDR at his disposal. When it comes to the clerkship task of steady administration of the law, Obama's success will be based on simple calculations of effectiveness. Interpretations of administration actions concerning the closing of the Guantánamo Bay detention facilities, trials of 9/11 terrorists, and the handling of the "underwear bomber" on Christmas Day 2009 may impact popular judgment—and it is no accident that such issues cross over functional categories to national security. Indeed, in the leadership tasks of crisis management and national security, the Obama administration has been able to alter and adjust its own goals in the wars in Iraq and Afghanistan, despite the grumbling of some within the Democratic coalition. It seems unlikely that changes in the status of unified or divided government will alter this dynamic much, barring an unforeseen catastrophe, such as sudden conflict with North Korea or Iran, or a natural disaster similar to the January 2010 earthquake in Haiti. But presidents throughout the modern era have been very successful in getting their way in security matters, whether facing unified or divided government. Structural features of the Constitution are more important in these areas.

Where Obama faces his biggest challenge is the leadership task of agenda setting—or, more properly, agenda enacting. Here, the opportunities Obama faces by virtue of the fact that he enjoys unified government are best understood when placed in the larger and more foundational historical context. The central question facing Obama's presidency is whether his victory in 2008 represented the opportunity for reconstruction or the constraint of opposition. As a candidate of the opposition party in an era that favored conservatism, Obama must be placed in one of these two categories. He is either a regime founder along the lines of Franklin Roosevelt and Ronald Reagan, or he is an opposition president along the lines of Dwight Eisenhower and Bill Clinton.

At the organizational level Obama has been quick to take advantage of the largest partisan majorities in Congress in thirty years. In fact, the *Congressional Quarterly*–computed score for Obama-supported legislation in Congress in 2009 was 96.7 percent—the highest score on record since such scores began to be calculated.[37] The previous record holder was Lyndon Johnson, who scored 93.1 percent in 1964 (see Table 5). Obama's mark certainly verifies the importance of enjoying unified government when pushing an agenda, and a short list of accomplishments includes protections against wage discrimination, expansion of the State Children's Health Insurance Program, an economic stimulus package, home mortgage reforms and foreclosure assistance, curbs on abusive credit card practices, and new tobacco regulations—all of which were signed before Democrats seated their sixtieth senator.

This figure, however, is almost completely an artifact of unified government, not an indication of long-term agenda success. Both Dwight Eisenhower and Bill Clinton enjoyed very high support scores in their first two years in office, when their parties controlled both houses of Congress, and neither proved able to redefine the fundamental political debate. Far more interesting in the early Obama presidency has been the near-obsession with filibuster-proof majorities. Because of the protracted nature of the Minnesota Senate race in 2008, Democrats did not achieve their filibuster-proof majority of sixty senators (counting two independents who caucus with Democrats) until Al Franken took his seat in July 2009. For the next six months Democrats enjoyed the ability to run Congress without deference to Republicans, assuming their caucus remained united. Then, in January 2010, Republican Scott Brown shocked the political world by winning the Massachusetts Senate seat that had been occupied for decades by the late Edward Kennedy. Democrats lost their filibuster-proof margin when Scott took his seat in early February, calling into question such large-scale agenda items as health-care reform and cap-and-trade energy legislation. The 2010 State of the Union address did not appear to reset the national conversation, and the president's budget, submitted in early February, sparked renewed concerns over skyrocketing deficits.

In some ways Obama's difficulties mirror those experienced by Bill Clinton in his first two years in office. Like Obama, Clinton had very high support scores in Congress, but his failure to enact his signature agenda item—health-care reform—paved the way for the Republican takeover of Congress in 1994. In 2009 Obama picked off a lot of low-hanging legislative fruit, but he struggled to achieve his signature agenda items. The reason for this trouble can be found in his historical context. In terms of secular time, Obama took power in a period of exceptionally high polarization in Congress, and he was ranked the most polarizing president in history in 2009.[38] Those two facts transformed the highest partisan majorities in the Senate since the 1970s into de facto divided government.

In terms of political time, it is becoming increasingly clear that Obama may not represent the vanguard of a new reconstructive era of progressive Democratic politics. His campaign of "change we can believe in" repudiated George W. Bush's management of the government, but not the core principles of the Reagan Revolution. Regime builders like Roosevelt and Reagan tend to achieve their regime-changing accomplishments early in their presidencies. The Obama administration's struggles passing health-care reform indicate that the Reagan era has not yet come to a close. Instead, one could fairly argue that the relatively unknown Obama, new to the national stage and largely disconnected from the central partisan battles of the Reagan era, ran a cautious and moderate post-partisan campaign that capitalized on his own charisma and style, as well as discontent with the governing party. By masking the core differences between the two parties Obama failed to lay the necessary foundation for dramatic and durable policy change, even with unified government. Taking power then as an opposition president, history suggests that a centrist course in agenda- setting is the most likely route to governing effectiveness. That was the route pursued by Eisenhower and eventually Clinton in a similar context.[39]

Obama clearly hoped for the role of reconstructor, but he consistently betrays uncertainty about his place in political time. Chief of Staff Rahm Emanuel is famous for bluntly declaring: "You never want a serious crisis to go to waste. . . . This crisis provides the opportunity for us to do things that you could not do before."[40] But while this quote can be seen as evidence of the administration's regime-changing plans, it also betrays an understanding that without the "Great Recession" such plans would be unacceptable. Health-care reform and cap-and-trade legislation represent sharp turns away from a conservative era, and the effort to end the "don't-ask, don't-tell" policy concerning service by homosexuals in the military can be seen as a similar attack on the social issues front. On the other hand, Obama's cabinet picks in the national security and economic policy fields did not come from the progressive wing of the Democratic Party, and the selection of Sonia Sotomayor for the Supreme Court was carefully crafted to mute at least some conservative dissent, and she avoided articulating a vigorous defense of progressive judicial philosophy during her confirmation hearings. Obama has retained or merely tweaked a variety of Bush administration security policies, and while promising tax hikes for some, he continues to operate according to Reagan's playbook by promising no tax increases for most. Even on his signature issue of health-care reform, Obama was more than willing to discard the public insurance option from his health-care plan, due to a loud if selective negative reaction by the public. Despite the high-profile nature of the health-care reform debate, Obama did not wave "health security" cards or veto pens in front of Congress and the public, as Clinton did. In the most revealing incident, at a post–State of the Union address meeting with congressional Republicans, Obama insisted, "I am not an ideologue."[41] One can hardly imagine a conservative Republican being forced to engage in such a denial. That alone indicates that the forces of political time will put far more constraints around Obama's agenda than divided government.

Ultimately, divided government is a fact of American constitutional life. It has made its presence felt 40 percent of the time in the past 222 years, and much more so in recent decades. While it certainly presents short-term strategic concerns for a president interested in personal political success, it has not proven to be an insurmountable impediment to presidential effectiveness, much less to system effectiveness as a whole. The president has plenty of constitutional and political tools to pursue his core functions under all sorts of scenarios. Perhaps the best advice is for new presidents to seek the sturdy old classical virtue of practical wisdom, adapting the president's functions to the historical, institutional, and organizational context of the time, while always respecting the functions of the other branches in the constitutional order. Such an attitude would recognize the inevitability of "separation" without experiencing the "anxiety" of those who forget what is required for healthy constitutional government.

Notes

1. Richard E. Neustadt, *Presidential Power and the Modern Presidents: The Politics of Leadership from Roosevelt to Reagan* (New York: Free Press, 1990), 29.

2. James L. Sundquist, *Constitutional Reform and Effective Government*, revised ed. (Washington, D.C.: Brookings Institution, 1992), 93–96.

3. David R. Mayhew, *Divided We Govern: Party Control, Lawmaking, and Investigations, 1946–1990* (New Haven: Yale University Press, 1991), 4.

4. Morris P. Fiorina, *Divided Government*, 2nd ed. (New York: Longman, 2003), 171.

5. Charles O. Jones, *The Presidency in a Separated System*, 2nd ed. (Washington, D.C.: Brookings Institution Press, 2005), 10–31.

6. Sundquist, *Constitutional Reform*, 90–92

7. Neustadt, *Presidential Power*, xxi.

8. Ibid., xx

9. Jones, *The Presidency in a Separated System*, 1, 12.

10. Ibid., 24–25

11. David A. Crockett, "The Layered Rhetorical Presidency." *Critical Review* 19, no. 2/3 (2007), 299–314.

12. Jeffrey K. Tulis, The *Rhetorical Presidency* (Princeton, N. J.: Princeton University Press, 1987), 41–45.

13. Neustadt, *Presidential Power*, 3–9.

14. Charles C. Thach Jr., *The Creation of the Presidency, 1775–1789: A Study in Constitutional History* (Baltimore: Johns Hopkins Press, 1923); Herbert J. Storing, "The Creation of the Presidency" and "A Plan for Studying the Presidency," in *Toward a More Perfect Union: Writings of Herbert J. Storing*, ed. Joseph M. Bessette (Washington, D.C.: American Enterprise Institute Press, 1995).

15. Alexander Hamilton, James Madison, and John Jay, *The Federalist Papers*, ed. Clinton Rossiter (New York: Mentor, 1999), 418.

16. Ibid., 391–95.

17. Mayhew, *Divided We Govern*.

18. Jones, *The Presidency in a Separated System*.

19. Stephen Skowronek, *The Politics Presidents Make: Leadership from John Adams to George Bush* (Cambridge: Harvard University Press, 1993).

20. Sarah A. Binder, *Stalemate: Causes and Consequences of Legislative Gridlock* (Washington, D.C.: Brookings Institution Press, 2003), 23–26, 67–69; James P. Pfiffner, "Partisan Polarization, Politics, and the Presidency: Structural Sources of Conflict," in *Rivals for Power: Presidential-Congressional Relations*, 3rd ed., ed. James A. Thurber (Lanham, Md.: Rowman and Littlefield, 2006), 39–41.

21. Tulis, *The Rhetorical Presidency*, 6–9.

22. David K. Nichols, *The Myth of the Modern Presidency* (University Park: Pennsylvania State University Press, 1994).

23. Erwin C. Hargrove and Michael Nelson, *Presidents, Politics, and Policy* (New York: Alfred A. Knopf, 1984), 12.

24. Sidney M. Milkis, *The President and the Parties: The Transformation of the American Party System since the New Deal* (New York: Oxford University Press, 1993), 125–46.

25. See Theodore J. Lowi, *The Personal President: Power Invested, Promise Unfulfilled* (Ithaca: Cornell University Press, 1985).

26. Terry M. Moe, "The Presidency and the Bureaucracy: The Presidential Advantage," in *The Presidency and the Political System*, 6th ed., ed. Michael Nelson (Washington, D.C.: Congressional Quarterly Press, 2000), 447–54.

27. Kenneth R. Mayer, *With the Stroke of a Pen: Executive Orders and Presidential Power* (Princeton, N.J.: Princeton University Press, 2001), 99–101; William G. Howell, *Power without Persuasion: The Politics of Direct Presidential Action* (Princeton, N.J.: Princeton University Press, 2003), 69–74, 89–100.

28. Phillip J. Cooper, *By Order of the President: The Use and Abuse of Executive Direct Action* (Lawrence: University Press of Kansas, 2002); James P. Pfiffner, *Power Play: The Bush Presidency and the Constitution* (Washington, D.C.: Brookings Institution Press, 2008).

29. Hamilton, Madison, and Jay, *The Federalist Papers*, 402.

30. Mayhew, *Divided We Govern*, and Jones, *The Presidency in a Separated System*; though see George C. Edwards III, Andrew Barrett, and Jeffrey Peake, "The Legislative Impact of Divided Government," *American Journal of Political Science* 41 (April 1997), 545–63, for an important qualification of this point.

31. Hamilton, Madison, and Jay, *The Federalist Papers*, 289–90.

32. Jones, *The Presidency in a Separated System*, 198.

33. Sundquist, *Constitutional Reform*, 106–109.

34. Hamilton, Madison, and Jay, *The Federalist Papers*, 425.

35. Benjamin Ginsberg and Martin Shefter, *Politics by Other Means: Politicians, Prosecutors, and the Press from Watergate to Whitewater*, 3rd ed. (New York: W. W. Norton, 2002).

36. Mayhew, *Divided We Govern*, 29–33.

37. Shawn Zeller, "Historic Success, at No Small Cost," *Congressional Quarterly Weekly* (January 11, 2010), 112–21.

38. Jeffrey M. Jones, "Obama's Approval Most Polarized for First-Year President," Gallup.com, January 25, 2010.

39. David A. Crockett, *The Opposition Presidency: Leadership and the Constraints of History* (College Station: Texas A&M University Press, 2002); David A. Crockett, *Running against the Grain: How Opposition Presidents Win the White House* (College Station: Texas A&M University Press, 2008).

40. Alex Spillius, "Economic Crisis is Chance for Big Changes, Says Aide," *Daily Telegraph*, November 22, 2008.

41. Peter Baker and Carl Hulse, "Off Script, Obama and the GOP Vent Politely," *New York Times*, January 30, 2010.

Fighting a War, or Managing a Problem?

How Presidents Approach Terrorism

CHRISTOPHER PREBLE

Nearly every U.S. president has dealt with the threat posed by individuals or groups who wage violence against civilians for the purposes of advancing a political agenda, but the shocking events of September 11, 2001, elevated the problem of terrorism to an entirely new level. Following the 9/11 attacks, President George W. Bush declared a "war on terror," a phrase that persisted even as his administration pursued al Qaeda by both military and non-military means. When critics suggested that the war metaphor was overwrought or misplaced, some Bush supporters all but accused the skeptics of aiding the enemy. More than eight years later, all Americans, but particularly those responsible for keeping the nation safe, worry about stopping the next attack. That was George Bush's primary mission for all but eight months of his presidency. On January 20, 2009, a new person stepped into this role.

What context frames Barack Obama's approach to the problem of terrorism? In today's overly simplified political discourse, there are only two. The first, consistent with past presidents' dealings with most national security threats, is of a serious problem to be managed. The other frame of reference, adopted by George W. Bush, portrays terrorism as an existential threat to the republic, a threat that is not merely the moral equivalent of war (as Jimmy Carter said of the energy crisis of 1979) nor the numerous functional equivalents of war (from Lyndon Johnson's war on poverty, to Gerald Ford's war on inflation, to every president since Ronald Reagan's war on drugs), but rather that this is an *actual* war, pitting every American against all persons or groups who would use terrorism to achieve their ends.

With one year of the Obama presidency in the books, it is clear that the Democrat continued many of his predecessor's methods, even as his administration tried to fashion its own strategy for combating terrorism. The key change pertains to tone: long before taking up residence at 1600 Pennsylvania Avenue, Barack Obama had distanced himself, specifically, from the phrase "war on terror." This approach served his political objectives, first in securing his party's nomination, and then in fashioning a new strategy of outreach to the global Muslim community. As this chapter will show, Democrats have been much less likely than Republicans to invoke the language of warfare when discussing counterterrorism. Despite warnings that the electorate would not take them seriously on matters of national security, the message of hope over fear resonated with a substantial share of the electorate. It was no surprise, therefore, that one of Obama's first initiatives as president was a deliberate reshaping of the language of counterterrorism.

But this move was more than just smart politics; it was also smart policy. This chapter concludes with a discussion of why the language of war is often inapt for dealing with the threat of terrorism. In considering a response to a terrorist attack, or in fashioning a proactive strategy to prevent future acts of terrorism, presidents must account for the possibility that short-term approaches might have counterproductive medium- to long-term effects. Though a strong, military response immediately following a terrorist attack might appeal to Americans hungry for revenge, a disproportionate response might have the unintended effect of further increasing the threat of terrorism.

How U.S. Presidents Have Responded to Terrorism in the Past

Since 9/11, terrorism has become a defining issue for many Americans, but it is hardly a new phenomenon. Consider, for example, how the U.S. government approached al Qaeda prior to 9/11. Some terrorist acts that seem almost irrelevant by comparison, or failed or disrupted plots that were chalked up as fortunate near misses, now seem all the more chilling in retrospect because of the parallels to the 9/11 attacks. For example, when a massive truck bomb exploded in the basement of the World Trade Center (WTC) in February 1993, killing six people and injuring an estimated thousand more, that attack did not precipitate a new war on terror.[1] After the attack, an FBI informant pointed investigators to other terrorist plots involving some of the people behind the WTC attack. The investigation eventually led to the blind Egyptian sheikh Omar Abdel Rahman. Rahman and several associates were arrested in June of 1993, and were subsequently tried and convicted for crimes related to the bombing as well as other terrorist plots.[2]

Ramzi Yousef, the mastermind of the 1993 WTC bombing, evaded capture by U.S. authorities for nearly two years. During that time, he joined forces with Khalid Sheikh Mohammed (KSM) in the Philippines, where the two men set to work on a plot to destroy twelve U.S. airliners in mid-flight over the Pacific Ocean. The so-called Bojinka Plot unraveled when Philippine authorities stumbled upon Yousef's bomb-making operation in a Manila apartment. Yousef was eventually captured in Islamabad, Pakistan, in February 1995. KSM escaped to Qatar, where he began to plan the 9/11 attacks in earnest—attacks that would combine elements of Yousef's 1993 attack (namely, the choice of target) as well as the Bojinka Plot's use of commercial aircraft.[3]

Other cases of terrorism in recent U.S. history fell even more clearly in the realm of domestic crimes, not acts of international war, because they were perpetrated primarily by U.S. citizens against other Americans. Two years after the first World Trade Center bombing, Timothy McVeigh used a truck bomb of similar design to destroy the Alfred P. Murrah Federal Building in Oklahoma City, killing 168 people, including 19 children. McVeigh's act of terror resulted in his conviction by U.S. federal courts and subsequent execution. His coconspirator Terry Nichols was convicted and sentenced to life in prison. Immediately after the attacks, the U.S. government stepped up its surveillance of white supremacist and antigovernment militia groups who seemed to share McVeigh and Nichols's views. But President Bill Clinton never called for, and the public likely would not have supported, a declaration of war on such groups or individuals.

Likewise, in the 1960s and 1970s, groups such as the Puerto Rican nationalist FALN (Armed Forces of National Liberation) and the radical leftist Weatherman detonated bombs and orchestrated jailbreaks and riots, but each act was seen as a criminal act, and the principal agencies for dealing with such threats were the FBI and local law enforcement officials, not the U.S. military or the National Guard.

George W. Bush's Response to 9/11

Past presidents avoided declaring war on the tactic of terrorism because doing so would have made no sense; one wages wars against adversaries, not the means they employ to achieve their ends. But given the sheer scale of the killing and destruction in the 9/11 attacks, the enormous psychological impact on all Americans, to say nothing of the damage to the U.S. economy, it is understandable that George W. Bush's response was different from that of his predecessors.

In the days immediately after the atrocities, the desire on the part of most Americans for revenge, the need to identify and bring the perpetrators to justice, was palpable. The nineteen hijackers were already dead, but Americans wanted to know who paid for them, who trained them, who inspired them. It would not have been enough to treat this search like that for a common criminal.

The country didn't have to look very long, or very hard, for those responsible. Well before 9/11, terrorism experts within the White House and elsewhere had fixed on al Qaeda and Osama bin Laden as the leading threats to the United States, and within a matter of a few hours these experts had connected al Qaeda to the attacks. Less than a week after the attacks, Vice President Richard Cheney appeared on NBC's "Meet the Press." Host Tim Russert asked the vice president to explain what steps the administration was prepared to take. "I'm going to be careful here, Tim," Cheney began, "because . . . it would be inappropriate for me to talk about operational matters, specific options or the kinds of activities we might undertake going forward."

He continued:

> We do . . . have, obviously, the world's finest military. They've got a broad range of capabilities. And they may well be given missions in connection with this overall task and strategy.
>
> We also have to work, though, sort of the dark side, if you will. We've got to spend time in the shadows in the intelligence world. A lot of what needs to be done here will have to be done quietly, without any discussion, using sources and methods that are available to our intelligence agencies, if we're going to be successful. That's the world these folks operate in, and so it's going to be vital for us to use any means at our disposal, basically, to achieve our objective.[4]

By the time that President Bush appeared before the nation four days later, his administration had already begun executing some of these plans, plans that went well beyond bin Laden and his tiny band of followers. "Our war on terror begins with al Qaeda, but it does not end there," Bush declared on the evening of September 20, 2001, before a joint session of Congress, with most of the nation watching on television. "It will not end until every terrorist group of global reach has been found, stopped and defeated."

And how would the "war on terror" be fought? The president answered the question on everyone's mind:

> We will direct every resource at our command—every means of diplomacy, every tool of intelligence, every instrument of law enforcement, every financial influence, and every necessary weapon of war—to the disruption and to the defeat of the global terror network.
>
> This war will not be like the war against Iraq a decade ago, with a decisive liberation of territory and a swift conclusion. It will not look like the air war above Kosovo two years ago, where no ground troops were used and not a single American was lost in combat.
>
> Our response involves far more than instant retaliation and isolated strikes. Americans should not expect one battle, but a lengthy campaign, unlike any other we have ever seen. It may include dramatic strikes, visible on TV, and covert operations, secret even in success. We will starve terrorists of funding, turn them one against another, drive them from place to place, until there is no refuge or no rest. And we will pursue nations that provide aid or safe haven to terrorism.[5]

For the balance of his presidency, and in keeping with these promises, George Bush adopted a multifaceted approach to fighting terrorism. There were elements from Cheney's "dark side": secret prisons, unlawful surveillance of American citizens, and, in some cases, torture. There was also traditional intelligence analysis, law enforcement, and the use of the U.S. military.[6] But while the actual conduct of the Bush administration's counterterrorism policies implied something different from a traditional war, the Bush White House seemed reluctant to give up the "war on terror" metaphor.

On at least two separate occasions, senior Bush administration officials and military leaders advanced alternate frames of reference, but neither gained traction. In the summer of 2005, Defense Secretary Donald Rumsfeld used "global struggle against violent extremism (GSAVE)" to describe the campaign against terror. According to national security officials, the label shift reflected the broader goal of combating extremism, rather than the military emphasis of the war frame.[7] The phrase, however, did not last, and in January 2006 President Bush introduced different terminology in the State of the Union address. "Our own generation is in a long war against a determined enemy," he said.[8] The Bush administration took steps to ensure that the new term would endure. The Pentagon's Quadrennial Defense Review of 2006 officially used the term "long war."[9] "Long war" was intended to convey a generational struggle between Islamic extremists and Americans, similar to the ideological fight of the Cold War. By April 2007, however, U.S. Central Command had dropped the term because it connoted an indefinite American military presence in the Middle East.[10] The phrase "global war on terror" lingered on, almost by default.

The 2008 Presidential Candidates: Continuity or Change?

The leading candidates for the presidency in 2008 all wrestled with the terrorism question, and they did so within the context framed in the days and weeks after 9/11. The fifteen men and one woman who seriously vied for the office all spoke of using many different tools, not just the military, in order to address the threat.[11] But there was a difference in emphasis between the two parties, and these differences were largely framed by their conceptions of the character and magnitude of the threat, which, in turn, determines which policies are best suited for combating it.

Republicans Charge Democrats with being Soft on Terror

After 9/11, the Democrats struggled to differentiate themselves from President Bush on the terrorism question. In the immediate aftermath of the attacks, with the country rallying around the president, and his approval ratings nearing 90 percent,[12] the few politicians who dared question the president's judgment or motives were punished or shunted aside. There was strong, bipartisan support for the military intervention in Afghanistan.

But relations between the White House and Democrats and Congress turned sour again in the spring and summer of 2002, as the two sides sparred over the forming of a commission to investigate the attacks, and also on the creation of a new Department of Homeland Security (DHS). Although he initially resisted both ideas, the president turned an apparent liability to his advantage when he reversed course, embraced the formation of a 9/11 commission, championed the creation of the DHS, and then taunted congressional Democrats for not being serious about the "war on terror" because they sought to limit the president's ability to circumvent certain work rules within the new department.

This proved a devastatingly effective political strategy. Television and radio advertisements by Republicans cast Democrats who had voted against the president's wishes as soft on terrorism, or worse. The most notable case involved Republican Saxby Chambliss's attacks on incumbent Democratic senator Max Cleland of Georgia. Cleland had volunteered for the army after college, and was sent to Vietnam in 1967 where he lost both legs and his right arm in a grenade explosion. His service and sacrifice for country were a compelling story, particularly when juxtaposed with Chambliss's four student deferments during the 1960s. Nonetheless, Chambliss implicitly assaulted Cleland's patriotism by running a television advertisement which showed pictures of Osama bin Laden, Saddam Hussein, and Cleland, and pointed out that Cleland had "voted against the President's vital homeland security efforts 11 times."[13] Chambliss won the seat with over 53 percent of the vote in a state that had been trending toward the Republicans for years. His victory, combined with GOP pickups in Minnesota and Missouri, handed control of the Senate back to the Republicans.

The pattern of Republicans accusing Democrats of not taking the terrorism threat seriously enough continued into the 2004 presidential campaign. Like Cleland, John Kerry sought to inoculate himself from attacks on his patriotism by invoking stories from his wartime service in Vietnam. But he had to confront questions about his activities as an antiwar protester, and Kerry also stumbled in explaining his contradictory votes on Iraq; he had voted in favor of the authorization to use force in Iraq in October 2002, but by the spring of 2004 he seemed to be having second thoughts. The Republican National Committee and the Bush campaign seized on Kerry's doubts with a vengeance.

They were even more aggressive in targeting Kerry's comments about the so-called war on terror. In a *New York Times Magazine* article, Kerry explained to reporter Matt Bai, "We have to get back to the place where we were, where terrorists are not the focus of our lives, but they're a nuisance." Kerry continued: "As a former law-enforcement person, I know we're never going to end prostitution. We're never going to end illegal gambling. But we're going to reduce it, organized crime, to a level where it isn't on the rise. It isn't threatening people's lives every day, and fundamentally, it's something that you continue to fight, but it's not threatening the fabric of your life."[14]

The Bush campaign pounced. Campaign chairman Marc Racicot castigated Kerry for his "pre-9/11 view of the world," and GOP chairman Ed Gillespie flatly asserted, "Terrorism is not a law enforcement matter, as John Kerry repeatedly says." Others suggested that Kerry was equating terrorism with petty crimes. A Bush-Cheney campaign commercial asked: "How can Kerry protect us when he doesn't understand the threat?"[15] Bush's reelection seemed to vindicate his decision to cast the fight against al Qaeda as a war to be won, as opposed to problems like crime or poverty that no government can ever truly eradicate.

The Democrats: No Longer Just Strong and Wrong

It took the Democrats a few years to shake off the bitter experiences of 2002 and 2004. In their book *Hard Power: The New Politics of National Security,* published in the spring of 2006, Kurt Campbell and Michael O'Hanlon called on Democrats to "regain their confidence and establish their bona fides" on "the first-order matters of traditional national security—that is, how and when to put force on targets."[16] According to Campbell and O'Hanlon, "former president Bill Clinton captured the post-9/11 mindset of the American people—and the existential problem of the Democratic Party—when he suggested that . . . the electorate would choose 'strong and wrong' over 'timid and right' every time."[17]

But the success of a number of candidates who generally eschewed the "hard-power" approach in the mid-term elections of 2006 encouraged a few adventurous politicians to break free from this orthodoxy. One of the more unorthodox contenders for the presidential nomination was the junior senator from Illinois, Barack Obama. During the campaign, Obama's "advisers told him he had a choice: he could try to out-Cheney Cheney and demonstrate that when it comes to national security, Democrats also have hairy chests, as one put it, or he could develop a new paradigm," writes Peter Baker of the *New York Times.* "Obama, typically, found the idea of a new paradigm more appealing."[18]

"It is time to turn the page," Obama declared in a speech at the Woodrow Wilson Center in Washington in August 2007. He explained that "America is at war with terrorists who killed on our soil; we are not at war with Islam."[19] Obama did not pay a political price for daring to reframe the discussion, or for opposing the Bush administration's policies. If anything, this boosted his long-shot candidacy at precisely the right moment.

By the time of the Iowa caucuses in January 2008, none of the eight declared candidates for the Democratic presidential nomination embraced the idea of a "war on terror." It took over three years, but John Kerry's sensible ideas about treating terrorism as a problem to be managed ultimately seemed less a liability than an opportunity for drawing distinctions between competitors.[20]

For example, former senator John Edwards dismissed the "war on terror" as "a bumper sticker, not a plan." "By framing this struggle against extremism as a war," Edwards wrote in an article in *Foreign Affairs,* the Bush administration "reinforced the jihadists' narrative that we want to conquer the Muslim world and that there is a 'clash of civilizations' pitting the West against Islam."[21]

Obama invoked similar themes in his campaign, knocking the Bush administration for responding "to the unconventional attacks of 9/11 with conventional thinking of the past, largely viewing problems as state-based and principally amenable to military solutions." In a related vein, Obama cast the removal of U.S. forces from Iraq as the crucial first step in fighting terrorism in a more effective way.[22]

Hillary Clinton, who like the other Democratic candidates generally refrained from using "war on terror" rhetoric in her speeches, stressed that the military had an important role. But she also focused on homeland security spending. "I firmly believe that we must do everything within our power to ensure that terrorist attacks never occur on our soil again," she said on her campaign website. "Indeed, the government must have the ability to take every legal measure necessary to root out terrorists. But that does not mean that we must sacrifice our laws and Constitution in the name of security."[23]

All of the leading Democratic candidates placed particular emphasis on improving intelligence gathering and assessment. Barack Obama's plans included "a program to bolster our ability to speak different languages, understand different cultures, and coordinate complex missions with our civilian agencies,"[24] while Hillary Clinton aimed "to restore morale in our intelligence community, increase the number of agents and analysts proficient in Arabic and other key languages, and raise their profile and status."[25] Obama also pledged to "strengthen these civilian capacities, recruiting our best and brightest to take on this challenge," and "increase both the numbers and capabilities of our diplomats, development experts, and other civilians who can work alongside our military."[26]

In terms of the military aspects of his counterterrorism strategy, Obama talked of increasing military support for Afghanistan, including "at least two additional brigades to Afghanistan to re-enforce our counterterrorism operations and support NATO's efforts against the Taliban," as well as an additional $1 billion in non-military aid to "fund projects at the local level to impact ordinary Afghans, including the development of alternative livelihoods for poppy farmers." Despite his stated enthusiasm for using the military from time to time in order to fight al Qaeda terrorists, however, Obama, like his fellow Democrats, generally refrained from calling such operations part of a "war on terror." He criticized claims of "unchecked presidential power" and vowed to roll back many of Bush's policies. "That means no more illegal wiretapping of American citizens, no more national-security letters to spy on citizens who are not suspected of a crime" and "no more ignoring the law when it is inconvenient." Obama also pledged "to close Guantánamo, reject the Military Commissions Act and adhere to the Geneva Conventions."[27]

Republicans and the "War on Terror"

By contrast, Republican candidates for the presidency were reluctant to criticize any aspect of Bush's counterterrorism policies. They were especially eager to embrace the "war on terror" as their frame of reference, even as their speeches and writings occasionally implied an understanding that the term itself was misleading and often counterproductive.[28] The GOP candidates' difficulty in distancing themselves from the language of war paralleled the Bush administration's failed attempts to back away from it.

Some embraced the "war on terror" frame with gusto, and none more so than Rudy Giuliani, who made 9/11 and the war against terrorism the central theme in his campaign.[29] Giuliani's implied rejection of the law enforcement frame stood in stark contrast with his approach to the problem during the 1990s; Giuliani rarely if ever mentioned terrorism as a major concern as a federal prosecutor in New York City, and later as mayor.[30]

Notwithstanding his conduct in both offices, however, Giuliani based his ultimately failed candidacy on his experience as mayor at the time of the 9/11 to make the case that he was better prepared than any of his rivals to wage, as he liked to describe it, "the terrorists' war on us." Still, even Giuliani candidly noted, "Much of that fight will take place in the shadows. It will be the work of intelligence operatives, paramilitary groups, and Special Operations forces."[31]

In a similar vein, former Arkansas governor Mike Huckabee pledged to use political, economic, intelligence, diplomatic, and military tools to fight the war. He envisioned "swift and surgical air strikes and commando raids," to be carried out by U.S. Special Forces, in order to remove terrorist cells in Pakistan, Afghanistan, and Iraq. Former Massachusetts governor Mitt Romney also advocated non-military engagement with Muslims, and suggested creating trade and economic opportunities in the Middle East to combat terrorism. "U.S. military action alone," he explained "cannot change the hearts and minds of hundreds of millions of Muslims."[32]

In other words, all of the leading GOP candidates, who were strongly supportive of the war in Iraq, and who cast that war as the central front in the war on terrorism, seemed to recognize that conventional instruments of military power were of limited utility against shadowy enemies like al Qaeda. And yet, all of the major Republican candidates justified continued high spending on the military, and in most cases considerable increases, on the grounds that conventional military power was needed to disrupt the state-terror nexus, that is, the state sponsors presumed to be behind most terrorist organizations.

Common Themes and Discontinuities

Beyond the competing frames—a problem to be managed versus a war to be won—the two parties shared many points of agreement. For example, a number of commentators took note when, during the course of the 2004 presidential campaign, Senator Kerry and President Bush agreed that the most urgent threat facing the United States was terrorists gaining control over a nuclear weapon.[33] In this vein, both Senators McCain and Obama pledged to pay more attention, and devote more resources, to programs aimed at locking down loose nuclear materials.[34] There was also strong bipartisan support for expanding the military on the grounds that a larger conventional force is essential to fighting terrorism.[35]

Despite these common themes, the campaign highlighted important differences between the two parties. The war in Iraq has received the most attention. President Bush cast the war as the central front in the war on terrorism, more important even than the war in Afghanistan. Defeat in Iraq, Bush explained on numerous occasions, would dramatically increase the danger of future terrorist attacks, whereas victory in Iraq would spell the beginning of the end for terrorists. In his final State of the Union address in January 2008, Bush implored, "It is in the vital interest of the United States that we succeed. A free Iraq will deny al Qaeda a safe haven."[36] By all accounts, John McCain shared Bush's view of the singular importance of the war in Iraq.

Most rank-and-file Democrats, and many party leaders in Washington, categorically rejected this point of view, however; they saw the war in Iraq as a distraction from the hunt for al Qaeda, and even counterproductive to it. Few Democrats in Congress believed, as a majority of Americans did at the time, that Saddam Hussein was connected to the events on 9/11.[37] Likewise, many Democrats doubted President Bush's claim that the creation of a democratic state in the center of the Middle East would deal a fatal blow to terrorism.

Over the course of the Democratic nominating process, candidates refined their messages on Iraq to better appeal to the sizable and vocal antiwar movement. New Mexico governor Bill Richardson, whose campaign never gained much traction, pledged to remove all U.S. troops from Iraq in less than a year, a position functionally identical to fringe antiwar candidates such as Congressman Dennis Kucinich and former Alaska senator Mike Gravel. Even the more mainstream candidates, including senators Clinton, Joseph Biden, and Christopher Dodd, and former senator Edwards, who had all voted for the Iraq war resolution in October 2002, supported the withdrawal of some U.S. troops from Iraq. By the time of the general election, many voters entered the polling booths convinced that an Obama presidency would bring a swift end to the war. The eventual winner's commitment to ending the war was more conditional than commonly thought. For example, in a *New York Times* op-ed published in July 2008, Obama pledged to remove all *combat* troops from Iraq within his first sixteen months in office, but he left room for "a residual force" that "would perform limited missions" over an undefined period of time.[38] It is true, however, that Obama had spoken out against the war as an Illinois state senator in 2002, and he had celebrated his opposition to the war to differentiate himself from his political rivals.

By contrast, the Republican presidential candidates—with the notable exception of Texas congressman Ron Paul—saw no need to run against a war that most Americans had come to oppose; the GOP hopefuls pledged to continue the fight in the face of public opposition. Some were quite candid as to what sacrifices might have to be made to achieve ultimate victory there. For example, Senator McCain, of all the Republican candidates the one most heavily invested in the mission, purportedly said that he "would rather lose an election than lose a war."[39] In another instance, McCain surmised that U.S. troops would have to remain in Iraq for decades, comparable to the long-term presence in Germany, Japan and Korea.[40]

The role of the Iraq war in the context of Washington's wider counterterrorism strategy would appear, therefore, to be a major point of difference between the two parties. As it happened, however, President Obama's plans for ending the U.S. military presence in Iraq were consistent with those of the outgoing Bush administration. Obama's path forward was cleared by a binding status of forces agreement (SOFA) negotiated by members of the Bush administrations with the Iraqi government. The SOFA provided political cover for Obama to execute a slow but deliberate withdrawal, even in the face of the danger that Iraq might collapse back into chaos, and in turn become a safe haven for al Qaeda or precipitate a wider regional war.[41]

The inability of the United States to bring the military occupation of Iraq to a swift end presented serious challenges in shaping a comprehensive counterterrorism strategy for both the Obama and Bush administrations. A number of experts note that stationing conventional forces in foreign lands is not conducive to fighting terrorism; indeed, it is often counterproductive. Even non-kinetic military operations can serve as a central grievance around which terrorist organizations can mobilize new recruits.[42] An understanding of this dynamic seems to have influenced Obama's determination to end the Iraq war, but fears of a political backlash from Republicans might have discouraged him from attempting a faster withdrawal.

Obama's First Year

Barack Obama's handling of the Iraq war parallels other policy initiatives undertaken during his first year in office, especially in that his efforts failed to satisfy partisans on either the right or the left. He delivered on several of his campaign promises, including, most significantly, a substantial deepening of U.S. military involvement in Afghanistan, and an expanded use of drone attacks against suspected al Qaeda targets in Pakistan.[43] These steps elicited grudging support from some Republicans, but an equal measure of criticism from many within his own party. He infuriated liberals by refusing to prosecute intelligence personnel who might have used torture against terror suspects, and he blocked an effort by the ACLU to publish inflammatory photographs of abuse by U.S. personnel at Iraq's Abu Ghraib prison. He annoyed conservatives by pledging to close the prison at Guantánamo Bay within his first year in office, and then frustrated those on the left when he failed to deliver. He rebuffed civil libertarians by invoking the need for military tribunals, indefinite detention of terror suspects, and the continued overuse of the state-secrets privilege, but frustrated critics on the right by proposing to try some terrorism cases—including Khalid Sheikh Mohammed and four others implicated in the September 11 attacks—in civilian courts. Surveying the new president's record after just a few months in office, former vice president Cheney observed during a speech at the American Enterprise Institute, "The administration seems to pride itself on searching for some kind of middle ground in policies addressing terrorism . . . But in the fight against terrorism, there is no middle ground, and half-measures keep you half exposed."[44]

Notwithstanding Cheney's sniping, however, Obama's counterterrorism initiatives were largely in step with those of the Bush administration. A number of Republicans highlighted this continuity. "The administration came in determined to undo a lot of the policies of the prior administration," explained Senator Susan Collins of Maine, the top Republican on the homeland security committee, but it found "that many of those policies were better-thought-out than they realized—or that doing away with them is a far more complex task." James Carafano of the Heritage Foundation amplified these sentiments. "I don't think it's even fair to call it Bush Lite," he said. "It's Bush. It's really, really hard to find a difference that's meaningful and not atmospheric."[45]

Such comments might be interpreted as partisan spin, but Obama essentially agreed with these assessments. In an interview with *New York Times* reporters several weeks after taking office, Obama explained that many of the worst practices he had objected to had already been corrected by the end of Bush's presidency.[46]

But Obama also worked assiduously to reframe the narrative. He was encouraged in this even by some members of the outgoing administration. "We're doing things very well," Michael Leiter, a Bush appointee who directed the National Counterterrorism Center, told the president-elect, "but we're losing the messaging war." A significant share of the global population thought America was at war against the rest of the world, Leiter maintained. "You have an opportunity to change that message, to change how the struggle is perceived," he said.[47]

Almost immediately, Obama set out to do just that. He especially hoped to convince Muslims around the world that the United States was not engaged in a war against their religion, but was instead focused on killing or capturing those few who had hijacked Islam as a vehicle for advancing secular political causes. Given that the harm from al Qaeda's terrorist attacks fell disproportionately on Muslims, Obama appealed for, and expected to receive, support from the wider Muslim community.[48]

This public relations initiative began with an interview with the Al Arabiya television network a week after he took office,[49] and continued with an April address in Ankara, Turkey, where the president reiterated that the United States was not "at war with Islam." Speaking before the Turkish parliament, Obama appealed for a "partnership with the Muslim world" that was critical to "rolling back the violent ideologies that people of all faiths reject.[50]

Obama delivered his most important speech, however, at Cairo University on June 4, 2009. "I have come here," the president explained to those in attendance, plus millions of viewers, listeners, and readers,[51] "to seek a new beginning between the United States and Muslims around the world; one based upon mutual interest and mutual respect; and one based upon the truth that America and Islam are not exclusive, and need not be in competition." He called on his audience to join with the United States in confronting the "violent extremists who pose a grave threat to our security." "None of us should tolerate these extremists," Obama continued. "They have killed in many countries. They have killed people of different faiths—more than any other, they have killed Muslims."

He explained America's response to the horrific 9/11 attacks, directly confronting the persistent ignorance and denial surrounding the atrocities:

> I'm aware that there [are] still some who would question or even justify the events of 9/11. But let us be clear: Al Qaeda killed nearly 3,000 people on that day. The victims were innocent men, women and children from America and many other nations who had done nothing to harm anybody. And yet al Qaeda chose to ruthlessly murder these people, claimed credit for the attack, and even now states their determination to kill on a massive scale. They have affiliates in many countries and are trying to expand their reach. These are not opinions to be debated; these are facts to be dealt with.
> [...]
> 9/11 was an enormous trauma to our country. The fear and anger that it provoked was understandable, but in some cases, it led us to act contrary to our ideals.

To those who questioned America's methods, therefore, he pledged to do better: "America will defend itself respectful of the sovereignty of nations and the rule of law. And we will do so in partnership with Muslim communities which are also threatened. The sooner the extremists are isolated and unwelcome in Muslim communities, the sooner we will all be safer."[52] But although Obama tried diligently to shape a new narrative in the hope of soliciting international support for his counterterrorism policies, his words occasionally came into conflict with his other goals. And sometimes events well beyond his control undermined this carefully crafted dialogue.

A shooting spree in November 2009 by Army Major Nidal Hasan at Fort Hood in Texas left thirteen service members dead. The killings shocked the nation, and the revelation that Hasan, an army psychologist and a Muslim who had spoken openly of his dissatisfaction with U.S. policies over the course of his checkered career, cast the massacre as an act of domestic terrorism. Subsequent investigations determined that Hasan was radicalized by the teachings of a Yemeni cleric with ties to al Qaeda.

The potential crisis deepened when a failed attempt to blow up a Northwest Airlines flight in Detroit on Christmas Day 2009 exposed crucial vulnerabilities in airline security. Umar Farouk Abdul Mutallab, a twenty-three-year old Nigerian with no prior connections to terrorism, had trained in Yemen. He first came to the attention of U.S. officials when his father visited the U.S. embassy in Abuja, Nigeria, with a warning that his son had become radicalized and was espousing extremist views, but was not barred from boarding a plane to the United States. Although Abdul Mutallab was unable to detonate the explosives hidden in his undergarments, al Qaeda in the Arabian Peninsula claimed credit for the failed attack.

Both incidents threatened to derail Obama's message that the United States was not at war with Islam. Opponents, led by former vice president Cheney, accused the president of complacency. "[W]e are at war," Cheney said in a statement to Politico.com, "and when President Obama pretends we aren't, it makes us less safe." Cheney further speculated that Obama didn't "want to admit we're at war" because "[i]t doesn't fit with the view of the world he brought with him to the Oval Office."[53]

Obama shot back:

> Over the past two weeks, we've been reminded again of the challenge we face in protecting our country against a foe that is bent on our destruction. And while passions and politics can often obscure the hard work before us, let's be clear about what this moment demands. We are at war. We are at war against al Qaeda ... And we will do whatever it takes to defeat them.

[...]

Here at home, we will strengthen our defenses, but we will not succumb to a siege mentality that sacrifices the open society and liberties and values that we cherish as Americans, because great and proud nations don't hunker down and hide behind walls of suspicion and mistrust. That is exactly what our adversaries want, and so long as I am president, we will never hand them that victory. We will define the character of our country, not some band of small men intent on killing innocent men, women and children.

With these words, Obama tried to reassure Americans and respond to his domestic critics. He also reaffirmed the importance of America's relations with the outside world. "We must communicate clearly to Muslims around the world that al Qaeda offers nothing except a bankrupt vision of misery and death—including the murder of fellow Muslims."[54]

Rhetoric versus Reality

As noted above, the rhetoric of warfare has been deployed on numerous occasions to convey the seriousness of a particular problem, even as few people expected that the fight would be conducted by the military. So it is with terrorism. But while President Bush's use of the war metaphor might have borne superficial similarities to Ford and Carter's jihad against high food and energy prices, Bush, unlike his predecessors, chose to highlight the use of the military as his primary means for combating the most important challenge of his presidency. He did this, in part, in order to draw distinctions between himself and his political opponents. This practice carried over into the Obama administration, when GOP critics scorned the president's outreach efforts, and bemoaned Obama's unwillingness to refer to a "war on terror." Thus, the terminology surrounding the fight against al Qaeda has been filtered through the lens of partisan politics.

This has not served us well. In the last year of the Bush administration, the Department of Homeland Security advised policy makers to "accurately identify the nature of the challenges that face our generation." "If senior government officials carefully select strategic terminology," the paper published by the Office of Civil Rights and Civil Liberties averred, "the government's public statements will encourage vigilance without unintentionally undermining security objectives."[55] A report by the Pentagon's Defense Science Board (DSB) amplified these recommendations.

Evocative phrases such as "global war on terror," and "fighting them there so we don't fight them here," the panelists admitted, "may have short-term benefits in motivating support at home." However, this "polarizing rhetoric," the DSB went on to say, "can have adverse long-term consequences that reduce the willingness of potential allies to collaborate, and give unwarranted legitimacy and unity of effort to dispersed adversaries."[56] These were not isolated instances. Indeed, a number of experts lamented the "war on terror" construct.[57]

This might be a semantic matter except for the fact that rhetoric, and the shaping of expectations, is more important in the context of counterterrorism operations than in traditional wars. Victory or defeat in most wars is determined by armies on the field of battle, or fleets of ships at sea. By contrast, because terrorists aim specifically at breaking the public will, measures intended at shoring up public resolve are a crucial element of effective counterterrorism strategy.

What Works?

Obama counterterrorism adviser John Brennan told Peter Baker of the *New York Times,* "This president recognizes that there's still a very serious terrorist threat that we face from organizations like Al Qaeda." "But at the same time," Brennan continued, "what we have to do is make sure that we're not pouring fuel on the flames by the things that we do."[58]

This was a sensible approach. Effective strategies for confronting terrorism, and of doing so in a manner that does not generate still more terrorism, begin by putting the problem into the proper perspective. The world survived two global hot wars in the twentieth century, and was poised on the brink of extinction during the long Cold War. The First and Second World Wars claimed perhaps one hundred million lives. The Cold War tied up vast resources in the military complexes of the Soviet Union and the United States, especially, and presumed to reduce hundreds of millions of people within the so-called Third World to little more than pawns on a global chessboard.

The violence and bloodshed that can be unleashed by modern industrial states is several orders of magnitude greater than that which could be caused by international terrorism in the twenty-first century—and this is true even if, sometime in the future, Osama bin Laden or his followers get their hands on a functioning nuclear device, and then manage to detonate it in a populated area.

To be sure, the scope of destruction from even a single act of nuclear terrorism would be greater than anything ever before witnessed on U.S. soil, and policy makers should take steps to ensure that nuclear material does not wind up in the hands of terrorists. Such efforts require diplomacy and cooperation with other countries, and might include additional measures to discourage further nuclear proliferation and to enhance the security of existing arsenals, but rarely military action. Al Qaeda might aspire to possess nuclear material, or even a nuclear device, but such designs can best be disrupted by targeted action based on timely intelligence.

While al Qaeda terrorists appear to take particular pleasure in causing pain and suffering on a massive scale, their violence does have a political purpose. For al Qaeda, the object is the overthrow of the established political order in the Muslim world. Bin Laden and his followers generally believe that they would move toward achieving that goal by expelling Westerners and all Western influences from the lands once dominated by Islam, from Morocco to Indonesia. President Bush asserted that the United States must stand up to al Qaeda and its ideological allies wherever they might rear their ugly heads. If we do not, Bush warned, if we failed in Iraq, or if we are seen as having retreated, this would pave the way for the Islamists to realize their vision of a new global Caliphate, "a violent political utopia across the Middle East . . . where all would be ruled according to their hateful ideology."[59]

This is not an isolated point of view. Mitt Romney intoned, "Radical Islam has one goal: to replace all modern Islamic states with a worldwide caliphate while destroying the United States and converting all nonbelievers, forcibly if necessary, to Islam."[60] Eventual GOP nominee John McCain envisioned "a fundamental change in the world where radical Islamic extremism dominates the entire world" if the United States didn't prevail in Iraq.[61] When *Fortune* magazine asked McCain what was "the gravest long-term threat to the U.S. economy," he responded: "I would think that the absolute gravest threat is the struggle that we're in against radical Islamic extremism, which can affect, if they prevail, our very existence."[62] None of these statements take into account the Islamists' actual capacity for achieving such absurdly grandiose ends.

That is a serious oversight. To portray the terrorists as posing a mortal threat to the United States, or more broadly the West, dramatically exaggerates their power and influence. The vast majority of Muslims reject bin Ladenism in all its forms, not least because most of the harm done by al Qaeda over the years has been felt by Muslims.

Not surprisingly, recent research has concluded that the threat of terrorism is already on the wane.[63] Andrew Mack and Zoe Nielsen determined that the incidences of global terrorism and the human costs of terrorist violence were in decline. Mack and Nielsen surmise, "In the long term, perhaps sooner, Islamist terror organizations will join the overwhelming majority of other terrorist groups that have failed to achieve their objectives."[64]

Other empirical studies comport with these findings. Max Abrahms looked at twenty-eight terrorist organizations and found that these groups failed to achieve their stated policy objectives 93 percent of the time. Abrahms further concluded that terrorism's "poor success rate is inherent to the tactic of terrorism itself." This challenge to the conventional wisdom that terrorism is uniquely effective has policy implications, the most important being that we should not adopt overly aggressive strategies against an enemy that is likely to do more harm to itself than to others. Indeed, Abrahms concludes his article by recommending further study into "why counterterrorism campaigns tend to breed even more terrorism."[65]

James Fallows of the *Atlantic* asked a similar question in the summer of 2006. After interviewing dozens of counterterrorism experts, Fallows concluded that al Qaeda's "hopes for fundamentally harming the United States ... rest less on what it can do itself than on what it can trick, tempt, or goad us into doing."[66]

A Clash of Civilizations?

A number of popular writers and columnists claim that radical Islam poses an existential threat to the West, and that nothing short of a clash of civilizations will be required to rescue ourselves from certain doom.[67] They further imply that radical Islam is widely popular, and is poised to displace moderate Islam as the leading current of Islamic thought.

Here again, Barack Obama has sought to correct such misperceptions. Indeed, in his Cairo speech, Obama declared it "part of my responsibility as president of the United States to fight against negative stereotypes of Islam wherever they appear."[68]

He has at the same time, however, called attention to the threat from al Qaeda, and urged Americans to remain vigilant. And, while he has eschewed the phrase "war on terror," he has not shied away from referring to a "war on al Qaeda."[69]

This distinction is crucial. But even Obama's high-profile public relations campaign has its limits. Non-Muslims have only a very limited capacity to shape the debate within Islam. As the 9/11 Commission report concluded: "We must encourage reform, freedom, democracy, and opportunity, even though our own promotion of these messages is limited in its effectiveness simply because we are its carriers. . . . The United States can promote moderation, but cannot ensure its ascendancy. Only Muslims can do this."[70]

On the other hand, and paradoxically, while we cannot "ensure the ascendancy" of moderate Muslims, we do have a great capacity for influencing the debate within Islam in a negative direction, empowering extremists and marginalizing moderates. The words and actions of the president of the United States are particularly crucial. In the days and weeks immediately after 9/11, President Bush differentiated the nineteen terrorists, who happened to all be Muslim, from the 1.4 billion other Muslims in the world. In his speech before Congress on September 20, 2001, he assured Muslims around the world that Americans respected their faith. "It's practiced freely by many millions of Americans and by millions more in countries that America counts as friends. Its teachings are good and peaceful, and those who commit evil in the name of Allah blaspheme the name of Allah."[71]

It was hardly a foregone conclusion that America's leaders would exhibit such resolve in preventing the war on terrorism from being cast as a war against Islam. Indeed, some suggested that a campaign of isolation against Muslim Americans along the lines of what was done to Japanese Americans during World War II would advance U.S. security.[72]

Fortunately, the U.S. government has not resorted to internment camps, and while bigots and hate-mongers have attempted to exacerbate the divide between Muslims and non-Muslims, most Americans have resisted even subtle forms of persecution and ostracism. We have not, as many European countries have done, systematically isolated and marginalized Muslim populations in ghettoes and enclaves. And this different approach has paid dividends as the American Muslim community has stepped forward to help fight Islamic extremism.

A Fresh Start

No modern president enters the Oval Office with a clean slate on which to inscribe his policy preferences. The names and faces in the West Wing changed in January 2009, but the rest of the world did not. In comparing how the two post-9/11 presidents approached the problem of terrorism, it is clear that President Obama took some early steps to differentiate his administration from the Bush White House. His executive orders banning the use of torture and a pledge to close the detention facility at Guantánamo Bay were focused on those policies that have created ill will within the Muslim community. The leading source of resentment—the U.S. war in Iraq—is drawing to a close, but the expansion of the war in Afghanistan raises new suspicions of U.S. motives. But as radical Islamism struggles to expand its reach, a U.S. president's words sometimes matter as much as his actions. Obama's high-profile public diplomacy and outreach initiatives aimed at improving America's standing have yet to bear fruit, and have elicited considerable domestic criticism. As of this writing, he has remained largely on message.

President Obama's quiet shedding of the term "war on terror" is both politically astute and strategically wise. By rightly resisting the language of war to describe U.S. counterterrorism efforts, President Obama hopes to erode the too widespread perception that the United States is engaged in a war against all of Islam. Further, the war metaphor itself conceals and confuses the nature of U.S. efforts to hunt down violent extremists. With the exception of the U.S. military operations to depose the Taliban and disrupt al Qaeda camps in Afghanistan, the most successful counterterrorism operations do not involve the U.S. military. The disastrous invasion and occupation of Iraq—cited in a National Intelligence Estimate as the "cause célèbre" for jihadists, "breeding a deep resentment of U.S. involvement in the Muslim world and cultivating supporters for the global jihad movement"[73]—stands in stark contrast to the successful nonmilitary operations that enabled the United States to capture such al Qaeda figures as Ramzi Binalshibh and Khalid Sheik Mohammed, the key plotters of the 9/11 attacks.

The Obama administration had an opportunity to build on the Bush administration's record, but also to make a sharp break where a dramatic change was warranted. President Obama appropriately recast the discussion away from that of a war to be won and toward thinking of terrorism as a problem to be managed. As the danger of traditional war has ceased to be a serious concern, the danger of terrorism has grown. Our enemies know the sheer futility of facing us in a field of battle, and have chosen other means for challenging our primacy. The logical recourse is terrorism, the preferred tactic of the weak against the strong. Terrorism has persisted throughout human history, and it will be with us in some form forever. President Bush candidly conceded this point during the 2004 campaign, when he said to *Today* host Matt Lauer "I don't think you can win it."[74] Claiming that our national survival hangs in the balance, or that the terrorists pose a threat comparable to that of the Nazis or the Soviets, builds pressure for policies that do not increase our security but instead erode the very liberties that define us as a nation.

There is more to be done to restore the balance between liberty and security that was upset by the 9/11 attacks. But the pendulum that had begun to swing during Bush's second term has accelerated somewhat under Barack Obama. Whether he can maintain a new equilibrium following another attack is still unknown, but one hopes that his efforts to tone down the rhetoric and reassure the American public will continue to pay dividends.

Notes

The author wishes to thank Matt Fay, Adam Lamothe, and Charles Zakaib for their assistance with this paper. The views expressed are those of the author.

1. Ironically, the FBI team investigating the attack took note of the size of the bomb and concluded that nothing could ever bring down the towers. Lawrence Wright, *The Looming Tower: Al-Qaeda and the Road to 9/11* (New York: Alfred A. Knopf, 2006).

2. *The 9/11 Commission Report* (Final Report of the National Commission on Terrorist Attacks upon the United States), official government edition (Washington, D.C.: Government Printing Office, 2004), 72.

3. Ibid., 147–48.

4. "The Vice President Appears on Meet the Press with Tim Russert," September 16, 2001, White House, http://georgewbush-whitehouse.archives.gov/vicepresident/news-speeches/speeches/vp20010916.html.

5. George W. Bush, "Address to a Joint Session of Congress and the American People," September 20, 2001, White House, http://georgewbush-whitehouse.archives.gov/news/releases/2001/09/20010920-8.html.

6. For a relatively balanced assessment by a Justice Department official within the Bush administration, see Jack Goldsmith, *The Terror Presidency: Law and Judgment Inside the Bush Administration* (New York: W. W. Norton, 2007).

7. Eric Schmitt and Thom Shanker, "U.S. Officials Retool Slogan for Terror War," *New York Times*, July 26, 2005.

8. George W. Bush, "President Bush Delivers State of the Union Address," January 31, 2006, White House, http://georgewbush-whitehouse.archives.gov/news/releases/2006/01/20060131–10.html.

9. Tim Harper, "New Name, Same Conflict," *Toronto Star,* February 12, 2006, available at GlobalSecurity.orghttp://www.globalsecurity.org/org/news/2006/060211-long-war.htm (accessed April 18, 2010).

10. Michael R. Gordon, "U.S. Command Shortens Life of 'Long War' as a Reference," *New York Times,* April 24, 2007.

11. There were sixteen viable candidates on the Democratic and Republican ballots at the time of the Iowa caucuses on January 3, 2008.

12. "President Bush's Approval Ratings," WashingtonPost.com, no date, http://www.washingtonpost.com/wp-dyn/content/graphic/2005/04/25/GR2005042500945.html (accessed April 18, 2010).

13. Michael Barone and Richard E. Cohen, *The Almanac of American Politics* (Washington, D.C.: National Journal Group, 2008), 460–61.

14. Matt Bai, "Kerry's Undeclared War," *New York Times Magazine,* October 10, 2004, 6.

15. "Bush Campaign to Base Ad on Kerry Terror Quote," CNN.com, October 11, 2004, http://www.cnn.com/2004/ALLPOLITICS/10/10/bush.kerry.terror.

16. Kurt M. Campbell and Michael E. O'Hanlon, *Hard Power: The New Politics of National Security* (New York: Basic Books, 2006), 7, 9.

17. Ibid., 2.

18. Peter Baker, "Inside Obama's War on Terrorism," *New York Times Magazine,* January 17, 2010.

19. Barack Obama, "Remarks of Senator Obama: The War We Need to Win," speech at the Wilson Center, Washington, D.C., August 1, 2007, available at http://www.barackobama.com/2007/08/01/remarks_of_senator_obama_the_w_1.php.

20. By then, even such reliably conservative commentators as George Will had concluded that John Kerry had been proved right. George F. Will, "The Triumph of Unrealism," *Washington Post,* August 15, 2006.

21. John Edwards, "Reengaging With the World: A Return to Moral Leadership," *Foreign Affairs* 86, no. 5 (September/October 2007), 2.

22. Barack Obama, "Renewing American Leadership," *Foreign Affairs* 86, no. 4 (July/August 2007):, 4.

23. Hillary Clinton, "Civil and Constitutional Rights," New York Senator Hillary Clinton Webpage, http://clinton.senate.gov/issues/civil (site discontinued April 18, 2010). See also Hillary Clinton, "Security and Opportunity for the Twenty First Century," *Foreign Affairs* 86, no. 6 (November/December 2007), 2.

24. Obama, "Remarks of Senator Obama: The War We Need to Win."

25. Clinton, "Security and Opportunity for the Twenty First Century," 4.

26. Obama, "Remarks of Senator Obama: The War We Need to Win."

27. Ibid.

28. Unless otherwise noted, Texas congressman Ron Paul was the notable exception among the GOP candidates, eschewing the term "war on terror," calling for a withdrawal of U.S. troops from Iraq, and advocating a policy of restraint in order to reduce the terrorist threat against the United States.

29. One of Giuliani's leading foreign policy advisers, Norman Podhoretz, wrote a best-selling book casting the challenge as "World War IV." See Norman Podhoretz, *World War IV: The Long Struggle against Islamofascism* (New York: Doubleday, 2007). For a critical appraisal, see Christopher Preble, review of Podhoretz, *World War IV*, in the *Cato Journal* 28, no. 2 (Spring/Summer 2008), 358–62. While the former New York City mayor stopped short of employing the "world war" frame on the campaign trail, the gist of his comments revealed the extent to which he seemed to agree with Podhoretz's central formulation.

30. An analysis of eighty speeches between 1993 and 2001 found that Giuliani "mentioned the danger of terrorism only once, in a brief reference to emergency preparedness." See Amanda Ripley, "Behind Giuliani's Tough Talk," *Time,* August 22, 2007, available at http://www.time.com/time/nation/article/0,8599,1655262,00. html (accessed April 18, 2010).

31. Rudy Giuliani, "Toward a Realistic Peace," *Foreign Affairs* 86, no. 5 (September/ October 2007), 2.

32. Mitt Romney, "Rising to a New Generation of Global Challenges," *Foreign Affairs* 86, no. 4 (July/August 2007), 5.

33. Commission on Presidential Debates, "The First Bush-Kerry Presidential Debate," September 30, 2004, at the University of Miami in Coral Gables, Florida. Transcript available at the Commission on Presidential Debates website: http://www. debates.org/pages/trans2004a.html.

34. Council for a Livable World, "2008 Presidential Candidates' Responses to Seven Key National Security Questions," August 16, 2007, http://www.clw.org/elections/2008/presidential/2008_presidential_candidates_questionnaire_responses.

35. See John McCain, "An Enduring Peace Built on Freedom," *Foreign Affairs* 86, no. 6 (November/December 2007), 23; and Barack Obama, "Renewing American Leadership," *Foreign Affairs* 86, no. 4 (July/August 2007), 7.

36. George W. Bush, "President Bush Delivers the State of the Union," January 28, 2008, White House, http://www.whitehouse.gov/news/releases/2008/01/20080128–13. html.

37. A *Washington Post* poll taken in August 2003 found that 69 percent of Americans believed that Saddam Hussein had a role in the 9/11 attacks. Dana Milbank and

Claudia Deane, "Hussein Link to 9/11 Lingers in Many Minds," *Washington Post,* September 6, 2003.

38. Barack Obama, "My Plan for Iraq," *New York Times,* July 14, 2008.

39. "Obama Would Swap Iraq War Loss for Election Win: McCain Camp," Agence France Press, July 4, 2008, http://afp.google.com/article/ALeqM5i6dhh7D-sKfF17534Cn0gaalXi9UQ.

40. Laura Meckler, "McCain Tries to Clarify '100 Year' Remark," *Wall Street Journal,* February 25, 2008.

41. Marc Lynch of George Washington University makes a similar point. See "Bush's Finest Moment on Iraq: SOFA, Not the Surge," ForeignPolicy.com, January 18, 2009, http://lynch.foreignpolicy.com/posts/2009/01/18/sofa_not_the_surge.

42. On the many different grievances and other risk factors that can drive an individual or group to employ terrorism, see Marc Sageman, *Leaderless Jihad: Terror Networks in the 21st Century* (Philadelphia: University of Pennsylvania Press, 2007); Louise Richardson, *What Terrorists Want: Understanding the Enemy, Containing the Threat* (New York: Random House, 2006); Mia Bloom, *Dying to Kill: The Allure of Suicide Terrorism* (New York: Columbia University Press, 2005); Robert Pape, *Dying to Win: The Strategic Logic of Suicide Terrorism* (New York: Random House, 2005); and Jessica Stern, *Terror in the Name of God: Why Religious Militants Kill* (New York: HarperCollins, 2003). Earlier studies noted the correlation between U.S. military intervention and incidents of terrorism against Americans. See Ivan Eland, "Does U.S. Intervention Overseas Breed Terrorism? The Historical Record," *Cato Foreign Policy Briefing* no. 50, December 17, 1998; and *The Defense Science Board 1997 Summer Study Task Force on DoD Responses to Transnational Threats,* vol. 1, Final Report (Washington: U.S. Department of Defense, October 1997).

43. Obama effectively tripled the number of U.S. soldiers deployed in Afghanistan during his first year in office. There were approximately 31,000 American military personnel in Afghanistan in January 2009; Obama approved several rounds of increases that would bring the total to more than 100,000 by spring 2010. With respect to drone strikes, Peter Bergen and Katherine Tiedemann at the New America Foundation concluded that the CIA had launched forty-four such strikes in the first nine months of 2009 (two while Bush was still in office), as compared with thirty-four in all of 2008. Peter Bergen, and Katherine Tiedermann, "Pakistan Drone War Takes a Toll on Militants—and Civilians," CNN, October 29, 2009, http://edition.cnn.com/2009/OPINION/10/29/bergen.drone.war. See also Baker, "Inside Obama's War on Terrorism"; Helene Cooper, "The Label Factor: Is Obama a Wimp or a Warrior?" *New York Times,* January 9, 2010; and Scott Wilson, "The Making of a Wartime Commander in Chief," *Washington Post,* January 19, 2010. Many in the media now routinely refer to the war in Afghanistan as "Obama's War." See, for example, "Obama's War," *Frontline,*

PBS, http://www.pbs.org/wgbh/pages/frontline/obamaswar; and "Obama's War," the ongoing coverage at WashingtonPost.com, http://www.washingtonpost.com/wp-srv/special/afghanistan-pakistan/index.html?sid=ST2010011803658.

44. "Remarks by Richard B. Cheney," American Enterprise Institute, Washington, D.C., May 21, 2009, http://www.aei.org/speech/100050.

45. Collins and Carafano quoted in Baker, "Inside Obama's War on Terrorism."

46. Ibid.

47. Quoted in ibid.

48. A study by the Combating Terrorism Center at West Point concluded that 85 percent of al Qaeda's victims between 2004–2008 were Muslim, and 98 percent of victims from 2006–2008 were from Muslim countries. Scott Helfstein, Nassir Abdullah, Muhammad al-Obaidi, "Deadly Vanguards: A Study of al-Qa'ida's Violence against Muslims," December 2009, Occasional Paper Series, Combating Terrorism Center.

49. "[TRANSCRIPT] Obama's Interview with Al Aribiya," January 27, 2009, http://www.alarabiya.net/Articles/2009/01/27/65096.html.

50. Barack Obama, "Remarks by President Obama to the Turkish Parliament," Turkish Grand National Assembly Complex, Ankara, Turkey, April 6, 2009, White House, http://www.whitehouse.gov/the_press_office/Remarks-By-President-Obama-To-The-Turkish-Parliament.

51. The German magazine *Der Spiegel* reported that "sixty million people watched, read or listened to the speech on the radio, on television, on the Internet or via text message." Christoph Schult, Gabor Steingart and Bernhard Zand, "A Peace Mission: Obama's Offer to the Islamic World," *Der Spiegel*, June 8, 2009, http://www.spiegel.de/international/world/0,1518,629207,00.html.

52. Barack Obama, "Remarks by the President on a New Beginning," June 4, 2009, Cairo University, Cairo, Egypt, White House, http://www.whitehouse.gov/the_press_office/Remarks-by-the-President-at-Cairo-University-6-04-09.

53. Mike Allen, "Dick Cheney: Barack Obama 'Trying To Pretend,'" Politico.com, December 30, 2009, http://www.politico.com/news/stories/1209/31054.html.

54. Barack Obama, "Remarks by the President on Strengthening Intelligence and Aviation Security," January 7, 2010, White House, http://www.whitehouse.gov/the-press-office/remarks-president-strengthening-intelligence-and-aviation-security.

55. "Terminology to Define the Terrorists: Recommendations from American Muslims," Office for Civil Rights and Civil Liberties, Department of Homeland Security, January 2008.

56. "Report of the Defense Science Board Task Force on Strategic Communication," Office of the Under Secretary of Defense for Acquisition, Technology, and Logistics, January 2008, 19, 43.

57. See, for example, Jeffrey Record, "Bounding the Global War on Terror," U.S. Army's Strategic Studies Institute Monograph Series, December 2003; and Michael Howard, "A Long War?" *Survival* 48 no. 4, 7–14.

58. Baker, "Inside Obama's War on Terrorism."

59. George W. Bush, "Remarks on the War on Terror," *Washington Post,* September 5, 2006.

60. Romney, "Rising to a New Generation of Global Challenges."

61. John McCain, Remarks at "Iraq: A Turning Point," American Enterprise Institute, January 5, 2007, http://www.aei.org/events/filter.all,eventID.1446/transcript.asp.

62. David Whitford, "The Evolution of John McCain," *Fortune,* June 23, 2008, http://money.cnn.com/2008/06/20/magazines/fortune/Evolution_McCain_Whitford.fortune/index.htm.

63. For a skeptical view of the terrorist threat, see John Mueller, *Overblown: How Politicians and the Terrorism Industry Inflate National Security Threats, and Why We Believe Them* (New York: Free Press, 2006); and Ian S. Lustick, *Trapped in the War on Terror* (Philadelphia: University of Pennsylvania Press, 2006).

64. Andrew Mack and Zoe Nielsen, *Human Security Brief, 2007,* Human Security Report Project, School for International Studies, Simon Fraser University, March 2008, 21.

65. Max Abrahms, "Why Terrorism Does Not Work," *International Security* 31, no. 2 (Fall 2006), 43. See also, Seth G. Jones and Martin C. Libicki, *How Terrorist Groups End: Lessons for Countering al Qa'ida* (Santa Monica, Calif.: RAND, 2008); and Audrey Kurth Cronin, *How Terrorism Ends: Understanding the Decline and Demise of Terrorist Campaigns* (Princeton, N.J.: Princeton University Press, 2009).

66. James Fallows, "Declaring Victory," *Atlantic,* September 2006, http://www.theatlantic.com/doc/200609/fallows_victory.

67. See, for example, Lee Harris, *The Suicide of Reason: Radical Islam's Threat to the West* (New York: Basic Books, 2007); and Bruce Bawer, *While Europe Slept: How Radical Islam is Destroying the West from Within* (New York: Doubleday, 2006). See also the writings of Robert Spencer, who has published several books maintaining that Islam is based on violence, and who maintains the popular website JihadWatch.org.

68. Obama, "Remarks by the President on a New Beginning."

69. See, for example, Obama, "Remarks by the President on Strengthening Intelligence and Aviation Security," January 7, 2010

70. *The 9/11 Commission Report,* 375–76.

71. Bush, "Address to a Joint Session of Congress and the American People," September 20, 2001.

72. See, for example, Michelle Malkin, *In Defense of Internment: The Case for 'Racial Profiling' in World War II and the War on Terror* (Washington, D.C.: Regnery, 2004).

73. National Intelligence Council, "Trends in Global Terrorism: Implications for the United States," April 2006, http://www.dni.gov/nic/special_global_terrorism. html.

74. Quoted in Bai, "Kerry's Undeclared War."

About the Contributors

MEENA BOSE is Director of the Peter S. Kalikow Center for the Study of the American Presidency at Hofstra University, Peter S. Kalikow Chair in Presidential Studies, and Professor of Political Science. She is the author of *Shaping and Signaling Presidential Policy: The National Security Decision Making of Eisenhower and Kennedy* (Texas A&M University Press, 1998), and editor of the reference volume *The New York Times on the Presidency* (CQ Press, 2009). She also is co-editor of several volumes in presidency studies and a reader in American politics, and she is a contributor to the textbook *American Government: Institutions and Policies,* 12th ed. (Wadsworth Cengage Learning, 2011), by James Q. Wilson and John J. DiIulio Jr. She taught for six years at the United States Military Academy at West Point, where she also served as Director of American Politics in 2006. Dr. Bose previously taught at Hofstra University from 1996–2000.

LARA M. BROWN is an assistant professor of political science at Villanova University. She is the author of *Jockeying for the American Presidency: The Political Opportunism of Aspirants* (Cambria Press, 2010). She has published articles in several scholarly journals, including *Congress and the Presidency, Presidential Studies Quarterly,* and the *Journal of Political Marketing.* Prior to completing her doctorate, she served in President William J. Clinton's administration as Coordinator, Corporate Outreach, at the U.S. Department of Education in Washington, D.C. She holds a PhD, MA, and BA from the University of California, Los Angeles, as well as an MA from the University of Arizona.

DAVID A. CROCKETT is associate professor of political science at Trinity University. He is the author of *The Opposition Presidency: Leadership and the Constraints of History* (Texas A&M University Press, 2002) and *Running against the Grain: How Opposition Presidents Win the White House* (Texas A&M University Press, 2008), as well as numerous articles on the presidency. From 1985 to 1991, he served as a communications officer in the United States Army, assigned to the Third Infantry Division in the Federal Republic of Germany and the 13th Corps Support Command at Fort Hood, Texas. He received his undergraduate degree from Georgetown University (1985), his master of public affairs degree from the Lyndon B. Johnson School of Public Affairs at the University of Texas at Austin (1993), and his doctorate from the University of Texas at Austin (1999).

VICTORIA A. FARRAR-MYERS is a Professor of Political Science at the University of Texas at Arlington. She specializes in the American presidency, presidential-congressional relations, separation of powers, and campaign finance reform. Among her many publications, Dr. Farrar-Myers is the author of *Scripted for Change: The Institutionalization of the American Presidency* (Texas A&M University Press, 2007) and the co-author of *Legislative Labyrinth: Congress and Campaign Finance Reform* (CQ Press, 2000) and *Limits and Loopholes: The Quest for Money, Free Speech and Fair Elections* (CQ Press, 2007). During 1997–1998, she served as an American Political Science Association Congressional Fellow. Among her honors, she was the recipient of the 2001 University of Texas at Arlington's Chancellor's Council Award for Excellence in Teaching, the 2005 *Arlington Star-Telegram* Service Learning Award, and the 2007 Honors College Faculty Award.

JOHN C. FORTIER is a Research Fellow at the American Enterprise Institute (AEI). He has been the principal contributor to the AEI-Brookings Election Reform Project since 2005 and has served as executive director of the Continuity of Government Commission since 2002. In July 2008, he was named the first director of the Center for the Study of American Democracy at Kenyon College. He writes a column for *Politico*, commenting on current events in U.S. politics, and is a contributor to *Politico.com*'s "The Arena" forum. He has testified before Congress on issues concerning continuity, representation for the District of Columbia, and absentee voting. He is the author of *Absentee and Early Voting: Trends, Promises, and Perils* (AEI Press, 2006); and editor of *Second-Term Blues: How George W. Bush Has Governed* (Brookings Institution Press, 2007); and *After the People Vote: A Guide to the Electoral College* (AEI Press, 2004). He received his BA from Georgetown University and his PhD in political science from Boston College.

DAVID GREENBERG is an associate professor of History and of Journalism & Media Studies at Rutgers University and the author of three books on U.S. political and history, including *Nixon's Shadow: The History of an Image* (W.W. Norton, 2003), which won the Washington Monthly Political Book Award, the American Journalism History Book Award, and, in dissertation form, Columbia University's Bancroft Dissertation Award. A former journalist who served as managing editor and acting editor of *The New Republic*, he is a columnist for Slate and a contributing editor to *The New Republic* and has written for the *New York Times, The New Yorker, The Atlantic, Raritan, Daedalus*, and other scholarly and popular publications. He holds a BA, summa cum laude and Phi Beta Kappa, from Yale University (1990) and a PhD in history from Columbia University (2001).

LORI COX HAN is professor of political science at Chapman University. She is the author of *Governing From Center Stage: White House Communication Strategies During the Television Age of Politics* (Hampton Press, 2001), and *Women and American Politics: The Challenges of Political Leadership* (McGraw-Hill, 2007). She is co-editor of *In the Public Domain: Presidents and the Challenge of Public Leadership* (SUNY Press, 2005); *The Presidency and the Challenge of Democracy* (Palgrave Macmillan, 2006,); *Rethinking Madam President: Is America Ready for a Woman in the White House?* (Lynne Rienner, 2007); *Encyclopedia of American Government and Civics* (Facts on File, 2008), and *Political Leadership, Vol. 2 of Leadership at the Crossroads* (Praeger, 2008). Prior to joining the faculty at Chapman, Dr. Austin taught at Austin College in Sherman, Texas.

DIANE J. HEITH is Associate Professor of Government and Politics at St. John's University. She is the author of several works on the presidency, public opinion and the media including, *Polling to Govern: Public Opinion and Presidential Leadership* (Stanford University Press, 2004) and is co-editor of *In the Public Domain: Presidents and the Challenges of Public Leadership* (State University of New York Press, 2005). Her work has appeared in *Public Opinion Quarterly, Presidential Studies Quarterly, Political Science Quarterly, The Journal of Health Politics, Policy and Law, The Journal of Women, Politics and Policy, White House Studies*, and *Congress and the Presidency*.

CHRISTOPHER A. PREBLE is the director of foreign policy studies at the Cato Institute in Washington, DC. He is the author of *The Power Problem: How American Military Dominance Makes Us Less Safe, Less Prosperous and Less Free* (Cornell University Press, 2009); *Exiting Iraq: How the U.S. Must End the Occupation and Renew the War against Al Qaeda* (Cato Institute, 2004); and *John F. Kennedy and the Missile Gap* (Northern Illinois University Press, 2004). Preble also has published more than 100 articles in major publications including *USA Today,* the *Financial Times,* the *Wall Street Journal,* the *Philadelphia Inquirer, Reason,* the *National Interest,* the *Foreign Service Journal,* and the *Harvard International Review.* He has appeared on many television and radio news networks including CNN, MSNBC, Fox News Channel, NPR, and the BBC. Before joining Cato in February 2003, he taught history at St. Cloud State University and Temple University. Preble was a commissioned officer in the U.S. Navy and is a veteran of the Gulf War, having served onboard USS *Ticonderoga* (CG-47) from 1990 to 1993. Preble holds a PhD in history from Temple University.

TIMOTHY J. RYAN is a graduate student in American politics at the University of Michigan. Prior to that, he was a Research Assistant with the American Enterprise Institute (AEI)-Brookings Election Reform Project. His senior thesis, "You Can Bring a Horse to Water . . . Youth Voting and the Personal Touch," won the 2006 best undergraduate thesis award from Pi Sigma Alpha, the national political science honor society. He is the author of "Public Confidence in Elections: Measurement and Implications," in *Voting in America,* vol. 3, ed. Morgan Felchner (Westport, Ct.: Praeger, 2008). He graduated from Tufts University in 2006.

SHIRLEY ANNE WARSHAW is professor of political science at Gettysburg College. She is the author of several books on the presidency, including *The Co-Presidency of Bush and Cheney* (Stanford University Press, 2009); *The Keys to Power: Managing the Presidency,* 2d ed. (Longman, 2004); *The Clinton Years: Presidential Profiles* (Facts on File, 2004); *The Domestic Presidency: Policy Making in the White House* (Longman, 1997); *Powersharing: White House-Cabinet Relations in the Modern Presidency* (State University of New York Press, 1996); and *Re-examining the Eisenhower Presidency* (Greenwood Press, 1993). She has been a consultant to the White House under three administrations and a consultant to the Public Broadcasting System. Before joining the Gettysburg College faculty, Dr. Warshaw worked in Pennsylvania state government, including the Governor's office during two different administrations.

LaVergne, TN USA
25 February 2011
217987LV00001B/6/P

9 781603 442275